Uncut Cords

Caring for our sons and daughters with learning disabilities

© Pauline Rogers, Linda Fletcher, Pat Nicholson, Anne McLaren, Susan Paterson, Gillian Payne and Liz Maynard, 2015

Published by Caring Expressions

A CIP catalogue record for this book is available from the British Library.

ISBN 978-0-9932857-0-7

Book layout and cover design by Clare Brayshaw

Cover background image © Tatisol | Dreamstime.com

Prepared and printed by:

York Publishing Services Ltd
64 Hallfield Road
Layerthorpe
York YO31 7ZQ

Tel: 01904 431213

Website: www.yps–publishing.co.uk

Stories of the lives of families caring for a son or daughter
with learning disabilities

Authors
Pauline Rogers
Linda Fletcher
Pat Nicholson
Anne McLaren
Susan Paterson
Gillian Payne
Liz Maynard

Published by
Caring Expressions

This book is dedicated to all our children

"Being a parent of a child with learning disability is often both challenging and extraordinary. It is not the disability which challenges, but the complexity and bureaucracy that still surrounds getting the right support – and ensuring that our children do enjoy fulfilling lives."

"The Care Act of April 2014 introduced for the first time the concept of 'whole family assessments' and whole family support and care planning, after a decade of personalisation and greater ambitions for 'ordinary lives' for people with learning disabilities and their families."

"*Uncut Cords* is a remarkable book produced by parents, but it is also for the much wider audience involved professionally, as well as personally in their lives."

Dame Philippa Russell is the mother of an adult son with learning disability and brain damage and the grandmother of a lovely grandson with an autistic spectrum disorder. She is the former Chair of the Government's Standing Commission on Carers and a member of the Cross Government Programme Board for the Carers Strategy.

CONTENTS

Introduction & Poem by Pauline Rogers   vii

Preface   xi

Introducing Ourselves   1

Introducing our Children   13

The Things People Say   25

Beginnings   31

Fork in the Road   46

A Day in the life   58

Snapshots and Threads   74

Graffiti Wall of Prejudice and Ignorance   86

Siblings   88

Special Occasions   98

Food and Eating   110

A Journey   121

Familiar Objects   133

The Photograph   143

Significant Words   154

Positive Encounters   166

Rites of Passage   179

Metamorphosis   191

Hopes and Fears for the Future   206

Notes on the Writing Process – by Dr. Laura Potts   221

Afterword – by Maureen Ryan   223

Glossary   225

Acknowledgements   229

INTRODUCTION – BY PAULINE ROGERS

Caring for a son or daughter with learning difficulties is a lifetime commitment for many families. Adequate support for parents and other family members is still sadly lacking, leaving them often frustrated and angry as they battle the system, trying to get the best possible quality of life for their sons or daughters. The stresses and strains of this unending struggle can, and often do, cause physical and emotional ill-health. Caring commitments can also lead to feelings of loneliness and isolation from mainstream society. Having a job and good opportunities for leisure activities, things most people take for granted, are, in many cases, impossible to achieve and impact tremendously on the psychological health of many family carers, sometimes leading to anxiety, depression, physical disease and even mental breakdown. As a family carer myself I have experienced first-hand some of the negative consequences of my caring role.

Having been actively involved with various groups in York, working towards improving the lives of people with learning difficulties and their families, I had become frustrated and demoralised by the bureaucratic process which involved meeting after meeting, with much being said, but with little real improvement in families' lives. More and more people will inevitably have to take on a caring role and I suspect that the majority of the general public has little idea of what the lives of unpaid family carers are like. It sometimes feels as though the most we should expect is to do it for 'love'. I believe that sharing our life experiences with the general public is vital to get family carers' issues and rights at the top of the government's agenda and to achieve a better life for all carers and families. I hope that professionals working in the field of learning disabilities will use these experiences to inform policy decision making and their own practice.

I wanted to find a new approach to getting the voice of family carers heard, one which would give carers involved something for themselves. Having always been interested in writing, I knew that as well as being an enjoyable activity, it can also have a powerful healing effect, and I felt a creative writing group, where family carers could write about their lives would have the capacity to become a valuable support network for the carers involved.

It is well-documented that creative writing can help to aid relaxation and reduce stress which every family carer I know is usually in need of. It also encourages self-reflection and self-appraisal which every one of us has found helpful in allowing us to explore feelings and finding ways forward. It has also helped us build up our self-confidence and given us new skills. Creative writing for this group of family carers has helped us to feel less alone, more supported and has helped with our sense of positive well-being.

In 2009 the BBC launched My Story, a writing competition, inviting anyone living in the UK to submit true life stories. This seemed to be a very good place for a writing group for carers to begin and with help from Maureen Ryan, the manager of Talkback North Yorkshire, a self-advocacy group for people with learning difficulties, and from York Carers Centre who provided a free venue, a group was launched. Initially, there were three carers, two of whom did submit a story for the competition. Linda, Pat and I continued to meet with Maureen talking through our ideas and forming ourselves into Caring Expressions. In 2011 we were delighted that our application for funding to Awards For All, part of the Big Lottery Fund, was approved for one year, and for our second year we are grateful to the Joseph Rowntree Foundation for funding. We have also received some funding from York Vikings Rotary Club.

For me this book is the culmination of a long-held dream. We have laughed and cried together as we revealed our stories to each other. It has been very rewarding to see each other's writing skills develop with the expert help of our tutor. We have each discovered our own unique voice, rediscovered lost dreams, uncovered hidden hopes and memories, developed fresh views and insights and begun to see past experiences differently. For me, as an older carer it has been an opportunity to revisit and re-evaluate the past. To see that all the struggles have been worth it after all, to celebrate the many things my daughter has achieved despite enormous difficulties, and to realise in spite of all the heartache along the way, I wouldn't swap my life for anyone else's.

Rainbow's End – by Pauline Rogers

harsh, hurtful, half-witted words
idiot, imbecile, inadequate
better ignored
sub-normal, subservient
should be suppressed
this heritage lingers long
kinder categories
mental handicap, special needs, learning disability
but social stigma's invasive, corrosive acid
still burns within the psyche
difference still cause for concern
not celebration
feared more than favoured
i am blessed
i am privileged
i have found my pot of gold
my daughter lights up my life
enriches me, enchants me
shows me love unconditionally
gives me lessons
in patience, in prejudice
in true prosperity
riches in a world which
does not value enough
the special gifts our children
bring to it

PREFACE

In 2011 a group of family carers of people with learning disabilities in Yorkshire joined together to set up a creative writing group, with a tutor to guide us, with the aim of enabling us to share experiences, our fears and anxieties for the future, and to celebrate the achievements and successes of the children. Our children range in age from mid teens to late 40s, and have varying diagnoses, and in one instance no diagnosis at all. Although we did not all know each other before the project started, we very quickly felt confident and able to trust each other with our innermost feelings about our children and the lives we lead.

We spent much of the first year honing our writing skills on topics which were not necessarily related to our caring roles. With persistence and practice, we have found our individual voices. We have organised our writing into this book, which we hope will not only be a comfort to other carers, but will give professionals, students, service providers and the general public an insight into the reality of our lives and to dispel some of the myths and stereotypes attached to the label "carer".

In revealing ourselves to each other, we have, it seems, revealed ourselves to ourselves. Raw truths have been exposed. Many tears have been shed. Compiling this book has also helped us to feel supported, acknowledged and validated. As Annie says, *"When you are a carer, you can feel isolated, lonely and overwhelmed by the constant and ongoing responsibilities. Sometimes you think you are going mad. The writing group enables me to share some of this burden and these feelings with other carers who are in similar circumstances. Being taught ways of expressing these thoughts on paper helps me address some issues which I had been suppressing and which, at times, were dragging me under. Realising that other people have experienced similar situations* and attitudes to my own and share the same concerns has been like finding an island in a seemingly endless rough sea."

Pat says, "During our early days as carers, we all came to slowly realize that we were embarking on an unknown, unplanned and unending life journey. Having a child with a learning disability forces you to re-assess your expectations of what your child's life might have been, and how you imagined and hoped it would be. You are taken down a very different path and you have to constantly re-programme your expectations as your precious child changes and develops over the years. The end product is a complete unknown. In writing this book as a group, it has given us the comfort, support and strength to re-visit and write about the sometimes painful experiences we have encountered during our lives as carers."

As the seven of us sat around the table, it became apparent that there were common threads in our lives, experiences, attitudes and emotions which naturally became the chapters in the book. In this way readers can choose whether to read it through or dip into certain aspects. We hope this will prove a more interesting read than seven autobiographies in one book.

Liz says, "Being part of the Caring Expressions Writing Group was simultaneously incredibly comforting and very stimulating. It was comforting because whatever our differences these were women with whom I shared what is the most central experience of my life: having a child with a learning disability, and there was complete understanding of the significance of this from all the other members. That alone was unique. It was also very stimulating. Firstly, the challenge of trying to express on paper all the struggles and complications and delights of my daughter. But I also learnt from the other women how they have lived their lives and this filled me with admiration. I also gained a lot of information about available resources to help our children to experience enjoyment and fulfilment. I came late to the group, but I only wish I had been there for the whole journey.

We have shared a common desire to ensure that our children retain their dignity and nothing is revealed about them that they would not wish others to know. In some instances, the names of the parents and children have been changed in order to protect their anonymity. No professionals, service providers or other individuals/institutions have been named in this book.

The confidence we have gained from sharing our experiences has been cathartic and life affirming, and has given us the strength to carry on fighting to ensure our children are receiving everything they need to enjoy a happy, fruitful and meaningful life. We hope that other carers will be able to identify with what is said and find comfort in the fact that they are not the only ones. For Susan, writing her story has helped her to find a voice, and to be able to express the frustrations, the anger and the joy she has experienced since her daughter was diagnosed with a learning disability. She reveals in this book how learning to use her anger in a constructive way, i.e. transforming anger into action, and speaking and acting on behalf of her daughter is empowering. *"Being the mother of a daughter with a learning disability and who is on the autistic spectrum has helped make me the person I am today, part of my journey of becoming who I am. My daughter is my greatest teacher – she has taught me and continues to teach me about love, compassion, acceptance, and patience. I have sometimes felt powerless, but find resilience and determination within myself when I really need them."*

The discovery your child has a learning disability is difficult enough, but each of us has experienced battles with bureaucracy which lead to feeling unsupported, undervalued, ignored or even held in contempt by the very people who are supposed to support us. However, we realise that we all sometimes get things wrong, despite good intentions.

For Linda, writing her contributions to this book has helped to heal some longstanding traumas by getting them down on paper and out of her head. *"The battles we have fought on Andrew's behalf have left me with a desire to make a difference, and I have been a School Governor throughout most of Andrew's school life, as well as sitting on various multi-disciplinary strategy groups. I value the opportunity to contribute a parent's point of view, but I needed some other means to express what life is like as a carer. I have always enjoyed writing, and one of my life ambitions is to write a book. This is why I was drawn to Caring Expressions, as it is such a refreshing change from going to meetings and taking part in consultations, and it gives me protected time to switch off from my* caring role for a few hours and focus on writing. Sharing our stories with each other has been a very special experience which I will never forget."

We remain the only constant in our children's lives. We recognize their vulnerability and are committed to getting a fair deal for them, a commitment which will, for us, never end.

All of us feel anxiety about the future for our disabled family members. Gillian says *"I'm worried that my son's disability is not immediately obvious, and he lives fairly independently in the community, with a minimum of supervision. This means that he is in reality very vulnerable, and open to mate crime from people he feels are his friends. I am concerned that he is a target for exploitation – financially, emotionally and sexually."*

We want those who deal with disabled children during their working lives to read this book and "walk around in our shoes" for a while. We hope that professionals and students alike will gain insight and modify their attitudes and approach to become more understanding. We hope they will agree with the sentiments of the civil rights poet, June Jordan: "Change will not come if we wait for some other person or some other time. We are the ones we've been waiting for. We are the change that we seek."

The wider public will be enlightened to read about the chaos, confusion, uncertainty and stress of our all-day and everyday lives. It is not a tidy existence, but there are some beautifully touching moments which can put things into perspective, pull us up and make us think, "what is life really about anyway and what is important?"

INTRODUCING OURSELVES

INTRODUCING LINDA

I was born in Sunderland in 1957, and have one younger brother. My parents met when my father was a railway signalman and my mother was sent to his signalbox as a relief signalwoman towards the end of the war. I love looking at photographs of them when they were young. Everyone seemed so glamorous and stylish compared to today, and to me they both looked like film stars. Dad was always told he was a dead ringer for Stewart Grainger, and mum could have been a model. When we were very young, my parents seriously considered emigrating to Australia, but in the end my mother could not face moving to the other side of the world and, when I was 7 years old, we ended up in York instead.

I have only one child, born when I was 39 years of age. My life prior to becoming a mother was a slightly nomadic existence of moving home six times, and changing career almost as many times. I attended three different primary schools – one in Sunderland and two in York – and was always the outsider who never really fitted in. I had a small circle of friends, but was very introverted and was the target of bullies throughout the whole of my school days.

Denied my childhood dream of going to drama school, I dutifully went to business college as directed by my parents and careers advisor. I started out my working life as a shorthand typist, progressing to become secretary to the Managing Director of a local manufacturer at the age of 20. I joined an amateur musical theatre group when I was 17, where I found the camaraderie I had never felt at school. The Theatre Director was a hard taskmaster, but he got the best out of people and, apart from my parents, he was the first person to believe in me. The group became the centre of my life for over 10 years and I played several major roles. This went some way to compensating for the loss of my ambition of being a professional actress. It also equipped me with the skill of appearing confident on the outside, when inside I felt anything but. Little did I know how useful this would become when fighting battles on behalf of my son! I met my first husband in the theatre group and we were married in 1982.

Becoming bored with the solitude of sitting in an office on my own all day, I felt drawn to work with people in a caring role, and qualified as a Registered General Nurse in 1989. My first marriage did not work out, and in 1991 I left my husband to be with John. It was the hardest thing I have ever done, and was a painful experience which scarred many other people, but it was the right decision for me. My only regret is that I did not handle the fallout in the kindest or most mature way. John and I have now been together for 23 years.

Our son, Andrew, was born in 1996. By now I was a Registered Midwife, and the shock at needing an emergency caesarean section at 32 weeks was exacerbated by my professional knowledge and experience; at that time ignorance may not have been bliss, but it would have made the situation a little less stressful. It was not evident at birth that Andrew had any problems, but his first year was plagued with ill health, culminating in a critical illness which almost claimed his life. This period took a severe toll on my physical and mental health, and still comes back to haunt me at times.

John was made redundant when our son was 3 years old, and through sheer luck we were offered the opportunity to manage a guest house for a friend. This heralded a new phase in our lives together, but it was not without its drawbacks. Unable to juggle caring for my son, being a nurse on shift work, and helping my husband to run the guest house, I had no option but to give up the only thing I could – nursing. It was a difficult decision but my son is my priority and I feel very lucky to have been given the opportunity to be self-employed. John's redundancy hit us hard, but it turned out to be a blessing in disguise as, with hindsight, I know I would not have been able to sustain my nursing career. Running a guest house is incredibly demanding, but no two days are ever the same, and seeing our guests leave us feeling relaxed and refreshed is very rewarding.

One of my failings is my inability to stop volunteering for things! I have been a school governor for the last 9 years, and a member of several multi-disciplinary committees and strategy groups which gives me the opportunity to offer a parent's point of view. This is something I value highly. My passion for advocating for my son remains constant, but I feel equally strongly about carers' rights. Around 5 years ago, Andrew and I bumped into a lady at a table top sale in our street and we discovered our mutual interest in carers' rights. This lady was Maureen Ryan, a Carers Development Worker, who has written a contribution to this book. It was eventually through Maureen that I heard about Pauline and was instantly drawn to her vision of creating a group which would offer family carers the opportunity to express what it is like to be a carer through creative writing. Along with Pauline and Pat, I became one of the founder members of Caring Expressions and I am incredibly proud to have played a role in this exciting project.

INTRODUCING ANNIE

I am the sort of person who, when swimming, will move aside in the pool in order to let someone else plough along in a straight line.

I am defined by my family. Growing up, the youngest of four children, our father was a renowned research metallurgist and we were all imbued with his work ethic. On my mother's side, there were generations of doctors, and I opted for this profession in my turn, as did my elder brother. After studying pre-clinical medicine and taking a natural sciences degree at Somerville College, Oxford, I completed the clinical part of my training in Edinburgh. During my house jobs in Edinburgh Royal Infirmary, I met a handsome and gentle Scotsman, who had ambitions to be a surgeon.

He is the sort who ploughs up and down the swimming pool in a straight line.

Following post-graduate medical training and having passed excruciatingly hard exams to become a Member of the Royal College of Physicians, we were married. I wanted a career in hospital medicine, but no sooner were we married than Gus accepted an excellent training rotation in rural North Wales. As it would have been impossible for me to do higher training as a Physician from this remote area, I started alternative training to become a GP. This change of intention was difficult to accept for a good few years.

During the next years, when we were moving annually with his jobs, I had Sophie, our daughter. I became a partner in a GP practice in Stoke, only to have to leave it after six short months due to Gus's promotion. Surgeons are an odd bunch, not blessed with great negotiation skills, rather tending to spearhead major decisions which they expect everyone else to support and fall in with. I am a faller-inner. We spent six months in Africa, when Sophie was 2, where I enjoyed not working for once. After we finally settled in York, I became a GP in a lovely practice, where I worked happily for twenty years.

Following many years of dashed hopes trying for a second child, Max arrived, but from the start he appeared compromised. He has autism, with learning and physical disabilities. When he was 13, I decided to retire early, to have time for myself whilst he is at school, and to look after him. Over the years, I found support services frequently let me down at the last minute and in our family the buck stops with me. As he became older, it was more difficult to find friends or babysitters that I could ask to look after him for a few hours, so it was easier when I stopped regular work. Now when the school has an unannounced training day, or finishes early, I know I will be able to relinquish other activities and look after Jack.

I am interested in creative pursuits. I am studying ceramics for a day a week at Art College, and am a member of a large community choir. I enjoy walking in the beautiful Yorkshire countryside, or playing bridge with friends. Gus has also retired early and we can spend some time together when we are not sharing the caring for Max. Sophie, our daughter, is an all-round high achiever and, raising her, there were plenty of high hoops she could jump through. An entirely new world has revealed itself to me through being Max's Mum. Now it's not so much jumping through high hoops, as struggling slowly over low bars. Although demanding, it is also enriching in many and varied ways.

I relish the involvement I have had with our writing group and am thrilled and proud to present our book.

INTRODUCING SUSAN

My parents met during the war when my father was training at the Ordnance Depot in Chilwell where my mother worked as a typist. They married in 1944 and I was born in 1948. I was an only child; there was a sister who had been born the previous year but she was stillborn and my parents were told that there was something severely wrong with her spine. My safe arrival was welcomed and I was loved and treasured. I spent many happy hours playing with friends and loved being outdoors. I was also happy doing things on my own such as reading, sewing and drawing. I loved writing stories and as a small child, I often lay in bed at night telling stories to my dolls and teddy bears.

I was bullied at primary school; I think the bullies sensed that I was useless at standing up for myself and made my life a misery. Verbal bullying happened at my grammar school too and consequently I had very little confidence or belief in myself and my abilities.

I left school at sixteen after sitting my O Levels and went to work in a department store in York. I wanted to do something creative rather than working in an office like most of my school friends so I trained to become a Window Dresser and attended a part time course at Art School. The following year, in 1965, an unplanned pregnancy put paid to my ideas of an artistic career. I married my boyfriend and my beautiful daughter, Karen, was born when I was seventeen and Paul was twenty. Two years later, Karen was joined by her brother Steven. The marriage was not made in heaven, my romantic ideas of love and marriage soon turned to dust and we separated when I was twenty. However, I am thankful that the relationship was blessed with two lovely children. I became a single parent struggling to make ends meet and support my children on my social security allowance. A year later, I found a job in the Civil Service and because my starting salary was fairly low, I was lucky to be offered free Day Nursery places for the children. Such provision existed in the 1960s and 70s.

In 1975, I met Tom and we married the following year. He accepted the children as if they were his own and we have had some wonderful family outings and holidays. We are very happy together.

I wanted to further my education and had always been an avid reader so I studied A Levels in English Literature and Sociology at evening classes. I started studying with the Open University in 1979. I took a number of psychology courses because I find the human mind and human behaviour fascinating. My OU courses also included "The Handicapped Person in the Community" and "Special Needs in Education" Karen had been diagnosed as being "mentally handicapped" when she was six years old and I wanted to understand more about this and to find out how I could best help and encourage her to reach her potential. I liked the way both courses focused on abilities rather than disabilities and helped me to have a positive outlook. I was awarded my BA (OU) in 1985 and in 2006, studied "Tradition, Modernity and Change", a sociology of religion course, to complete my Honours degree.

I joined the PTA of Karen's ESN school where I first met Pauline. Later, we both campaigned against the closure of a workshop for people with learning disabilities that our daughters attended. I was also involved in a another campaign against the closure of a similar workshop. These experiences along with advocating on behalf of Karen, helped me to develop skills that were useful for my workplace Trade Union role such as campaigning to save jobs and negotiating on behalf of members and speaking at conferences. I have always found it easier to speak out on others behalf rather than my own but my style is negotiation rather than confrontation.

I am now retired and enjoy walking in the countryside or by the coast with my husband, singing songs from around the world with a community choir, reading and visiting the theatre and cinema. I love dancing and go to circle dancing classes and classes in Egyptian and Arabic folkloric dance and have taken part in dance performances at community events and on stage. I am also a volunteer "Befriender" for Age UK. Being part of the Caring Expressions creative writing group has given me a chance to rediscover the satisfaction of expressing myself in writing and telling a story. I have often felt that I have a story to tell.

INTRODUCING PAULINE

I was born in 1939 in India where my father was stationed in the British Army and my mother was a children's nanny. I have two younger sisters and a brother. I was married for almost 25 years and I have a son and a daughter who I love dearly. I met my husband in the 1960's at Guy's Hospital, when he was a patient on the ward I was working on, as a newly qualified staff nurse. We moved from London to York when the children were quite young to be nearer my family. I carried on with my nursing career until Alison was diagnosed as mentally handicapped. I decided then that I would give it up to take care of my daughter myself, rather than have a succession of child-minders, as I thought she had enough to cope with. My husband and I built up a successful electrical contracting company, which enabled me to work from home and to take care of my daughter.

I developed dependency on alcohol and tranquillisers, which eventually resulted in hospital treatment, and from which I have recovered. After my divorce in 1987 I suffered a mental breakdown which again resulted in admission to hospital for several months.

Following discharge from hospital and on-going psychotherapy, and able to live my own life at last, I applied to go to university as a mature student – something I had always wanted to do. I gained a degree in English Literature and Social Science at York St John University.

I went on to work for various charitable organisations and got more involved with groups working to improve the lives of people with learning disabilities and family carers. This proved to be invaluable in increasing my self-confidence and gave me a real sense of purpose.

My hobbies include organic gardening – I grow my own fruit and vegetables, reading, circle dancing and more recently Zumba Gold. Now I am retired I am fulfilling my lifelong dream of writing.

INTRODUCING LIZ

I was born in 1946, the first most welcome child of my parents who had only been married the year before and my father was yet to be demobbed. Two brothers followed and we spent our early years in rural Suffolk. A lot of time was spent on windswept beaches, which has left me with an enduring fondness for plunging in the icy sea and an ability to enjoy myself against the odds. I went to two convent schools and with hindsight I am amazed how much I loved it. I would like to report that this produced a rebellious critical spirit, but I was happy with the nuns and the spinsters who taught us. I was the kind of child who was always Mary or the Angel Gabriel in the nativity plays and sadly, I am still the kind of person who won't cross a pedestrian crossing when the red man is there.

After university, as many of my friends did in those days, I got married in a very proper manner with lots of bridesmaids and lots of pyrex casseroles for presents. My husband is a very competent guy. In contrast to myself who is messy and disorganised and loses keys and purses and mobile phones, he has never even scratched a car in decades of driving, never spills his soup down his shirt and always looks, as his mother would have put it 'well turned out'. He is probably a workaholic, but as we progress towards old age, we are like a pair of old slippers, comfortable in our forty five year old marriage.

After working in higher education for years, now my only academic activity is attending an evening class with two friends and a thermos of coffee to keep us awake. Shamefully I spend a fortune on gym membership and this can mean that a single swim can cost up to £50 if other things get in the way. We inherited a dog from one son's marriage break-up and never having had a dog before we are amazed at our mutual devotion: the dog loves us and we love her. Much of my time is spent trying to keep Sally, our daughter, occupied, but a lot of time is also spent helping our other three children through various difficulties. I sometimes console Sally by pointing out the incredible muddles her siblings have created for themselves, despite their supposed greater intelligence. The things I used to teach about in sociology I have now experienced through my kids: illness, depression, addiction, divorce and unemployment. Life has been far from smooth, but it has always been so very, very interesting.

INTRODUCING PAT

I was born in Egypt. My father was serving in the Royal Air Force at that time, during the 1950's. Much of my early life, obviously not remembered by me, was spent moving around the UK, my mother, older brother and me following my father around each time a new posting came up.

My early education was overshadowed by the fact that a regular move every 1 to 2 years or so resulted in me being put into, and taken out of various primary schools at least 6 times. It included two separate short sessions in a Bristol Primary School, my grandparents in Bristol being where my mother would be deposited along with us children to await a suitable house to be allocated at the Air Force base my father had moved to. I always remember being the 'new girl' in the playground and found it hard to make new friends and be accepted by my peer group. No wonder I was always shy and introverted. I accepted being 'excluded' from peer group friendships as the norm. We moved during my 11 plus year, and I ended up being subjected to the most appalling emotional bullying by a group of girls who lived on the base, which continued throughout my secondary education. Looking back, I don't know how I survived; it's so true, the saying that what doesn't kill you makes you stronger!

I met my future husband whilst studying for 'A' Levels. He was a serviceman, and despite all my misgivings about marrying into service life we married 18 months after meeting. Shortly after marrying, we moved to Kenya, East Africa, where we lived in Nairobi for 3 years. It was a wonderful experience learning to live in a strange beautiful country, with its diverse population. The wildlife was breathtaking and I think we saw the country at it's best in those times. Even in the 1970s Nairobi was very much a cosmopolitan and polyglot city, with not only its native African and Indian population, but also many ex-patriots from different countries living and working together. I learnt a lot about poverty amongst the indigenous population, and sadly became aware of undercurrents of corruption within the Kikuyu African Government. During this time, unable to get a work permit, I continued to study part-time and polished up on my qualifications to enable me to get a better job and develop a career.

On returning to UK I went back to full time work, and 10 years after marrying, I felt I had reached a point in my working life that, at that time in the late 1970's, was about as far as I felt I could go as a married woman. I was the Personal Assistant to the Managing Director of a company in York, and I loved my job. However, destiny had different plans, and although I was never very interested in becoming a mother in the earlier years of my marriage, I found myself caught up in an overwhelming maternal instinct in my late 20's.

My son was born in May 1979, and three and a half (relatively peaceful) years later, my daughter was born in December 1982. It was like being hit by a brick wall. My son had been a happy, content and compliant baby. Not so my daughter! Colic and ear infections were just the beginning of years of uncertainty and struggling to cope with what appeared to be a difficult, uncooperative and frustrated child. At around 18 months old she was initially diagnosed with general delayed development. Thus my life was taken down a very different path to the one I had imagined for my family and myself. Finally, years later she was diagnosed as being on the Autism spectrum, with Aspergers Syndrome at aged 19. It was such a relief to have a label and a reason at last behind all the difficult times, although naturally mixed with feelings of great sadness and loss.

As a family we love traveling and have visited many parts of the world. As well as working part-time once my daughter was settled into school, I also continued with my education on a part-time basis over the years, and enjoyed studying a variety of subjects and also gaining qualifications along the way. This has enabled me to finish my working life as a Schools Business Manager. Combining the studying at home, with a responsible job, motherhood and domestic chores was not easy, but made possible with a very supportive husband. I often think it was a kind of coping mechanism to keep me going, and also enabled me to be in control of at least one area of my life. My early education had been very messy to say the least and I never felt my true potential had been reached. On eventually gaining my Diploma in Business Management, I felt a real sense of achievement.

I think my early childhood years of constant change and, later, having to cope with bullying in my early teens, helped me to learn to be resilient. Learning to cope with being the parent of a child with a learning disability was not easy, and I fought many battles with the establishment along the way to ensure my daughter got the best available help at every stage in her life. Being a parent of a child, and now young adult daughter with Aspergers, has been a long slow painful process of constant readjustment and reassessment of life. I believe I am a very different person to the one I might have been had I not had this path in life. I will never know, of course, but I like to think it has made me a more empathetic, caring and selfless person than I might otherwise have been, and possibly once was.

INTRODUCING GILLIAN

I have always enjoyed working out how other people tick. My early childhood as a daughter of academics was spent in the USA, with a year in Europe, attending schools in England and France when I was six. My British parents had friends from when they lived in an International House in California, and their time in Australia, where I was born. Thus I was brought up in the midst of many nationalities and cultures, and needed to adapt to new ideas. I was a clumsy child, with an eye patch, and never felt that I was living up to my mothers' expectations. Nowadays I would be labelled as having dyspraxia (difficulty in coordinating and sequencing movements). I spent a lot of time immersed in books, as this was something I could do easily. When I was eleven we moved to Britain permanently so that I could start secondary school at the right age.

I chose a career in Speech and Language Therapy because of my interest in language and communication. After five years of working mainly with children and adults with disabilities I took a career break for seven years to raise my three children, two of whom have special needs. Subsequently I only worked part-time because of my role as a carer. My older son has dyspraxia, and needed very little help apart from additional time to complete exams because he writes very slowly. He now works in a senior position for an international aid charity. His brother continues to need support, but leads a full life in the community. My daughter has two little girls, and I enjoy watching their development as well as joining in their enthusiastic play. I feel my daughter has had to live in the shadow of her brothers.

When I heard that there was a group of carers planning to write about their lives with their adult children and young people with learning disabilities, I felt that this would be an opportunity to explore my experiences and emotions now that my boys have left home. I had previously contributed to a book about my experience of having a child with disabilities. My motivation is also to encourage other parents of "different" children to celebrate their achievements. I would like to give a flavour of what it is like to grow up as a child with difficulties, and of how hard it is to gain the courage to attempt new challenges when anxious that one may get it wrong yet again. It has taken me a long time to learn to trust myself, and I am still fragile and easily knocked down.

I would like to give members of the public, including professionals, an understanding of the impact that their attitudes and actions can have on people with disabilities and their families.

INTRODUCING OUR CHILDREN

INTRODUCING SALLY

I was happy to be pregnant for the third time. I was young and fit and my two sons were thriving and we were happily settled. All seemed to go well during the pregnancy, although I occasionally wondered if this baby was less vigorous than the other two. I was certainly annoyed and disconcerted when she was nineteen days late when the other two had been an obliging four days earlier than the expected date. However the birth at home was straightforward and she was the hoped-for daughter. She was a beautiful baby with lots of black hair and big blue eyes. The realisation that something was not right crept up on us slowly. She was late in reaching all the milestones. Finally, when another mother whose child had been labelled 'learning disabled' told me her daughter did not walk until she was two, which was the same age as Sally, I forced myself to recognise what I had known for a while, that for my daughter life would never be the same as it was for her siblings.

Education in most of its forms was hard for Sally. In mainstream primary school she struggled in vain to keep up with her peers. In special school she struggled with the stigma of not being in mainstream school. She also struggled with the unwanted attentions of male pupils. In boarding school she struggled with being away from home. On her 'Independence' course she just struggled.

However she did eventually learn to do most of the things that other people learned at much earlier ages. She learned to read and write although she never did grasp any arithmetic. At home she learned to tie her shoe laces and wash her hair. She learned to swim and ride a bike. She learned to cope with injections and blood tests and how to swallow pills. She also learned many of the skills needed for living in twenty first century Britain. She can find her way around the Internet, use a mobile phone, use an ATM (all too well!). She can pay cheques into the bank using a machine and use a self- service check out.

Nevertheless there are many things which are impossible or challenging for her. Although she can read, she would find it hard to read a whole book. She can ride a bike but wouldn't be safe on a busy road or riding through the city. She can find her way around the shops but would not be able to give the exact money for something costing six pounds thirty four or to check her change. She can write but filling in a housing benefit form would be beyond her. She can withdraw money from a bank but could not readily give the fourth digit of her security code. Her writing is difficult to read and her spelling idiosyncratic, yet she is the mistress of the elegant written apology. Her dexterity with mobile phones has quite often landed her in trouble as she texts people constantly and expresses frustration to her bosses in extremely inappropriate language. Even as she nears forty we are constantly surprised at the things she can do and the things she cannot do.

Liz

INTRODUCING WILLIAM

William is a friendly young man of 31, who thoroughly enjoys being the life and soul of the party. He collects friends and loves connecting with them through social media. His main peer support group springs from the congregation of a lively church, of which he is an enthusiastic member.

William lives in a whirl of constant activity – he cycles long distances with friends, enjoys swimming, and regularly goes to the cinema, catching all the latest action movies. He is also a willing volunteer at an international student café and with a "Besom" project, where he loves delivering furniture and decorating homes for people in need. Work is another component to William's busy life. He has held down a part-time job at a coffee shop for seven years – when he makes a commitment, he sticks to it!

William lives fairly independently in a privately rented shared flat with four others. He has limited contact with his support workers, restricting this mainly to times when he needs help with official paperwork. William gets stressed and distressed when unexpected things happen or when he has not fully understood what he has been told. He finds it hard to see things from other people's perspectives, which can lead to anger or grumpiness, but usually he bounces back quickly. He hates having unstructured time, and has become expert at filling any gaps in his schedule, sometimes double-booking himself because he has forgotten to use his diary.

William is rarely at home because of his multitude of passions. Having done a performing arts course at college, William has taken part in the York Mystery Plays and other community dramas. His interest in sport has led to a qualification in sports leadership and as a swimming pool lifeguard. He is disappointed that these have not led to employment, but adequate support has not been available. William has also achieved his gold Duke of Edinburgh award.

Did I remember to mention that William has been diagnosed as having dyslexia, dyspraxia, ADHD and Asperger's Syndrome?

Gillian

INTRODUCING CLAIRE

Claire was born in December 1982, after a normal labour and delivery. She struggled to feed, suffering from colic, and was not a happy baby. As time went by, it became apparent to me, and my husband, that she was not developing at what could be perceived a 'normal' rate. She was my second child and although I tried hard not to make comparisons, her development was questionable.

After moving to York when she was 18 months old, she was referred to the Child Development Centre. Initially diagnosed with general delayed development and a speech and language learning difficulty, she entered mainstream primary school, with some support, and struggled with all aspects of school life. She never seemed to be able to make much contact with her peers and consequently was perceived very early on as being 'different'. When she was 10 we made a conscious decision to move her to a special school, and she attended a school for moderate learning difficulties until she was 16 years old. She was one of the brighter children in her class, and in contrast to how she was in mainstream school, she blossomed and benefited a great deal from being one of the higher achievers. Her self esteem and confidence grew. At 16 she went to York College, where she did a foundation course for special needs pupils, finishing up with an NVQ2 in Hospitality. When she was 19, she was finally diagnosed as being on the Autism spectrum, with Asperger's Syndrome.

She is a complex character. Sometimes she astounds us with her astuteness and absolute black and white view of the world. If something isn't right, she is quick to point out any anomalies, sometimes oblivious to the complexities of socially acceptable boundaries. She has a great sense of humour and is great company on holidays. She loves to travel. She has phases of obsessions. For several years she adored all classical music, and collected masses of CDs, listening avidly to Classic FM. During this phase, and even now, she can name either the piece or the composer of most pieces of classical music that she hears. She also enjoys pop music, and has a great deal of knowledge about current trends in popular music genre. She is loving and affectionate and needs constant reassurance that she is loved. She still sometimes finds it hard to control her emotions and can be warm and loving one minute and then engulfed in anger about some small issue over which she has no control. The tantrums have lessened with maturity thankfully, and we have learned to cope by heading off any impending 'explosions' whenever we can. Not easy at times!

She was fortunate to find employment with Sainsburys, which started when she was 18 with a Saturday job, until she finished her 3 year course at York College. Unfortunately, eczema and an allergy to certain cleaning products spoilt her chances of pursuing her job in catering, working in Sainsburys public cafe, which she enjoyed and hoped to continue. She had to move out of the café environment and became a general store assistant, working in various departments.

Sadly, she became ill in 2005 with Ulcerative Colitis, an autoimmune disease, which affects the large bowel, and in severe cases such as Claire's, radical abdominal surgery is the last resort as a means of controlling the condition and preventing a rupture of the bowel, which can be fatal. The surgery took place when she was 25 and has limited her choices in life: the after effects of the radical surgery means she has required periods of constant nursing care, both at home and in hospital. Plans for supported independent living away from home have had to be put on hold. In the meantime she remains living at home. Further surgery in 2012 improved the situation and we are hopeful that she can continue with her life. After a lot of time off work ill during 2012, she has recently managed to resume her full 18 hours at work a week.

I feel humbled at the way in which Claire has coped with the consequences of all the surgery she has had. I think that being Asperger's has somehow helped her to accept what has happened to her body, and proves how much strength of character she has. She has no sense of vanity at all – unlike most young women of her age. Yes, we still grieve for the life she might have had, had she not suffered with Asperger's, but we are very proud of the way she still remains cheerful and positive about life, despite all that has happened to her. I know that being a carer has changed me as a person, and I am convinced for the better. We will never know what our lives might have been like had she not been 'special', but she will always be our ray of sunshine.

Pat

INTRODUCING ANDREW

At the time of writing this book Andrew is 18 years old – a typical teenage boy, full of 'attitude', oppositional and trying to find where he fits in this world. He generally wakes up smiling and stays that way most of the day, but he certainly has no problem with letting people know when he is not happy. He has a winning smile, a wicked sense of humour and he is an outrageous flirt who appears entirely content in his own skin.

Andrew really enjoys watching DVDs, weekend stays with his friends, after school sports club, going out for walks to look at nature (he particularly likes trees), and going out on his trike. He has lots of friends at school, and several girls in particular who vie for his attention while he remains cool and aloof. A far cry from his mother at 17 – a shrinking violet who would apologise to a lamppost for bumping into it.

One thing Andrew really loves is travel – whether it be by car, train, boat or aeroplane. He particularly loves flying, and gets very excited as we approach the airport and see the planes.

Andrew has no medical diagnosis, but was given the label "Global Developmental Delay" around the age of 2. He has been deemed to have profound and multiple learning disabilities, but the terminology keeps changing. We have no idea whether he has a genetic disorder, whether his problems were present before birth, caused during his delivery by caesarean section 8 weeks early, a result of the fits he suffered when he was 8 weeks old, or the bronchiolitis which nearly claimed his life at the age of 8 months. I have written several pieces in this book about Andrew's early years and his health issues, of which there were many.

Andrew has had a gastrostomy for the last 16 years, and stopped eating altogether at the age of 8, for reasons which were never fully established, but which we believe could have been related to a change in the lunchtime routine at school. In 2012 he started eating again, thanks to the patience, persistence and ingenuity of his class teacher.

The only time he seems to get angry or upset is when he is trying to let us know he is unhappy or unwell, when we take him into shops, or when we stop him from indulging one of his favourite pastimes – swinging curtains or vertical blinds. Andrew has no speech and no effective means of communication. He is entirely dependent on adults for all his physical care, to keep him safe and to interpret his needs as best they can. On the whole he is very tolerant of our shortcomings.

Andrew is essentially a wheelchair user, although he has always been able to walk with a frame, or by holding onto someone's hand. Our local supermarket raised money to buy him a custom built tricycle in 2009, and it was less than 3 months later that Andrew, aged 13, initiated his first independent steps. Andrew still needs his wheelchair for distances, but he can walk around inside school with close supervision. Notwithstanding the years of physiotherapy, surgery to both his feet, various complementary therapies, and the support and encouragement of school and medical staff, we feel certain that the trike was the catalyst to finally get Andrew on his feet. Watch this space!

Linda

INTRODUCING ALISON

My daughter Alison was born in 1964 and is 49 years old. The only diagnosis she had ever had is that of mental handicap, until last year, when she was finally assessed as being on the autistic spectrum.

Alison is a very warm, loving woman with a personality which attracts people to her. She doesn't however, get on with other people with learning disabilities, who she finds difficult to understand or empathise with. She much prefers to be around "normal" people.

The most difficult aspect of life for Alison is dealing with change of any kind. It has a serious adverse emotional effect on her. She prefers the status quo, familiarity of people, places and objects as these give her some sense of security in a world she finds difficult to understand. She can be quite courageous, and generally speaks her mind, as she sees it, but she can be incredibly worried about upsetting people. If she is disappointed or upset, she can become very distressed and agitated and verbally aggressive, which is difficult to deal with.

She is interested in wildlife, avidly watching TV programmes like Spring Watch or David Attenborough's documentaries. Her particular love is dolphins, and many of our holidays have been in Scotland in an effort to find somewhere she could actually see live ones. To our great delight, she finally saw them from the shore at Chanonry Point in Scotland. She also loves bird-watching and visiting RSPB reserves. She reads a little and enjoys word search puzzles. Growing plants – flowers, tomatoes and strawberries is another activity she gets pleasure from. Her love of pop music is centred on Robbie Williams and TakeThat and she regularly goes to TakeThat tribute concerts. Her most recent passion is for Zumba Gold fitness classes, which she enjoys immensely and has made lots of new friends there.

Her post school education gave her an NVQ qualification in catering and lots of certificates in creative activities from Askham Bryan College.

Some years ago she was given the opportunity of some part-time work in a delicatessen but unfortunately this didn't last for long. Since then she has done voluntary work at York Hospital first in the WRVS coffee shop and after that closed, in the hospital restaurant for one morning a week.

After many changes of accommodation which you will hear about, finally we seem to have found the right place for her. She has been fortunate to be able to buy her own bungalow under a shared ownership scheme and is very proud and happy in her own home. She lives on her own with some support during the day, with support staff coming on at 9pm and staying overnight.

Alison has a 'circle of support' which meets every two or three months at her home and is very important to her. Members of her circle help her to socialise with meals out, visits to their homes and accompanying her to activities such as card-making classes. They also help to encourage and support her with whatever is going on in her life.

Alison has a full life, with activities to do during the day, good support from her care providers and her family, and interaction with people in the community. However, she still lacks basic self-confidence and all this is achieved with an enormous amount of emotional and physical support and constant reassurance and encouragement.

Pauline

INTRODUCING KAREN

When Karen is happy, she smiles a lot and many people have commented on her lovely smile and beautiful eyes. She has a laugh that is both loud and infectious. If she has a good day, she will excitedly tell people what she has been doing. If she is unhappy, she will become withdrawn and may drop her head and avoid making eye contact. She can have problems interacting with others and finds it more comfortable to be in one-to-one situations with people. She needs time and encouragement to express how she feels. Sometimes, if she is being asked a question, she will not look at the person asking the question but will address the answer to someone else, to me if I am there. Sometimes, she does not respond and may not have heard the question, possibly because she is thinking about something else and finds it hard to deal with more than one thing at a time. Or she may start talking about a completely different topic and tends to talk at people as she does not understand about taking turns in conversation.

Karen can find changes in routine or staff upsetting. If she knows that someone is leaving that she has formed a close relationship with, such as a Key Worker, she becomes very anxious and there will be a period of grieving. If she knows she is going to meet someone new, a professional person for example, she can feel quite worried about meeting a "stranger". Once she has met the new person and got to know them a little, she is happy to be in their company. Meeting people spontaneously is not a problem: for example, if we bump into a friend of mine that Karen has not met before, she is relaxed and chatty. Crowded or noisy environments can also make her feel anxious but she does enjoy being in congenial company such as a family gathering and enjoys going out for a meal or a hot chocolate and cake. Karen enjoys going to the theatre to see a show, ballet or pantomime. Sometimes it can be difficult to encourage her go on an outing or to a party, but if she does go, she invariably enjoys herself and has a really good time.

Although Karen is forty seven years old, she still needs to be reminded to clean her teeth, change her clothes or have a bath. Occasionally, this might result in an outburst because she feels that she is being treated like a child. If she feels stressed, she can become very "shouty" and she can sometimes become verbally aggressive with people. Usually, she says sorry afterwards and will hug the other person. Her residential home has introduced a system using charts and symbols to help her express herself and this has resulted in less anxiety and hence less shouting. She is awarded with stars for remembering to clean her teeth, change her underwear and for not shouting.

Having set routines and working on a one-to-one basis helps her to feel secure and she enjoys going to her day centre each weekday where she has a regular timetable of activities. She is quite creative and has designed greetings cards that are sold in the shop. She particularly enjoys her two woodwork days when she helps to make items such as boxes for plant pots and to carry out repairs. She notices if things such as shelves need repairing and will keep reminding people that they need fixing. She is very proud of her tool box and enjoys looking at and buying tools in DIY shops and she is fascinated by tool sheds. She also enjoys using a computer to do some typing and also look at websites, perhaps at places or exhibitions she has visited or information about a film, ballet or show.

Karen loves animals, particularly dogs, cats and donkeys and is interested in wildlife, especially birds and is good at recognising them and remembering their names. For instance, she knows the difference between a coot and a moorhen and will remember the names of different types of geese that she sees on the river or in the park: greylag, barnacle or canada. She likes frogs too and becomes very excited when she sees tadpoles or frogs. She has a collection of frog ornaments and toys. She also enjoys visiting a donkey sanctuary near Leeds where she sponsors a rescue donkey called "Billy".

Karen has a learning disability and in 2011, she was diagnosed as having autistic spectrum disorder. She lives in a residential home and during the week attends a centre for people with special needs.

Susan

INTRODUCING MAX

As with so many things in life, when you give up trying for it, it happens. So it was with Max, who kept his family waiting for eight long years, then surprised us by arriving at the last chance saloon, when all hope of having a second child had gone.

He was born four weeks prematurely, and what a joyous occasion it was when we heard his first gentle crying. The midwife allowed Sophie, his sister, who was 10, to fix a clip to his umbilical cord and dress him in his first tiny vest. He smiled his way through everything and when not smiling, was sleeping. His breathing seemed erratic and with long gaps. We took him to hospital after one of these apnoeic attacks and were reassured. He had tiny pin-point pupils and white irises, only to turn a lovely gentle green colour much later. He could only see shades of light for the first 10 months and would look at the border of my head against the background, not at any of my features. This, we were told was called delayed visual maturation and in fact, all of him was delayed. 'Delayed development is not like a delayed train, which will eventually arrive,' the paediatrician said, 'sometimes, the train never arrives.'

He is now in the learning support section of mainstream school, aiming for music GCSE as well as several softer GCSEs in life-skills, and personal and social development. He is handsome, placid and undemanding, with a sunny disposition which endears him to all. 'In the air, there is love,' he says to me and 'if there's one thing about you, it's love.' Apart from an interest in expressing love, he is riveted by planes, birds, animals, trains, flowers, butterflies, moths, vintage vehicles, the weather, the second world war and the songs thereof, other music-mainly big band, jazz, swing, Sinatra, Bing and musicals. Then there is his singing, which is so beautiful, tuneful and word perfect too. Singing is a pastime he and I both enjoy and can share, especially on our long and usually slow countryside rambles. In the family, we all go together on many 'big days out' or 'BDOs' which usually incorporate something of interest and, as he volunteers plenty of facts and opinions, he is good company to have around. Seemingly even-handedly, he shares many of his natural history obsessions with Gus, his Dad, so they have plenty in common. They even attend RSPB York and York Ornithology club together: little and large. He has one main school friend and on the way to youth club, they will chat in the car, keeping each other right about school happenings like two old men in a café.

In addition to autism, and learning disability, he is unable to write, due to a bilateral hand tremor, but he can use a keyboard. Max needs help with self-care activities such as washing, brushing teeth, showering, and fastening buttons. He has poor road sense, as unexpected sounds make him jump and shake with fear, especially barking dogs, or revving engines. It is unlikely he could live independently and he will require life-long support. 'I'm fine,' he says, 'I can manage,' and then you find he doesn't manage, which tugs at your heart. Sophie will oversee his living arrangements, but she will have her own family and work commitments. I often think, 'Who will love him and care for him as we do, when we are gone?'

Annie

THE THINGS PEOPLE SAY

SUSAN AND KAREN

"She'll Never Be Brilliant"

After her first year of schooling, Karen was transferred from a mainstream school to a school for children with physical disabilities. Shortly before the end of the summer term, I attended a review meeting at the school with Karen's class teacher, the head teacher and a paediatrician. I was told that she had made very little progress. "But she's bright in some ways" I said. "In what ways, because we haven't noticed it?" responded the head teacher. "She's good at remembering people and places" I said. The paediatrician told me bluntly that Karen was retarded. When I asked what the outlook was and what progress she might make, he said "Well, she'll never be brilliant" The rug had been pulled from under my feet and my hopes shattered.

"Why on earth did she have another child?"

Shortly after Tom and I married in 1976, Tom submitted a written request, to the area office of the bank that employed him, requesting that he would not be transferred to a branch outside the York area because his eleven year old stepdaughter attended a special school for educationally subnormal children and was very happy and settled there. A week or two later, Tom's boss, the bank manager, called him into his office for an interview and told him that the bank had agreed to this and a note would be put on his file. He then asked how old Karen's brother was and whether he was "normal". "He's almost nine and yes, he is" Tom replied. "Why on earth did she have another child?" his boss asked.

GILLIAN AND WILLIAM

1982 – From birth, William had a particularly penetrating cry, which all the staff and Mums in the hospital ward quickly learned to recognise. He seemed to save up the most ear-shattering screeches for mealtimes, when we were all sitting together in the middle of the ward for Mums who needed extra care following delivery of their babies. Nobody could fail to notice the loud screams, and the ward sister christened him "the demon William," which everyone but me found hilarious. What a label for a baby to receive before being a week old! I did have to agree secretly with the nurse's "diagnosis", but was not impressed by William's new title.

1983 – William was referred to a gastro-enterologist when he was 14 months old, for investigation of possible coeliac disease or cystic fibrosis, as he was failing to thrive. The dietician was called in. "It's a pity you haven't been feeding him biscuits and chocolate – he'd have put on weight then." I was startled to hear this from a dietician.

At this same admission to hospital, William's cry drew attention. One of the nurses requested, "Please will you shut your child up – he's disturbing all the other parents and children." This was an impossible ask, but I started taking him to the parents' room in an attempt to keep him away from those who were trying to rest. This was also frowned upon, as I was exposing my child to additional sources of infection. It was three days before one of the nurses offered to look after William to give me a chance to go down to the hospital canteen to have a meal. I was distinctly hungry by then!

1992 – "If you hadn't worked so hard with him and masked his problems, we would have realised the extent of his special needs a long time ago." This was at a medical assessment for ten-year-old William to determine whether he should have a statement of special educational needs, something I had tried to negotiate for several years. Why on earth would I not support my own child in an attempt to overcome at least some of his difficulties? I had already been told by a child psychiatrist that William was neither autistic nor hyperactive. Eight years later I was actually delighted when he was finally diagnosed as having Asperger's Syndrome and ADHD.

ANNIE AND MAX

The Paediatrician

The paediatrician said, 'You know this term developmental delay? We often think of delay being like a delayed train, which will eventually arrive. But sometimes, you know, the train never arrives. Have you any questions?' And with that, he glanced at his watch. He looked at me with an expression similar to that of a clergyman who thinks you've fallen from God's favour in some way and shook his head sadly. He patted me on the back as if to say, 'keep up the good work, you'll certainly need to with THAT child.' I was then ushered quickly from the room, as he had obviously run out of any other helpful things to say.

The Friend

One of my friends said with an air of commiseration and pity:"I do feel so sorry for you Annie. It must be so hard having Max, especially after having Sophie who is just a golden girl. He's a delightful little chap, of course, but it must be very demanding. I always say to everybody, 'Annie and Gus used to be the Posh and Becks of the village and THEN they had Max.'"

We now have to cope not only with a disabled child, but with loss of status too it seems.

The Ticket Sales Person

I asked for a concessionary ticket to go into a children's farm near York. I said, 'My child is disabled and I'm his carer.' She looked at me, then at him and saw nothing untoward in his appearance. 'What's wrong with him then?' she retorted scathingly. 'He's autistic and has physical disabilities as well,' I had to explain. Max, and the rest of the queue were listening to all this. I wonder how the child felt. In a reject box with 'faulty' written on it? Now I have a carer's card, which if I'm lucky, or have thought ahead, will be in my bag when needed. Usually, I am not lucky or have failed to think ahead, but this grilling has only happened to me once. However, I am always nervous when approaching the ticket booth and pathetically grateful to be believed without question by the attendant.

PAT AND CLAIRE

This is a comment made to me by the Headteacher of my daughter's first Primary School in 1988.

It was 1988. My daughter was aged 6 and had started school the year before with a Statement of Educational Needs, at the local Primary School. I had gone in to see the Headteacher following a particularly nasty act of bullying carried out in the playground, by twin boys who were extremely unruly and badly behaved, and, not for the first time, sensed my daughter's vulnerability as she struggled to fit in with school life. Her new leather Clarks shoes had been ruined. The previous day the boys had stamped on her shoes at the toe end so badly that one was left permanently indented, and her toes badly bruised. I had to keep her off school until they had healed.

Following a brief discussion about the incident in which he seemed to be questioning the accusation of 'bullying', the Headteacher commented, "Of course, Claire is a little peculiar isn't she"? Needless to say I was speechless and walked out in disgust, aghast at the ignorance of someone in such a position of trust. He was implying that Claire had "asked for it" because she didn't quite fit the "norm". Thankfully, since then I have recovered my confidence and voice which at that vulnerable time had deserted me. He would not have been allowed to get away with making that remark had I been my usual self, without serious consequences. As far as I know, no action was taken against the two boys by this headteacher, and no apology made. The class teacher, thankfully, was more sympathetic. I was relieved when this 'dinosaur' eventually retired!

Although the gentleman concerned is no longer living, I wonder if he ever thought about the effect it would have on me as a parent by making such a comment. Claire already had a 'Statement of Educational Needs' indicating she had moderate learning difficulties, so surely he must have realised how inappropriate his comment was. I have certainly never forgotten it, and my lasting memory of him is unfortunately this incident.

LINDA AND ANDREW

1998

"What's his prognosis?" asks one of my midwifery colleagues. Andrew is 2 years old, and I have only just returned to work following a year's sick leave with post-traumatic stress. I am shocked by the bluntness of her question. Fighting back the tears I tell her I don't know. I really should have said, "I have no idea, what's yours?"

2000

"What's wrong with him?" We are in a gift shop in Pitlochry. Andrew is 4 years old and is in a McLaren pushchair. To me, he looks like any other child in a pushchair, but a complete stranger has just come up to me and uttered those words. I am incensed at this intrusion, and I want to say "Absolutely nothing. He is perfect", but instead I hear myself saying "He has global developmental delay".

2013

I received an email today from an old friend I haven't seen since Andrew was a baby. She has a son two years older, and a daughter who was born a few months after Andrew. "Hi, how are you? Rob is at Uni now and Cathy is hoping to take a nursing degree. It feels like there is finally a light at the end of the tunnel. Now I have got more time on my hands, it would be lovely to meet up. Let me know when you are free". The reality hits home very hard. For me, Andrew's transition to adulthood means more responsibility for us as he will need support to access social, educational and occupational opportunities, and to forge a future without us. There is certainly no light visible at the end of this tunnel.

PAULINE AND ALISON

"But she needs to be somewhere she can be looked after". I gazed at my ex-husband in disbelief. Since Alison was first diagnosed as having learning disabilities, and all the way through our marriage of almost 25 years I had tried to help Alison be as independent as possible in order to avoid 'being looked after'. I wanted above all for her to live a life as happy and as normal as possible. She was now in her 30's and had just moved into a bungalow, sharing with three other girls, but with fairly minimal support. The bungalow was set in the grounds of a residential care home, with about 15 residents, both male and female, which was staffed 24 hours every day. "They have a fantastic time there. They're taken for days out, have group holidays – everything she could wish for". I shook my head in despair. Didn't he know his daughter at all? I knew it was what she would hate, and I also knew that type of accommodation was what he wanted for his own peace of mind.

BEGINNINGS

SUSAN AND KAREN

My first thought on seeing my baby girl was "Oh, she looks like Uncle Maurice", I was astonished that she looked more like my father's brother than either myself or Paul, her father. Karen was tiny and exquisite. I felt euphoric, full of love and joy after giving birth. However, I had not been overjoyed when I realised I was pregnant. It was 1965, I was sixteen years old and I felt ashamed and scared. I was particularly afraid of my father's reaction as he had an explosive temper.

A friend told me that there was a hormonal pregnancy testing drug that would bring on a period if a woman was not pregnant; if a period did not materialise, this indicated pregnancy. In desperation but feeling too embarrassed to visit the family GP, I went to a different surgery and signed on as a new patient under a false name. Amazingly, the GP I saw prescribed the tablets. I took one that day and another the following day but the tablets failed to produce the longed for period. I had no option but to tell my parents.

My mother was in the kitchen by herself and I told her the news; she was upset but stoical, "I thought so" she declared, "you've got dark circles under your eyes. Where did this happen, was it in our house?" Paul and I had sometimes gone into the dining room to play records and shut the door; it was possible that it had happened in there. "Well you had better tell your dad because I'm not going to tell him for you." She called him into the kitchen. "I'm pregnant" I said and burst into tears. My father hit the roof as I knew he would. "What will the neighbours say?" he ranted, and "It's a good job your Nanny's not alive to see this" Nanny was my paternal grandmother who had died from an overdose of barbiturates when I was fourteen "Well I suppose you could have an abortion" he added. My mother accused him of being a hypocrite, "How on earth can you say that and you a Catholic?". My father then said that he would ask his priest about a home for unmarried mothers, "You could have the baby adopted", he added. "No", I wept, "I don't want to go to a home for unmarried mothers, we want to get married, we want the baby. I don't want to give it away". "Yes you will get married and as soon as possible" he said grimly.

A few weeks later when I was three months pregnant, I married Paul in St Clements Church where I had been baptised and confirmed. Our parents and a few relatives and friends attended; the church seemed rather large for such a small wedding party. I wore a long white broderie anglais dress my mother made and Paul wore a suit, winkle picker shoes and a Beatles hair cut. We had the reception at my parents' house and Uncle Maurice brought some bottles of champagne. Mary, one of my school friends, drank too much bubbly and was violently sick.

We lived in a furnished bedsit for a few weeks before moving into a rented, unfurnished flat. I was delighted that we had a place of our own and enjoyed making it look homely. Once they'd accepted the fact that I was pregnant, my parents were very supportive and donated some pieces of old furniture and their Ada washing machine that had a wringer. Our friends found the fact that I was pregnant quite exciting but I thought I noticed a change in attitude among some of the staff at the department store where I worked, especially the managers and older staff. In the 1960s, there was still a stigma about unmarried mothers and teenage pregnancies. "Nice" girls did not get pregnant and I sensed that, in their eyes, I was no longer a "nice" girl. For years afterwards, I carried a sense of shame and found it difficult to talk about.

I began to look forward to the arrival of the baby, attended ante-natal classes and carried out my pelvic floor and pelvic tilt exercises. The pregnancy seemed to progress normally but I developed high blood pressure when I was six months pregnant and was advised to rest more. Shortly after this, I stopped work and my blood pressure dropped a little. However, it rose again about a month before the baby was due and I was told that I might have to be admitted into hospital because of this. An examination showed that the baby was in breech position and I had a small operation known, as a "version", carried out under anaesthetic to turn the baby. When I came out of the anaesthetic, I was having abdominal pains that were dismissed as "false labour pains". These settled down and I was discharged the following day, a Thursday.

Over the next couple of days, I had some intermittent pains but thought these were false pains again; after all, there were another four weeks to go. On Saturday evening, Paul and I went to the Odeon to see "The Knack" and by the time the film ended, the pains had returned and were more insistent; it was clear that I was in labour. We went home and Paul called an ambulance from a phone box to take me to the maternity hospital; we were living on a low income and did not own a car or a telephone. I felt very calm travelling to the hospital but Paul was in a state of panic.

Karen was born about ten the following morning. It was a normal delivery, aided only by gas and air. Karen was placed in an incubator for a few hours. I assumed it was because she only weighed 4lbs 15 ounces. She was in a nursery in the premature baby unit and I was in a ward down the corridor but I could pick out her crying from the other babies. I wanted to breast feed her but she would not suck and would keep falling asleep, it took ages to feed her. "Flick the bottom of her foot to wake her" one of the nurses said. I tried, but she still kept falling asleep; I felt a failure, inadequate. One of the nurses seemed a bit abrupt and I thought that some of the other mothers were judging me. After a few days, I started to feel depressed and longed to be out of the hospital. I was discharged after a fortnight but Karen remained in hospital for another two weeks. I felt better being at home in our flat but I missed my baby and I felt guilty about leaving her. I expressed milk to send to the hospital and tried to visit her each day.

We brought Karen home when she was four weeks old. She was feeding better but quite often, followed by explosive vomiting. Her "milestones" were late; she was about ten months old when she began to sit unaided and did not walk until she had just turned two. The Health

Visitor assured me that premature babies' development was often delayed. "Don't worry" she said. So I didn't. Karen had missed out the crawling stage and instead shuffled along on her bottom with one foot tucked under her; she could move at the rate of knots. My mother told me I'd been a "bottom shuffler" too.

Karen started having speech therapy when she was three because her speech was delayed. When she was about three, she had an attack of febrile convulsions which was very frightening at the time because I did not know what was happening. It was apparently caused by a high temperature due to an ear infection and it happened again about a year later. She was admitted into hospital for tests that included a lumbar puncture and she was diagnosed as having "arrested hydrocephalus". Karen's head is larger than normal and she walks with an uneven gait. Hydrocephalus may be caused by a brain defect that is present at birth and sometimes occurs in premature babies. There is a build up of cerebrospinal fluid, (CSF) causing the cavities of the brain to enlarge leading to pressure on the skull. My GP said that Karen's brain damage was congenital and had caused spasticity in her lower limbs. I agonised as to what may her caused the brain damage. Was it the pregnancy testing drug? Was it the high blood pressure during pregnancy? Was it the anaesthetic or manipulation during the version? Was it too much oxygen when she was in the incubator? Or was it something I'd done wrong?

I have sometimes wondered whether Karen's brain damage could have been avoided or diminished if the hydrocephalus had been discovered at birth or shortly after.

ANNIE AND MAX

For Anne (that's me) and Gus (that's my husband) the genetic roulette wheel started spinning in the A&E department of the Royal Infirmary of Edinburgh. He was a surgical SHO and I was a medical houseman.

I said to him, 'You probably don't have to cajole the nurses to do things, like I do, because they're probably all in love with you and will do whatever you say, however you say it!'

I remember him gazing deeply into my eyes in surprise and with interest.

I thought, 'Oh dear, I've shocked him': yet another example of my voicing thoughts that Scottish people just wouldn't express, too personal, and also I had used the word "love", which was rarely, if ever stated within the cut and dried atmosphere of the prestigious teaching hospital.

In retrospect, I think he was really thinking 'If I asked her out, she might say "yes". Also, she's not wearing glasses or, (staring more deeply), contact lenses, so is likely to be of good breeding stock for a chap, like me, crippled by moderately severe short-sightedness.'

Thoughts about breeding are not usually at the forefront of a man's mind on meeting a young lady, but you have to realise that Gus is from a lineage of Scottish farmers. Considering pedigree points for humans, as for animals, comes as easily to them as wondering the time of day.

When we started going out, and I became aware of his musings on my excellent visual refraction and my fine ankles, I was understandably nervous about telling Gus about my brother, Peter. Having a schizophrenic brother, even though it had been triggered by LSD drugs taken at Cambridge during the psychedelic 70's, would surely not qualify as a positive breeding point in a potential wife. Perhaps by the time I told him, he had fallen for me. I like to think so. Maybe he reasoned the potential genetic vulnerability was only on one side therefore his sane genes would compensate and naturally be dominant, who knows? Although I was told later that Gus's own father had been diagnosed with possible manic depression, not severe enough to require treatment, neither of us realised the genetic significance of this.

When our son, Max was 3, we were questioned as part of the autism diagnostic process. We informed the psychiatrists about Gus's father. They probably thought all surgeons are a bit odd and therefore likely to have odd fathers. They were still looking serious and puzzled as if it didn't quite add up. However, when my brother's psychosis was revealed, the dice in their eyes showed double sixes.

Both Gus and I had had a major psychiatric condition in our families, and genetically, this apparently predisposed us towards having an autistic child. All doubt gone, they shared a glance of relief and triumph. The genetic cards had been laid down and the diagnostic game bid and made.

The latest theory is that a pregnant mother of such a susceptible baby would just have to inhale an agricultural pesticide, at a crucial stage of pregnancy, for the great croupier in the sky to bias the roulette wheel and pocket the ball into the autism slot.

As yet it is unknown which pesticide this may be. I wish a prominent celebrity's child, or even a royal baby would be born autistic and this would provoke research into finding out what particular chemical it is. Once found, public opinion would surely push for a ban. Dark thoughts indeed, but if you lived alongside someone with this affliction, you might think them too.

On the other hand you might, like Temple Grandin, think 'If you got rid of all the autism genetics you wouldn't have science or art. All you would have is a bunch of social "yak-yaks"'.

On yet another hand you might, like Gus and I, know the little genetic miracle that is Max, our small one, and love him to bits, just the way he is.

PAT AND CLAIRE

We have often pondered the wonders of the mysteries of inheritance, and looked into both our families. Claire was eventually diagnosed with Asperger's Syndrome, aged 19, after years of us struggling to come to terms with the fact that she had been identified as having delayed development with a speech and language learning difficulty. Was there someone else in the past with a similar, but undiagnosed condition? Will we ever find out?

At the beginning it was 1982, around Easter time. The Falklands War had begun. We had watched on television the armed forces being waved off to begin the long journey south to the Falklands Islands. My husband was at that time in the Royal Air Force and we didn't really appreciate how big an impact on our lives this war would have. We were living in a remote village in Shropshire, about 15 miles from the RAF base where my husband had been stationed for a short time. I had just discovered I was pregnant with my second child. My first born, a son, was just coming on for 3, and we had felt that the time would be about right to have a brother or sister for him to complete our family. Within a few weeks of the pregnancy being confirmed, my husband had been despatched to play his part in the war, and I was left on my own, for the next 6 months, in a fairly new environment, not knowing many people at all. All our friends had been left behind in Yorkshire where we had lived happily for four years before this enforced move, and I was finding the locals somewhat less than welcoming. Many times during those months alone I asked myself the question "Why now?" It's fair to say that I often wished the pregnancy hadn't happened at that time.

The pregnancy was difficult in the beginning: being on my own with a toddler who wasn't sleeping very well; 'morning' (more like all day) sickness most of the time; a nasty tummy bug which both my son and I caught; and at 12 weeks pregnant, an electric shock when a lightning bolt struck the house at the end of the cul de sac causing their roof to cave in. I happened to have my hand on the fridge in my kitchen at that precise moment, when the surge occurred in all electrical equipment, causing me to receive an electric shock, leaving blisters on both arms and across my back. I think possibly my rubber flip flops saved me from more serious injury that day. "You'll be fine," said the country doctor when I went to him for reassurance. "The current didn't pass through your tummy but across your arms and back." And then, "No I can't hear a heartbeat but you are only 12 weeks". (They didn't do scans as the norm 'in those days' only if they thought something was amiss.) Could this incident have been responsible for Claire's condition? That's something else I've often wondered about, as well as the gene pool.

When I was pregnant both times I didn't mind which gender I would have. My son had been a lovely natured and contented baby, and I rather liked the idea of another boy. However, there is always the premise that it would be nice to have 'one of each'. What would he or she be like this time? On the inheritance issue, my son had my fair colouring, blue eyes and very fair hair. He had been a biggish baby though – and quite a little 'Michelin' man and, although a week early, weighing 8lb 5oz, had looked more like a month old baby (so I was told!). He was developing into quite a tall toddler, and in fact has grown to over 6ft as an adult, a good few inches taller than his dad.

When our daughter was born in December, at the end of what seemed a very long year, she arrived with blackish/brown hair, with brown eyes, and has always been quite petite although she was a good weight at full term, 7lb 6ozs. But she wasn't a happy baby; she cried a lot and had colic for a long while. Had she sensed my anxiety during those difficult days I had spent alone? As it turned out, that was just another beginning.

LINDA AND ANDREW

Ever since I was a little girl, playing with my dolls, I always assumed I would one day have a child of my own. Two in fact. A boy and a girl. I would live in a nice house with a tall, dark handsome husband and we would all live happily ever after. As I grew older, I vowed that when I had my children they would both be brought up equally. I would teach them both to look after themselves. My son would not be the sort of man who expected his wife to do all the housework and wait on him hand and foot. Before they started school, they would both be able to read, to write their own names and tie their shoelaces. At the age of 18, my son can still do none of these things, and possibly never will. The irony is not lost on me that Andrew will always need somebody to look after him throughout his life.

I was 38 years old when I finally became pregnant. My second husband has two daughters from his first marriage, and had undergone a vasectomy. He had a reversal of his vasectomy after we had been together for 5 years. The surgeon told John that due to the length of time since his original vasectomy, there was only a 25% chance of success and that the reversal would be considerably more painful than the original operation. He was right on the second count, as John will testify, but wrong on the first. Within 6 months of the reversal, I discovered I was expecting a baby. My period was late and we were in Blackpool for the weekend, just the two of us. I bought a pregnancy testing kit from Boots and we went back to the guest house. We sat on the bed together, both staring at the test strip between my fingers. I can still remember the disbelief when it showed positive. I had been bracing myself for disappointment, the surgeon's words ringing in my ears: it was unlikely we would conceive. We turned to look at each other and clearly John was as stunned as I was. I was not the same person who walked from the bathroom to sit on the bed with a test stick in my hand. I was going to be a mother. A new life was growing inside me. I was no longer just me.

Due to my age, the chance of my child having Down Syndrome was already high, and there was no point in having a blood test to determine the need for an amniocentesis. I was left with the choice whether to have that procedure or not. In the end, I opted to go ahead, but as I lay on the couch, I was hit by a wave of panic. To this day, I wish I had stopped them from going ahead, but before I knew it, the needle had entered my abdomen and my baby's safe cocoon had been violated. I spent the rest of that day in tears, feeling so guilty that I had allowed this to happen, and knowing that it wouldn't make any difference even if the result was positive. This was my precious baby and I would not consider an abortion. Why on earth did I do it? And so the guilt started. I still wonder to this day whether the amniocentesis played any part in causing Andrew's problems.

We were asked at the 20 week scan if we wanted to know the sex of the baby. John was keen to know. He has two lovely daughters whom he adores and is hugely proud of, but there was no mistaking his joy when he was told he was also going to have a son. I was over the moon, and the bond grew even stronger with my unborn child. John and I were both concerned about the effect the new arrival was going to have on his teenage girls, and he was very keen to reassure them that the new baby would not usurp them in his affections.

Looking back on my pregnancy, it was a very anxious time. That anxiety has continued to this day, sometimes simmering on a backburner, sometimes in the form of acute episodes, sometimes flashbacks. I have no doubt the anxiety whilst I was pregnant was fuelled by my midwifery knowledge. I think I knew there was something not quite right but I can't place what triggered the feeling. Whatever the reason for my anxiety, I feel guilty that Andrew was marinated in stress hormones.

I developed pre-eclampsia at 28 weeks and was admitted to hospital straight from the GP surgery. I was supposed to be on a late shift that afternoon, and here I was leaving them one staff member short and one patient extra! Over the next four weeks I was in and out of hospital several times, and was admitted for the final time on my birthday. Our plans for a birthday meal were scotched. The doctors were concerned that Andrew would need to be delivered early and so I was given steroid injections to help mature his lungs.

On the morning of 26th April 1996 I had a shower and washed my hair, planning on styling it after the routine daily cardiotocograph tracing of Andrew's heart. Within a minute of the start of the tracing, Andrew's heart slowed down to a dangerously low rate and I was taken straight to the operating theatre to have an emergency caesarian section, 32 weeks into my pregnancy. Although I knew it was critical that they deliver him immediately, my damp hair and unmade-up face was an external sign that I wasn't prepared. It wasn't meant to be like this. But ready or not, my child was about to be born.

PAULINE AND ALISON

The year is 1961. I'm 21 years old, living in London, working as a student nurse at Guy's Hospital, on a male medical ward. I'm supremely happy, doing a job I love, despite the long hours and poor pay, and will soon be taking my final exams. London, compared to my home in a quiet, rural North Yorkshire village, is vibrant and exciting. Sometimes it's hard to believe this is real and I'm not still in the throes of a long-held dream.

I do most of my socialising with my fellow students, all female – the era of the male nurse isn't even on the horizon. We drink, at a Thames-side pub nearby where the other customers very generously buy us drinks. Guy's nurses are held in great affection by the local population.

Occasionally, if we are late back, we have to run the gauntlet of getting back to our rooms, without being spotted by the hospital gate porters. Some of us are jazz aficionados and head for a jazz club in Oxford Street as often as we can afford it. The hospital hosts a monthly dance for all the staff, so we do get dates from time to time. I went out for a while with a black medical student, which in London was OK, but I knew in my home village would cause great consternation. So far, I haven't met the man of my dreams.

On the ward, I'm responsible for the patients in an annex, which is used for patients with infectious diseases, so spend most of my time wearing a gown, a mask and gloves. A new patient is admitted, with a fairly advanced case of tuberculosis. He's a merchant seaman, who had been on a year's contract sailing round South America. At some point, he'd started to feel unwell, but had to wait months without proper treatment until the ship sailed back to the UK. My eyes are immediately drawn to him. He's tanned and very fit looking, compared to my other patients. He comes into the small ward kitchen when I'm doing the washing up and helps to dry the dishes. It's his way of being able to talk to me without everyone else listening. He soon makes it obvious he is interested in me, even though there isn't much of me to be seen. I'm flattered. He asks me to go out with him when he's discharged. Thinking that that could be a very long way off, I agree. Little did I realise then, that this man, is destined to become my future husband.

Genetic Inheritance

"Promise not to tell anyone, but the fact is I'm pregnant", I announced in rather a dramatic fashion. My two sisters looked stunned. "What are you going to do?" Carole stammered. "What d'you think I'm going to do. Get married and have the baby of course" I snapped. They were the first to know, and it had been an ordeal to tell anyone, so I was stressed but also relieved and my emotions were hard to control. "Do you want a girl or a boy? Jenny asked tentatively. I'd hardly had time to think about the baby because I'd come back home to arrange the wedding and I was keeping that as my focus. The baby wasn't something I wanted to think about just yet. "Well of course I want a boy" was my reply. I'd always wanted my children to be boys. I'd wanted to be a boy myself and in the pretend games of childhood I'd always played a male part. My mother had always wanted sons and had often bewailed her fate when three girls had arrived in succession, to be followed at the last gasp, when she was in her forties by the "hallowed" boy. It is debatable whether my inclination for boys was because of my mother's preference, or my own personality.

I love the mystery of birth. The not-knowing which sex the baby will be – the total randomness of which sperm will fertilise the egg, which genes and chromosomes it will have, the uniqueness of every person on the planet. Even twins, who are identical physically, develop different personalities. We are all miracles. I don't remember wondering about what each of my babies would be like. It was enough for me that they were conceived in love, and would be our children. We would be a proper family, something I'd longed for as I was growing up.

I've never thought that either of my children look especially like either of us, although Alison has her father's black hair and blue eyes, and as Mike was very bright and forward as a baby, secretly, I thought that he had inherited my intelligence – but that was only vanity talking. In terms of my own genetic inheritance and that of my siblings, I'm not pleased that I look like my mother – not that she was ugly or anything, but I don't want to be the kind of person she was. I have many of her characteristics, but because in the lottery we call life, I was her first-born and as her circumstances meant she had to bring up four children single-handedly, a lot of responsibility was laid on my shoulders. I used to resent this, but as the years have passed, my resentment has turned into gratitude, because it helped to make me the person I am today. Although I know very little about my father, what I do know isn't good. He had a problem with alcohol, which two of us may have inherited, and he deserted his wife and his four children. I'm surprised, given his genetic make-up that at least some of us didn't turn out to be bad 'uns.

Some instinct seems to kick in when people see a new born baby. They have to find something to identify them as being from one side of the family or the other. "Ooooh, she/he looks just like ……." they coo over the pram. Whether this is still the case when an obviously disabled child is born I don't know.

I have a jumble of mixed feelings when I think about the birth of my daughter She was born on a trolley outside the delivery room, despite my urgent pleas that she was going to be born immediately, so none of the vital equipment for newborns was on hand. Little did I know then, that this would be an ongoing pattern, with professionals taking little or no notice of my opinions.

Alison is autistic and has moderate learning disabilities, and having her certainly changed my life completely, but by and large, I wouldn't have had it any other way. I don't know for certain if she had these conditions in the womb, or if they were due to a lack of oxygen at birth, and I guess in the bigger picture it doesn't matter how it occurred – no amount of blame or recriminations will change it. However, we as family carers will always wonder why? Was it something we had done during our pregnancy, was it inherited and if so, which side of the family had it come from?

I have sometimes felt guilty that I didn't do anything to find out more about the circumstances of her birth. If, indeed, Alison was starved of oxygen, as a former nurse, I feel I should have followed it up and even maybe sued the hospital for negligence.

For at least the first 12 months of Alison's life we weren't aware that anything was different. She was a very placid baby and although she didn't reach the first year milestones at the same rate that her brother had, I put it down to the fact that babies do develop at different rates. When I did start to worry that something was wrong, Alison was almost two, and wasn't walking, talking or feeding herself. Eventually, our GP referred us to a paediatrician who, after various tests, told us to go to our GP to find out the results. The prognosis was grim, and we were told Alison would be unable to do anything for herself and would be little more than a cabbage. How wrong that diagnosis would turn out to be.

Having Alison in my life has been a most rewarding experience, whilst also being a long, gruelling battle to try to ensure she has the best life she can possibly have. The only regret I have is that she will never be able to experience many life events most of us take for granted.

GILLIAN AND WILLIAM

Three of us were finishing the washing up after serving drinks at mothers and toddlers group. The chat moved to our expected babies. Ellen's and Kate's were due in six weeks, and they both sported tidy bumps. Ellen said, "I'm sure mine will be a boy 'cos I'm the same shape as I was with my son, with the bump at the front. People don't notice that I'm expecting until I turn round." Katrina agreed – "With the girls my bump was sideways, but not as far out at the front, so maybe I'm having a boy too." They both turned to inspect my figure, which had a less prominent bump, as my baby was not due for another four months. After some speculation they came to the conclusion that I was just an unusual shape. "Well, I guess I'll just have to wait and see what happens." The other two duly delivered sons as predicted.

A month later I visited a friend and her new son. I complained that my baby was going to be either an elephant because of its size, or a kangaroo, as it seemed to be enjoying performing a lot of boxing, kicking and other gymnastic activities. I joked that this was probably the result of my having been born in Australia. We laughed, and carried on cooing at the new arrival.

At thirty-five weeks into the pregnancy, I worried that there might be too much amniotic fluid surrounding the baby, possibly a sign of distress. Not for nothing had I spent years taking ante-natal case histories from mothers with children who had speech and language disorders or special needs. I had all the text books at home to help me form theories about what would be wrong with this unborn child. I expressed my concerns to the G.P. He reassured me that there was no excess fluid and that the baby seemed to be a normal size, even a bit on the small side. Then his expression changed as he continued to prod my belly. "I think I've found another head." He noticed my alarm. "No, I mean that I think you might be having twins! I'll arrange a scan for you."

The next week, I was able to show him a photograph of the twins' heads next to each other, and I was booked in to see an obstetrician. A fortnight later I gave birth to a new son and daughter. William appeared head first, and Margaret one foot first, followed by a forceps delivery after the doctor tried unsuccessfully to turn her the right way round. Contrary to my "knowledge," it was the twin with the normal delivery who turned out to be disabled, and the one who was blue and did not breathe straight away who had no subsequent problems.

A fortnight later at toddler group Ellen, Kate and I reminisced about our earlier conversation, and decided that it was odd that nobody had at any point ever considered the possibility of twins.

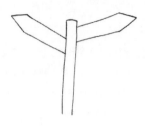

A FORK IN THE ROAD

SUSAN AND KAREN

After I left Paul, I was determined to find a job so that I could support my two children, Karen and Steven, be independent and not need to rely on benefits. I knew that I would be unlikely to receive any maintenance money from Paul as he was unemployed. I applied for places at the local Day Nursery and I was told that in order to take up the places, I would need to be employed. In 1970, I was offered two places at the Day Nursery and was given two weeks to find a job. I wondered how on earth I would be able to find work in such a short time but synchronicity took a hand. My dad knew someone in the Civil Service who told him that there was an urgent vacancy as a Machine Operator in the machine room (this was pre mainframe computers). The job application process was not as longwinded as that for clerical staff and incredibly, I was offered the job. Not long afterwards, there was a recruitment drive for Clerical Officers. As I had the required GCE qualifications, I applied, and was offered a post and a slightly higher salary.

Although I did not have the artistic career I had once dreamed about, I found that I enjoyed my job and the camaraderie in the office and I made a number of friends there. In July 1975, when I was twenty seven, Pam, one of my workplace friends invited me to a party at her flat. I worked as a barmaid at a nightclub on Saturday nights to earn some extra money that helped me to run my car. My parents usually had the children to stay overnight on a weekend. I had a night off from the club and, donning a black halter neck top, a long wine coloured skirt I had made and platform soled sandals, I went to the party. And that is where I met Tom. I spotted him across the room with his halo of long curly hair. He came over and asked me to dance and I said yes, trying not to sound too eager. He told me that he had bumped into Pam by chance a few weeks before the party and had almost forgotten about it. He had remembered at the last minute and come along because he was at a loose end. We danced and chatted and he asked me to meet him at a pub the following evening. "Oh gosh, he looks so young, about nineteen," I thought. However, I agreed to meet him and arranged a baby sitter. Tom was about to leave the pub when I walked in about twenty minutes late. It turned out that he was twenty four and single. I told him I was the mother of two children, aged nine and seven, one of them with a learning disability. Some men I had dated found this off-putting but it did not seem to worry Tom and he called at my house the following week and met them. He got on well with them and they took to him straight away, particularly because he was fun to be with and made them laugh.

We had been seeing each other for a few weeks when one evening, unbeknown to me, whilst Tom was downstairs with the children and I was upstairs getting changed, Steven said "are you going to marry mummy?" Very embarrassed and not knowing where to put himself, Tom mumbled "I don't know" and quickly changed the subject. I think Steven had secretly longed to have a father in his life and had set his heart on Tom fulfilling this role. He was only a year old when I left Paul who had not bothered to keep in contact with the children. After Steven had started school in1972, he asked me why he didn't have a daddy. "You do have a father," I said, "but he and I did not get on with each other".

Both Steven and Karen were very happy when Tom moved in with us. He bought me a ring which I wore on my ring finger. Although I had told everyone that it was not an engagement ring, engagement congratulation cards arrived in the post from my aunts. My mum had written to them to say that I'd got engaged. My mum and dad had not been keen on Paul but liked Tom and were delighted when we got married. It was the year of the long hot summer of 1976, but on the September day that we wed, it poured with rain and my wide brimmed, cream hat blew off when I stepped out of the taxi to walk into the registry office. Luckily someone caught it so it didn't get dirty. Because it was a registry office ceremony, we didn't have bridesmaids but Karen was very proud of the long flowered dress that mum made her. Tom and I are very happy together and Tom has always felt like a real father to his two stepchildren.

ANNIE AND MAX

'I took the path less travelled on, and that has made all the difference.'

Or rather, in my case, the path took me. It is my destiny, no turning back, deviating or opting out, caring for a disabled child, soon to be adult. It is suddenly a path that two are following, all the time and tread of life walked in tandem, each decision done double. I visualise that it will always be this way: he will grow and I will shrink as we cobble along together, but the one will always be the shepherd to the other.

Sometimes, the reality of living with a disabled person is like slapping into an unexpected glass door, hidden from superficial inspection, but there anyway and suddenly apparent.

Whilst on holiday in Greece one summer, I was so abruptly made aware of one negative aspect of my situation, that it caused me to weep silently on the beach. That morning, I had carefully placed my new Kindle in my bag, so I could read on the beach. The book was very exciting and, as the book club meeting was shortly after my return from holiday, I was keen to settle down to it that day. Unfortunately, when the device was removed from the bag, it was obvious that the screen was broken. This must have happened when I went to the loo, briefly, before leaving our room that morning. Max, our son, must have sat upon the rucksack, whilst it was perched upright on the bed. Usually people would not do this, but he would not have realised there was anything wrong with sitting on someone's bag. Of course, I should have taken more care. Being prepared for the unexpected outcome is the bread and butter of having a disabled child, and if you aren't good at it, you will have accidents with that child and plenty of broken possessions.

The sort of thinking one does with a tiny toddler: he might sweep that glass off the table with his elbow, or bang his head if he falls against that table corner, or swallow that small bead, or even drown if not supervised closely next to that garden pond; this sort of thinking must go on forever with a disabled child and I can tell you, it is tiring.

My tears were not just self-pity for the loss of my new reading device and book, but frustration with myself for failing to foresee that this mishap might occur, and exasperation at my always having to think through every situation in detail and all possible ramifications. Other people on that beach seemed so carefree. It seemed they could own and enjoy special possessions. Their precious objects would remain intact. As the German proverb says: 'Envy eats nothing but its own heart.' I did some heart-eating, weeping on that beach, that morning.

At these times, the negative aspects catch me like the jerk and recoil of a bungee wire which keeps kicking me back. I seem to bob up and down forever, attached to the umbilical cord of that wire, which will never free me. I will never have the freedom to just decide to go away for a few days, make decisions solely for myself or on a whim.

Aristotle had good aphorisms. One is 'happiness depends on ourselves' and another 'happiness is the meaning and the purpose of life, the whole aim and end of human existence.' We are all surely craving for our own share of happiness in life. For me, some happiness can be found enjoying aspects of my son's disability: his loving and cuddly nature, his total lack of competitive or malicious thoughts, his whacky specialist interest areas, which provide some texture to days out, and the alternative way he can perceive the world with his super-senses. Just knowing that I am responsible for him long term is also a spur to keep healthy and positive within myself, and to try to find sweet experiences that we may share and enjoy together or as a family. I do not want for us to be eaten by negativism whilst on our path through life. I guess I might as well accept my lot, and lump it. What's more, as a family, I hope that we can induce that lumpen lot into shedding every iota of happiness that it contains.

PAT AND CLAIRE

When I look back on my life I can honestly say with hindsight and years of experience later, that I may well have taken different roads – if only I had known then what I know now, as the well-known saying goes.

However, I am going to write about an incident that occurred when I was a small child, which could have had mega consequences on my future. The reasons for this statement will, I believe, become clear on reading this piece.

I was living at the time with my parents and brother at the edge of a small sleepy country village in Somerset. I was only about five and attended a small primary school. My father was in the Royal Air Force, and we were living in a cottage away from the base. I remember it was on part of a farm and I have happy memories of the hens, and in particular the cock crowing in the mornings, and my mother picking rhubarb before breakfast to cook for me. (Presumably to assist my lazy digestive system!) I recall the strong smell of the butter on hot toast in the mornings.

Our cottage was sited within a large garden, backing onto which was a small country pub. In order to get to the pub you had to go out of the garden at the far end and then walk back along the length of the hedge which bordered the garden and the cottage. The small country road on which the pub stood saw very little traffic in those days. The pub had a small hatch which opened up onto the outside wall next to the road, which enabled people to buy crisps, peanuts or drinks, without having to go inside. This was a rare treat for my elder brother and myself, which often occurred on a Sunday late morning.

This particular Sunday morning I was allowed to go on my own to get my crisps. I remember my grandparents from Bristol were staying with us. Having bought my crisps, I started to walk back to the garden gate along the small country road. I remember a white car slowing down as it came near me and the window wound down. A man leered out of the window and started chatting to me. He asked me to go for a ride in his car with him, and told me that he knew my daddy and that my daddy had said I could go. I hesitated for a split second – I had always been told never to go with strangers, but thought that if he knew my dad it would be OK, wouldn't it? I instinctively began to feel uncomfortable as he became more persistent. I ran the last part of the way home and dived into the gateway. He sped off in the car at great speed. I ran in crying out to my parents. I was very afraid that I'd done something bad. My dad and grandfather ran up the road after the car, but couldn't see it. I remember a policeman coming to see us on a bike later on, presumably after my parents reported it.

When I think about what might have happened to me if I'd got into that car it makes me shudder. I might have just become another statistic, a missing child, or even worse. I wonder if he ever succeeded in luring any other small children into his car, and can only hope he never did. I can only be thankful that something, instinct or whatever, saved me from what could have been a terrible fate and that I have been able to enjoy a fulfilling life, with all its ups and downs and sorrow, but most of all, joy.

LINDA AND ANDREW

"Wouldn't it be great if we could live in a parallel universe?" she thought. "I could jump from one reality to another and experience the infinite versions of the 'me' that could have been". As a child she had yearned to be an actress – a dream thwarted by her parents and the Careers Advisor. "Go to college and train to be a secretary, you are good at English and you will never be short of a job", she was told. "Acting is a very precarious profession and you need to be lucky to be able to make it". So, she toed the line and went to business college. She joined an amateur musical theatre group which helped to soften the blow a little.

After 10 years, bored with the monotony of being cooped up in her solitary office, she took a leap of faith and trained as a nurse. Emboldened by this change of career, she went on to become a midwife, and also trained as a massage therapist and a reflexologist. Looking back now, she wonders, "How different would my life have been if my parents had gone ahead with their plan to emigrate to Australia, if I had become an actress, if I hadn't changed careers, if I had stayed single, if my first marriage hadn't failed, or if I had never become a mother".

The real catalyst for change happened when she fell in love with someone who had been an acquaintance for several years. He was already married. So was she. The change of direction was inevitable but this was a painful and destructive fork in the road.

After five years with her new partner, she became pregnant. With a mixture of joy, excitement and anxiety, she realised her life would alter forever. What she did not know was that her child would have a severe learning disability. Her son was born eight weeks early by emergency caesarean section. Despite the foetal distress which brought about his delivery, he was born in good condition and she had no reason to believe that her son was going to have any major problems.

The day they finally brought him home from hospital six weeks later, she was full of optimism and excitement. Her euphoria was short-lived. Over the next 8 months he suffered many health problems and failed to meet his milestones. At 8 months old, he became critically ill with bronchiolitis, and spent four weeks on a ventilator. She spent virtually every waking hour in a bedside vigil, praying for him to pull through, no matter what his quality of life would be if he survived. When he came home six weeks later, she tried to tell herself he had just had a difficult first year and he would catch up, but the midwife in her knew there was something wrong.

The real wake-up call was when she took him to a mother and baby group just after his first birthday – the differences between her son and the other children were painfully apparent and she could no longer delude herself. Nobody was unkind to her, but she felt there was a big bubble around them, separating them from the other mums and babies. She had experienced many forks in the road in her life so far, but most had been of her own volition. The birth of her longed for child brought uninvited challenges, but it would be the making of her.

PAULINE AND ALISON

Musing on this concept, I begin to reflect that many things which affect or alter our lives happen seemingly by chance. Words come to me, so I look up their meaning: *serendipity* – 'the faculty of making happy discoveries by accident; *coincidence* – the remarkable concurrence of events without apparent causal connection; and *synchronicity* – the meeting of two unrelated causal chains in a coincidental event which appears both highly improbable and highly significant.

I wonder which of these terms best describes my first meeting with Cherry Bryden, a wonderful woman who completely changed my life. I guess it would have to be synchronicity, as it was both highly improbable and highly significant to me.

In my late forties, I was at an all time low-point in my life. After 25 years together, my marriage had disintegrated and I was divorcing my husband. Moving out of the marital home had been traumatic, and I had been hospitalised with severe depression for several months. In the difficult process of trying to put my life back together, it was hard, after being in a couple for so long, to motivate myself to do things on my own. Going to the library had re-established my passion for reading, although now fiction had given way to non-fiction and I was devouring books on psychology and self-development. This reading encouraged me to try to make sense of my past experiences, and with this introspection, a feeling began to develop that I was on some kind of journey, with some direction, which was preferable to feeling totally lost and not having a clue about how or what I wanted my new life to be. Subconsciously, I think I knew how important it was that I must be authentic. It was time to stop hiding behind the myriad of roles I had used to obscure the real me. I hardly knew where to begin and I was still so fragile mentally and emotionally that progress necessarily had to be slow.

Looking at the notice board in the library one day, my attention was drawn by a poster advertising an evening of circle dancing. I'd heard of circle dance before, from different people. Some extolled its virtues passionately, others viewed it as airy-fairy, self-conscious prancing about and I felt pretty certain that I would fall into the latter group. Dancing was something I had always enjoyed, but favoured what I saw as the more sophisticated ballroom type or the wild let your hair down rock 'n' roll or jive. Folk and square dancing just left me cold and I reckoned circle dancing would too. However, as I was trying to do things differently, I decided to find out for myself and went along with great nervousness and trepidation.

My first impression of the other people gathered there was that circle dance obviously attracted 'alternative' types – men with long hair chatting happily to women wearing long brightly coloured skirts or way-out patterned trousers. As usual I didn't feel as if I belonged and hovered uncomfortably on the edge of things. The person leading the dancing was a tiny, animated, white-haired woman, with sparkling eyes with whom I immediately sensed an affinity. I started to relax. She called us to form a circle and join hands and gave us a brief overview of the history of circle dance and showed the correct handhold which connected us to each others' energy. We didn't need a partner, and we didn't need to know the dance as she would teach each dance slowly before we danced to the music – so far, so good. The first steps were fairly simple and I soon got the hang of it and then the music started. I think I fell in love with circle dance and loved Cherry there and then.

My love for Cherry and hers for me was one of the most precious experiences of my life. Cherry became a surrogate Mum to me, someone I could always be <u>me</u> with, someone who never judged me, but supported and encouraged me always. We became great friends and travelled all over Yorkshire to circle dance events. I loved visiting her at home, as her garden was a magical space with little paths meandering in all directions, leading to half-hidden grottos and quiet corners with a seat for reflection and meditation.

She opened up a whole new world to me. It was like having my own life coach. She was vegan and an expert in nutrition, she loved her garden and taught me so much about plants, and she was warm and affectionate. Gradually I started to open up like one of her flowers. She wrote poetry, was an environmentalist, taught yoga and everything she did, she did with joy and passion. On some things we differed. I was sceptical about her belief in past lives, and when she told me she believed we had met in a former life as wise women in the time of the witch hunts, I found it difficult to see myself in that way. I eventually plucked up the courage to tell her I was gay, and I'm so pleased I did, as she had an estranged lesbian daughter who had moved to Australia. Being able to talk to me about it did help, and eventually Cherry travelled to Australia for a reunion with her daughter and I was delighted that I had been able in a small way to reciprocate some of what she had given me.

Sadly, Cherry is no longer with us, but I have such happy memories of our times together and feel enormous gratitude to her for being part of my life. I would like to think that some day we will meet again in some future lives. I do now believe that many people come into our lives for a reason and it helps to think I am not alone, that there is a greater force for good which is accessible to us all if we are open to it.

GILLIAN AND WILLIAM

This experience was an adventure I had on my last day at my older son's workplace in Hong Kong. Crossroads is an international charity that distributes aid to people in need, and also offers educational experiences to schools, universities and volunteers at the organisation.

The phone rang in the schoolroom at half past two. "Gillian, will you come down to the Volunteer Office at four? There's a group from the United Nations High Commission for Refugees (UNHCR) coming over, and we'd like you to join them." I was supervising the children instead of packing to return home later that evening. As soon as the teacher returned, I said my farewells to the class, and rushed to the flat to sort out my bags before heading for the office.

At the office, we were briefed for the Refugee Run simulation exercise. "Here are your identity cards, family information, and some money." Women were issued with headscarves, and I was informed that mine was the only red one, to indicate that I was vulnerable, to ensure I would not be treated too brutally, as I had mobility problems. We were all sent to "Afghanistan" (the comfortable room which was the starting point for the Refugee Run) to await our adventure, chatting nervously as we walked up the steep slope and two flights of stairs at the commencement of our journey.

My friends Joe and Ray suddenly burst into the room. They were now soldiers rounding up the group, ending our previously predictable lives. "Stand up, and move over here. Hurry up." They reinforced their message by herding us at gunpoint to the next room. We walked through a pitch-black uneven minefield; some of us were issued with bandages to indicate that we had been injured. Other soldiers pushed us about, screaming and shouting at us until we arrived at our refugee camp. We were forced to stand as the camp commander ordered us to find our family groups, from whom we had been separated, and erect makeshift tents from large sheets of canvas. We followed his instructions, threatened by the presence of the military. Joe suddenly approached me and pushed me with his gun. "Cover your hair, woman. You are not respectful." An anxious giggle bubbled up and escaped. "This is a serious situation, and laughter is not appropriate." That was what shocked me into making the transition from knowing gentle, kind Joe as a good friend to realising that I was now a vulnerable refugee in a life-threatening situation.

The next order came. "Send someone from your family to collect food and water." We bartered for the limited number of containers available for our bread and water, and some of us resorted to theft. That "night", we were woken up several times, and moved from our shelters so that we and the tents could be searched. In the morning, those of us who had been injured by mines were seen by the Red Cross. In my role as a journalist, I asked for help to leave the camp so that I could tell the world what was happening to us, but this idea was dismissed. I was herded into another tent, which was a makeshift classroom. "You need to learn Urdu as you are now in Pakistan." Ella, the Indian teacher I had been working with for a month and had parted from just over an hour previously, was showing me how to write numbers in Urdu to prepare for my new life in Pakistan. Now it was becoming easier to remember that I was a refugee.

When I left the classroom at the refugee camp this time, Phil approached me, and offered to help me escape. I handed over the money he demanded, and was taken to yet another tent, where I discovered that I should have been more wary of my friend from Kazakhstan, as he had just sold me into prostitution. I was given a piece of dog-eared paper to read, which informed of my duties in this establishment.

We refugees were ushered into the last room at 6:30 for a final de-briefing led by Joe, with the help of Ray, who had experienced life as a refugee before coming to Hong Kong. We discussed how, even in a simulated activity, we had resorted to cheating, lying and stealing to fulfil our basic human needs. This gave me time to reflect on how odd it was to live as a refugee for two hours, and to see friends in a new light, with the different personalities they had assumed for the simulation. It also gave me a chance to reflect on how odd it felt to take a step into the unknown and unpredictable, and to realise that this had links with the new, overturned world of disability into which my family and I had been plunged when my son was young. It also demonstrated that one can become resourceful and develop new skills and characteristics to gain more control of unanticipated situations.

A DAY IN THE LIFE

SUSAN AND KAREN

Sometimes, on a weekend, I will pick Karen up in the morning at around eleven to go and visit the Donkey Sanctuary at Eccup, near Leeds. They have donkeys that have been rescued from neglect or ill treatment and the centre provides riding therapy for children with "additional needs and disabilities". It is open to visitors most days a week and they have fund raising days too.

The first time we had visited the centre, in 2011, Karen "adopted" an elderly donkey called Rosie. This cost seventeen pounds and Karen received a large photograph of Rosie and a certificate and some information about her. On a subsequent visit, a helper told us "Rosie has retired and had gone to another centre because she was ready for a rest". She then turned towards me, mouthing "She's died". She was sensitive to the fact that Karen might be upset at this news. There were some young donkeys available for adoption and they were in stalls inside the large, barn like building where we had been talking to the helper. We spent some time patting them and talking to them. Karen said she would like to adopt "Billy O". I think she liked the name and was amused at being told that he is quite mischievous. He likes to run off with a bucket in his mouth and sometimes tips wheelbarrows up.

One Saturday in September, Karen and I drove to the Donkey Sanctuary. Usually, I drive on a fairly direct route that includes a dual carriageway. I knew the main road would be busy that day so I drove along quiet roads through the villages instead. It was a lovely day and the drive was pleasant and relaxing. I chatted to Karen who told me all about her week at work and what she had been up to. "I've been mending a fence" she said proudly. Helping to fix a fence had been a highlight of the week for her.

There is a café at the donkey sanctuary and sometimes we have a lunch of jacket potatoes and salad but this time we stopped for a meal at a small bistro in Tadcaster. Karen loves going out for lunch and we both enjoyed a very nice goat cheese salad. This meant that we arrived at the centre a bit later than usual and all the visitors had left. We drove up the farm road and could see some of the donkeys in the field behind the buildings. Previously when we have visited, some of the donkeys have been in the stables and we have been admitted into the stable yard. When we went through to the stable yard, there were no donkeys in the stables. Karen looked disappointed. One of the helpers came over and told us that the donkeys had been in the stalls but when the visitors left, they had gone to the field. "Karen's a bit upset, she sponsors Billy O and was really looking forward to seeing him," I said. "I'll tell you what," the helper said, "I'll go and see if I can entice him into the stable yard". She asked us to wait behind the gate and then she took some carrots out of a bucket and walked through the far gate into the field. A few minutes later, we saw a line of about ten donkeys heading towards the stable yard with Billy O in the lead. The other donkeys had decided they wanted some carrot too and obviously thought it was a good idea to follow Billy O. All the donkeys congregated round the gate where we were standing. Karen was thrilled to bits and enjoyed stroking Billy O and some of the other donkeys. Then she had a look round the little shop and bought a mug with Billy O's picture on it.

On the way back, we stopped at a café at Boston Spa. Karen had hot chocolate and a buttered scone which she loves, and I had a coffee and cake. It was a perfect ending to the afternoon.

LIZ AND SALLY

7 am I wake up before my alarm. It is cold and dark but I slowly get up so I can get ready for work. I text my mum so she knows I am up. I tidy the kitchen as I hate living in a mess.

8 am I walk to work, let myself in and start cleaning. I like having a job, but I don't like it when other people tell me I am getting in the way when I try to fill my mop bucket or tell me I am slow.

11 am Back at my mum's. She is cleaning up but we have a cup of tea and wonder what we should do for the rest of the day. I would like to see my sister, but she works and has four children, so I don't see as much of her as I would like, even though she lives quite close to me. I text her in case she wants to come round.

11.30 am One of my mum's friends comes for coffee. I sit and listen while they go on and on about something. It is very boring. After a while I go on the computer and look for voluntary jobs or new computer games or DVDs that I want.

12.30 pm Finally my mum's friend goes and we have some lunch. My mum wants to go swimming but I am not in the mood and I am tired from work. My mum does a bit more cleaning and I help her move the furniture around and hoover the stairs for her. This is very tiresome but when I complain my mum says 'We should have gone for a swim.'

3 pm We take the dog out. She pulls a lot and nearly pulls your arm off if there is a cat anywhere. Someone always says, 'Who's taking who for a walk?' We tie the dog outside the charity shop and go and look for bargains. We nearly always find something. The dog makes a terrible racket when we get back outside.

4 pm Time for another cup of tea and if I'm lucky a piece of cake too. My dad is home now and this is always a bit of a surprise as he has only just retired and we are not used to him being around so much.

5 pm I text the brother that I live with, to see if we have anything for tea. We haven't. I go to the Co-op to buy something. Neither of us is very good at cooking so we often have a 'ready meal'. I also buy some coke and yogurts with bits of chocolate in them. I go home.

6 pm I watch some soaps. Then my brother and I eat our tea and watch the Simpsons.

7.30 pm I have a shower and then I watch telly or a DVD in my room until I go to sleep about 9 pm. Just before I go to sleep I text my mum to see if I can buy some new computer games.

GILLIAN AND WILLIAM

The beginning of the day – Monday morning

"Oh gosh, it's ten to six! Come on everyone, show a leg. We're in a rush!"

All three children had to be out of the house by half past seven. Michael had to be shaken awake several times, as he was at the stage of teenager-hood when he would just continue to slumber, which would mean potentially missing his train to school. Margaret was independent, and would get herself out of the house in time for the bus at 7:15. She was going through a phase during which she wanted to travel on her own, although she and Michael actually attended the same school. I would have preferred them to go together, as early mornings were so dark, but also felt that she should be allowed some autonomy.

William was a different kettle of fish. He had no difficulty in rising. In fact he had to be encouraged to remain in bed and avoid disturbing his siblings. However he needed to be prompted at every stage of the getting up process, or he would divert to a more exciting activity instead of washing and dressing. The children sorted out their own breakfasts of cereal, toast and fruit. This was an attempt to give them responsibility for looking after their own needs, and was a task William completed without prompting. The resulting chaos indicated that as yet, the children had not fully finished learning their jobs!

As well as keeping tabs on the children I had to frisk William's bag to check that he had not smuggled contraband to take to his school, which was a specialist weekly boarding school for boys with dyslexia. If we had been out on Friday evening and the washing had not been done until Saturday, I might even have to pack clothes that had only just dried. William's mission in life seemed to be to swap clothes, and fit in as many toys and cassette tapes as he could manage without me noticing. We finally reached a satisfactory compromise – he could take his teddy (a large cuddly gorilla) and five tapes, one for each day, and my remit was to promise not to listen to the unselected ones during his absence (very unlikely!) and to hide them from Margaret.

William's taxi arrived at quarter to seven, and I bundled his bag and him into the car with the two bleary-eyed boys who had been picked up even earlier. I took another opportunity to monitor the contents of the bag – if it was suspiciously heavy there was likely to be a surplus item on board. This routine took place every school Monday for five years, and William became more and more adept at getting things past my watchful eyes.

The end of the day – Friday evening.

It was half past six. William was due home any minute now. I could truthfully report that nobody else had listened to any of his tapes, and he could spend twenty minutes with his music, winding down after his week at school. Until this had happened, he was unable to tell me about what he had been up to. Michael and Margaret would be arriving at the station and bus stop in half an hour, and I could make sure that dinner would be ready once everybody was home.

"William, we're getting into the car in ten minutes. Turn the tape off when that track is finished," was greeted by a grunt. "Five minute warning now, William. It's time to go to the loo before we collect the other two." He appeared in the doorway, keen to see his siblings. While we were waiting for the train he would tell me about his week, eager words spilling out. This routine and script seemed important to him, as was the speculation as to who would arrive first. Margaret was usually the winner on the bus, as Michael's trains were so often late. During his first term at secondary school he had written a long essay outlining the variety of excuses for tardiness given by British Rail. His English teacher was amused by the number of things found on the line – cattle, leaves, snow, and chewing gum to name a few, and it was remarkable that there were so often no staff available to operate the 6:30 train. William and I could always invent ways of passing time, usually embarking on making lists. These could be makes of car, his favourite bands, or animals. He would also use this time to talk about anything that was worrying him.

After dinner, Michael and Margaret would start their homework, which would come with them if we went out to a music group I attended.

William and I did the washing up, his participation best described as enthusiastic water play. At the group William "helped" by supervising the adults, and untuning my cello if he could get away with it while I was playing the piano instead of keeping an eye on him. We would get home by ten, and nobody needed to be encouraged to go to bed, especially as Michael and Margaret went to school on Saturday mornings.

ANNIE AND MAX

Each day looking after Max is like an episode of 'Wheel of Fortune.' The beginnings and endings are mostly the same, but the middle sections can vary, and this mainly relates to if it's a school day or if it's not.

All days start at 7am when Max wakes in a happy frame of mind to face a new day. As if inspired by the 'flying crooked' gift of the cabbage white butterfly, jerky and lurching, he pitches into our room.

'Good morning! How did you sleep?' he says.

'Oh, fine, open the curtains, Max….Pull that one the other way…'

Eventually a small slice of sky appears. 'Yep, it's a cloudy day today.'

Kneeling on my shin bones he flops in between us and shuffles himself under the duvet cuddling down.

'Mummy is very loved', he says, kissing my cheek.

Gus, my husband, will then rise; shower, dress and go downstairs to have his breakfast and lay out Max's. After a little cuddle, Max is ejected from bed and told to go to the toilet. I get up, run the shower, adjust the temperature and make him stand in it. At 15, I can barely reach up to his head, but manage to wash his hair and face with 'Head and Shoulders' shampoo, which I've found helps to prevent his teenage spots. I hand Max a flannel to wash his 'down belows,' but if he's had diarrhoea, which is fairly common with his condition, I need to wash him myself.

I towel dry his hair and send him off to dry the rest of himself on the landing, a large carpeted space with no external windows, ideal for the purpose. In fact, it was whilst standing on the landing, twenty-four years ago, that I knew this was the house we should choose to live in. I saw the large back stairway wall, covered with pictures, as now, and there was something else about the large floor area. Was I envisioning the space being of such use to us in the future?

Max dabs absently at various parts of his body. He puts on pants and socks, which I've left out over the banister, or fetches them from his drawer. He puts on his school shirt, sometimes inside out or upside down.

'Can you help me?'

'You can do it, Max. Take it off and try again, as taught.'

He bangs his fist at his forehead.

'There's no need to do your nut, just try again, calm down.'

It takes forever, with me advising and trying to help him work it out and persist.

I need to do up his buttons, but he drags on elastic waisted trousers and shoves his feet into velcroed shoes. He hauls on the pullover swirling it like a woolly necklace round his neck several times before he notices the school badge which goes at the front. I attach his clip-on tie, brush his hair flat and send him down to Gus for breakfast.

Gus makes him help to assemble the breakfast things. This is usually gluten-free cereal, rice milk, fruit puree, an apple, juice and toast. The knife is waved about like an ineffective wand, unable to spirit the margarine onto the toast. They eat breakfast, Max reading his aviation or train magazine, Gus, the paper. If there's time, Max will leaf through the paper afterwards spotting interesting articles, checking the weather, and the Radio 2 listings. I might be asked to record a jazz programme or 'the Big Band Special.'

I am now dressed, and make the pack-up for school. It's usually ham sandwiches, banana, elderflower cordial in water and a cube of apple juice. After breakfast, we send him to the loo for a poo. I am called through, and, as he can't use his hands very effectively, I hold the toilet roll. He tears off six pieces, as taught, and lies them down flattish on bunched up knees, then uses them to wipe. I have taught him to repeat this process.

'Well? Pass or fail?' he asks.

'Pass. Well done. What do we do now?'

Ignoring the checklist on the wall, he dangles his fingers in tap water, forgetting to flush the toilet or use soap. When reminded, he carries out the tasks, and then tries to leave the room.

'Where are you going? What haven't we done?'

'Teef!'

Why doesn't the New Oxford English Dictionary simply change all these words to fit in with the diction of all young people and be proactive in the evolution of our language….'teef, firty, fird, tenf, etc' ?

Max was blind for the first ten months of life and still has little body awareness, especially round the head area. He's already had some fillings under general anaesthetic, so I do his teeth, with a strange new disability toothbrush. He might need a shave, and I use Gus' electric razor. As he's got teenage spots, I scour his face with a scratch mitt and pore cleanser, followed by spot gel and cover-up. I brush his hair and make him neaten himself in the mirror: straighten trousers, tuck in shirt, flatten collar of blazer.

We go to school, usually in the car, occasionally on the buddy bike or walking. When we get there, I walk him in through the automatic doors at reception and we both say,

'Bye, see you at pick-up!'

On a school day, I pick him up six hours later, at 3.30pm. At home, I am a rounders player with no bat, continually racing around and around the four bases, washing, drying, ironing, sorting, game without end. I will cook Max's tea, sometimes the same as our own, a casserole, or fish. As he is on a gluten-free and dairy-free diet, I might make an entirely separate meal. If Max has gluten, he develops tummy swelling and pain and his behaviour becomes more absent. He will also get diarrhoea. In the evening, if there's no homework, tele will be watched, or radio shows listened to, whilst I tidy up. He likes Michael Portillo railway journeys, Pointless, Eggheads, The One Show, Antiques Roadshow, or old movies. Sometimes he will drift to the garden to visit his collection of footballs assembled on the trampoline and kick them against the net, or just lie amongst them staring up at the sky.

Two nights a week, we take Max to a youth club, one night he has a maths lesson, and one night a respite carer comes from Crossroads for three hours.

We run through much the same bathroom routine in the evenings. Most nights he goes to bed at 7 or 8pm, seemingly exhausted and needing plenty of sleep to function the next day.

In the holidays, routines are relaxed and often we will grind down into a state of torpor and apathy. I like to have some days out planned for us, as a means of staving off inactivity, but house tasks still need doing, and there is much mooching about at home.

I have to stop all of my activities during the holidays to organise Max. Gus is still working many hours, but will help when he can. For our family life, the quote 'Who chooseth me, must give and hazard all he hath,' has certainly proved to be true. However, Gus and I must be aware that we are lucky to have each other in this enterprise.

As Max's tiny boat bobs along on life's wild and strange seas, Gus and I are his rudder and his tiller, keeping him on a good tack and ever hopeful of finding a fair wind.

PAT AND CLAIRE

It was a long day. At 7.30pm in the evening I was sitting in a bed bay in the A & E department of our local hospital, with my daughter Claire. She was lying on a bed, and in a lot of pain. We had been brought in by an ambulance, which had been summoned following my call to NHS Direct for some advice on what to do. Claire's symptoms had been getting progressively worse as each day went by in that week. She has ongoing problems with her digestive system following years of surgery and complications, which have left her having difficulty eating and suffering bouts of extreme pain at times. At this time she was awaiting some scan appointments already as an outpatient and I hadn't wanted to over react, but her symptoms had become so bad she could not attempt to eat or even drink.

Two different on-call doctors examined her. The first one, around 8pm, a very nice young man (who, I couldn't help noticing, looked hardly old enough to be out of school, let alone so far down the track of training to become a doctor), informed me that he was not familiar with any of the possible causes of the symptoms Claire was presenting with, and was not able or prepared to answer any of my questions following his examination. He announced that he needed to take bloods; various other bodily function samples; an X-ray and to consult a more senior colleague. These were duly carried out. We were both very upset, but not surprised, to learn that she was going to have to be admitted, particularly as she was dehydrated – (I could have told them that!). She needed to be on a fluid intravenous drip at once, and admitted to a surgical ward, we were informed. However, following an examination by a second, more experienced doctor later on (around 10.30pm by now) I was informed that he wasn't sure where she needed to be admitted to, and under which 'umbrella'. I told him once again, that she was waiting tests for various possible causes for her pain, but that seemed to fall on deaf ears. "She needs to be examined by the duty surgeon to ascertain whether she needs more urgent surgery" he said. "When might that be?" I asked tentatively. "Don't know" he replied, we would "just have to wait until the on duty surgeon could come down as currently they were in theatre." So we waited, and waited …

Poor Claire. She was very upset as it was, and I didn't want to make things worse by seeming too anxious, so we tried to pass the time by speculating what was going on in the other cubicles, as we could hear every word when other poor souls were being examined. She picks up so easily on vibes so it was important to try and maintain a calm atmosphere. Around midnight I sent my husband home, as he had to go to work quite early the following morning, and told him I would get a taxi home when Claire was settled onto whichever ward she was going to. I didn't want to leave her, as she was frightened. The fact that she was Asperger's didn't help and nor did it seem to register with any of the staff she came into contact with that she has limited understanding of complex situations and needs lots of reassurance. Claire is out of her depth in unfamiliar surroundings and can become anxious and distressed very easily. Did they even know what 'Asperger's' was I wondered? One – entertaining to us – although quite serious incident took place as we sat peeping through the curtains into the rest of the A & E cubicle area. This occurred after midnight; when, presumably as a result of the pubs closing, an array of sorry souls with a variety of injuries were being ushered into the inner sanctum area. It was easy to assume that the injuries were most likely the result of a fall or fight caused as a result of over-imbibing of the demon alcohol. (From the state some of them were in and the slurred speech that came tumbling out of their mouths, it was not difficult to make that assumption.) Two young men suddenly decided to continue their fight in A & E and all hell broke lose. Nurses were running around, security men were called, and one senior nurse shouted, "Call the Police! Get Security to get them out NOW!" It brought some much needed light relief to a dark few hours and even Claire, though feeling so unwell and in pain, saw the funny side to it. "It's like an episode of Holby City" she giggled. (I'm so pleased she can still have a sense a humour at times like this!)

Her open wound dressing (from recent surgery three months earlier) was soaked through, and needed changing. "Mum it's really wet and I can feel the packing coming out," she wailed. I had been trained to do it at home from Christmas, and we hadn't thought to bring any packs with us as everything had happened so quickly. As we had no dressings with us, I asked the staff nurse in A & E about it. "We can't do dressings down here as we don't have the materials," she trilled. "Someone on the Ward will do it when she gets there". Funny, I thought, isn't this an A & E Department – with no facilities for packing and dressing wounds? Finally at 3am the duty surgeon appeared, full of apologies for keeping us waiting. (By now we had been there for almost 9 hours from the time we arrived and both of us had, ironically, almost lost the will to live). He quickly examined Claire and was satisfied that she didn't need to be rushed into surgery, and could go to a medical ward. All we had to do now was wait for a bed on the admissions ward. Finally, at 4am she was wheeled up to the medical admissions ward. On arriving at the ward with the nurse from A & E and a porter there was a frosty reception from the ward nurse, who indignantly declared she didn't know anything about anyone being admitted. There followed some telephone calls back down to A & E to establish who had spoken to who (could this night get any worse?) Finally she was shown to a bed. I reluctantly had to leave her, and got home at almost 5am on Friday morning, feeling exhausted.

Claire rang me from her mobile phone at 8am quite distressed. "Mum" she wailed, "I've had had no sleep at all. The dressing has only just been changed and it was so wet and soggy". Unbelievably they had had to get someone 'trained' on to the ward to do it. (Aren't they all trained nurses?) She still wasn't on a drip, nearly 12 hours after being told she was dehydrated and was by now retching so badly with terrible stomach spasms, she was crying down the phone. She was waiting for a bed on the women's medical ward. Although her dressing had been changed she still had not been put on a fluid drip. She rang again at around 12 noon. "They're putting me on a drip and I'm on Ward ….." The drip had taken over 12 hours to implement after it had been established she needed it – and more painkillers finally administered. The following twelve days she spent in hospital, with us visiting twice daily, are probably worthy of another chapter to themselves.

PAULINE AND ALISON

Journal Entry February 27th 2013

I got a phone call from Alison's care manager today to arrange a date for her annual review. I started wondering what issues around Alison's support I needed to bring up at this meeting. In many ways Alison is happier and more confident than she has been for years. At long last I feel that I can relax somewhat, and leave the people who are paid to support her to get on with it. I have a measure of trust in the agency which provides Alison's support and indeed over the last year they have gone to great lengths to improve the social lives of their clients. Alison has been to see Take That tribute bands three times this year with either a support worker or with friends. They are now encouraged to visit the homes of their friends, and often a group of them will go out for Sunday lunch together. All things most of us take for granted, but which very rarely used to happen for people with learning disabilities.

Alison rang me at 6pm as usual and started complaining about a support worker who does some of her sleepovers. Apparently she comes on at 9pm, when Alison is usually watching television, sits on the sofa with her and falls asleep. I tried to check this out as I know from experience that Alison sometimes gets muddled. "Are you sure she was asleep?" I asked. "Yes Mum, she was snoring" was the reply. "She often does it and I'm sick of it!" Well you can't get clearer than that! Perhaps this was something I could bring up at the review. I have always been Alison's advocate and it is hard work letting go and encouraging her to be her own advocate. I have been trying to show Alison that if there are things she wants to change, she can do it for herself. I decided that as the agency is probably as good as it gets, it would be better to give them a chance to sort it out before her review, as their reputation could be damaged unnecessarily if it had to be discussed in front of the care manager. Alison is worried that if she complains the staff will be angry with her and I patiently explain that she has every right to complain if a member of staff falls asleep when she should be working, even if that is only to talk to Alison about her day. I suggested that she rings the office and talks to one of the managers in the morning.

After dinner, I started to think about how things used to be, and for Alison how much better things are now. She has her own home, which she is buying under a shared-ownership scheme and this has transformed her life, but how fragile this state of affairs is. The fruition of our careful life planning is constantly subject to the vagaries of governmental whim. The current government is undermining much of the good work that has been achieved for people with learning disabilities, leaving them and us, their parents and carers, feeling very insecure. The alterations to the benefits system are starting to come into force, and I wonder what other nasty surprises David Cameron and the Tories have in store for us. I have long held the view that people with lifelong disabilities should have a separate benefits system. In most cases their disability will not change or improve, it is not something they have inflicted upon themselves; they will not magically one day be able to work. Surely, at the very least they deserve to have the means to lead comfortable, interesting and fulfilling lives, when so many other things are denied them.

LINDA AND ANDREW

Saturday 7th September 2013

7.15 am The alarm goes off as it does every day of the week apart from the four days we close the guest house for Christmas, and on our holidays. The good thing is that we never have that sinking feeling on a Sunday that the weekend is nearly over. The downside is that we never have that "Thank God it's Friday" feeling.

8.00 am John prepares the guest breakfasts while I see to Andrew who has been woken up by the alarm on his feed pump, alerting me to the fact that the overnight feed is finished. I ask Andrew if he would like to watch a DVD, and give him a choice between Shrek and SpongeBob, holding Shrek in my left hand and SpongeBob in the other. He makes a grab for Shrek and throws it to the floor. This does not mean he is rejecting Shrek – he would do the same to SpongeBob if I let him get hold of it. To Andrew, everything is a missile. We go through this routine in an attempt to encourage Andrew to make choices, so I put SpongeBob on. As soon as the opening credits start, he makes a sound which I know means he is not happy with my choice. Andrew has a rather impressive collection of 84 DVDs, which are stored in a cupboard above his bed. After four more failed attempts at finding a DVD Andrew wants to watch, I revert to the failsafe option, 'Andre Rieu Live in Melbourne'. This is a 2 hour concert which keeps Andrew engrossed throughout. Andre, what would we do without you!

8.30 am We have six guests in, and the dining room is buzzing with conversation as two Australian couples compare notes about their travels and life back at home. The other couple are from the USA and seem a little reserved at first, but by the time the empty plates have been cleared, they too are deeply involved in a conversation with the Australians. Our dining room is a bit like the United Nations some mornings and the best part of running a guest house is meeting new people every day and gaining a glimpse into their lives.

9.00 am Check on Andrew. Andre Rieu is halfway through his concert, and Andrew is watching it from the floor, surrounded by 84 DVDs. Pick up 84 DVDs and put them on a higher shelf.

9.30 am I give Andrew a shower, dress him and walk him into the dining room so I can keep an eye on him while I finish clearing up. He likes to sit in the window and watch the world go by, especially on a windy day when he will watch the trees and shrubs swaying in the breeze. There is not a breath of wind today, and while I am in the kitchen he takes up another favourite pastime – swinging the curtains.

9.32 am I return to the dining room, remove Andrew from his seat by the window, and pick up 22 curtain hooks from the floor. I let John know he has one curtain to put back up.

9.45 am I put the washing machine on and Andrew bottom shuffles into the kitchen as soon as he hears it start. He will sit engrossed through the full cycle which gives us an hour to crack on with the rooms. We take it in turns to keep checking on Andrew, but he is transfixed and doesn't notice us.

10.50 am I return to the kitchen to find the washing machine door open and freshly washed towels scattered across the floor. Note to self – we need to see if we can teach Andrew to unload the washer into a laundry basket.

12 noon No guests due until 4pm so we take Andrew out for a walk in his wheelchair.

1 pm We are sitting in the park tree-watching when my phone rings. We divert the landline to the mobile when we go out. "Hi." It is one of our guests. "We are on your front door step but no–one is answering the bell". It transpires they caught an earlier train. John walks back to let them in and then re-joins us in town for a late lunch.

3.30 pm I arrive back at home to deal with the emails and update the diary and our online availability. John and Andrew continue their afternoon out.

6 pm The guests due at 4pm ring to say they will now be arriving around 7pm. The 5pm guests have still not turned up. We sit down to our evening meal.

6.05 pm The doorbell rings, and my dinner goes back in the oven as I show the 5pm guests to their room.

7 pm Watching Shrek with Andrew, while I dream of the soak in the bath I have promised myself after the last guests arrive.

9.15 pm The doorbell rings heralding the arrival of the 7pm (originally 4pm) guests. "We decided to take in Hadrian's Wall on our way from Edinburgh, and we hadn't realised how long it would take" is the very sheepish apology.

9.30 pm Dress Andrew for bed and start his overnight feed. I give up on the idea of a bath and fall into bed.

The only analogy I can use to describe running a guest house is to imagine waiting in for the gas engineer every day of your life, and having your relatives stay all year round. Although the daily routine can make it feel like groundhog day, the positives far outweigh the negatives. It is fascinating meeting new people every day and being self-employed gives us a sense of autonomy we never had as employees.

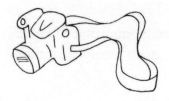

SNAPSHOTS AND THREADS

SUSAN AND KAREN

When I was growing up in the nineteen fifties, there were two children with disabilities who lived in our street. Sheila, who lived in the house opposite, was profoundly handicapped both physically and mentally. On warm days, she would sit in her wheelchair in the small front garden watching comings and goings in the street. She had no speech but when I walked across the road to talk to her and show her my dolls, she would make happy sounding noises, a bit like a baby. Then there was John, about the same age as me, a cheerful, friendly Downs Syndrome boy, who lived at the top of the street. He would run up to me whenever he saw me and I would chat to him. He liked playing at cowboys and Indians and sometimes he would sing pop songs. My parents were always warm and friendly towards John and Sheila too so I think I must have learnt from their example. When I was nine years old, my dad went to work as a charge hand at Remploy, a factory for people with disabilities. Occasionally, he took me into the factory and I met some of the workers there. To me, they seemed no different to other people except that they might be in a wheelchair or speak more slowly.

When Karen was born, everything appeared to be normal apart from her low birth weight. She was a month premature and weighed just under five pounds but was a beautiful baby. She gained weight and thrived and when her "milestones", such as sitting unaided, were late, I was assured by the health visitor that premature babies were often "slow to catch up". I was not worried: she smiled and laughed and gurgled. She loved having her tummy tickled and would take an alert interest in what was going on around her. She was two years old when she started walking and I assumed that this was because she was able to shuffle around on her bottom at a rate of knots. It did not occur to me at the time that there might be something wrong with her.

Karen was labelled "Educationally Subnormal" at the age of six; it was a shock and felt like a bitter blow. My beautiful daughter was labelled as "retarded". "Why my daughter? Why has this happened to me?" I asked myself. I went through a kind of mourning process, grieving for what might have been, the loss of my idea of a normal child and fearing what Karen's future might hold. The GP said that Karen may have had a brain infection either shortly before or during birth or a lack of or too much oxygen. It may have been because she had been born premature. Was it the high blood pressure during my final weeks of pregnancy or was it the anaesthetic used when I was eight months pregnant during the operation to turn her round in the womb because she was in breech position? Could I have caused the brain damage in some way?

Later, I realised that the reasons for Karen's brain damage were not important and I began to accept her for the beautiful and unique person that she is she is just as I had accepted Sheila and John for who they were, without judgement. Amazing to think that in our short street of some 26 houses, there were these two "special" children who could be totally in the moment and were teaching me a valuable lesson about acceptance and communication and love. Looking back, I feel gratitude that I grew up with no prejudice or embarrassment or fear about being around people with disabilities and I know now that my early encounters with Sheila and John were helping to prepare me for bringing up a child with a learning disability.

LIZ AND SALLY

I waited for the too small figure of my daughter to emerge from school. Gradually I realised that she wasn't coming out, so headed into school to find her, only to be told by her teacher that she hadn't been there all afternoon. Always inclined to panic, my mind ranged over all sorts of likely scenarios : she had been kidnapped; Sally had run away from her classmates from whom she was increasingly separated by long division, skipping, speaking, to name but a few. I rushed home and found a calm daughter watching telly with the cat, Ribena spread around the room. This child who was always firmly protected from everything, had walked home, crossed two busy roads and heaved up a heavy sash window to get in and then sat there serenely awaiting the arrival of her frantic mother. Apparently she had forgotten her packed lunch and since she rarely chose to speak in school to tell anyone about this, had decided to go home instead. Her headmaster's comment was, "Sally is much more capable than any of us give her credit for".

The end of the afternoon. We had trailed happily around the city and now my daughter-in-law wanted to slip into Mothercare and I went with her. We left the baby parked in the precinct with her father, my son Tom, and Sally.

After a few minutes we were joined in Mothercare by a bored Sally. We spent our money and then went back to the baby and Tom. But Tom joined us before we reached the baby whereupon my daughter-in-law screamed, 'Where is the baby?' We all rushed to find her and found her sleeping peacefully amid the shopping crowds.

In the inquest that followed, it transpired that Tom had left the child in the care of its aunt, only for her to abandon her post when it got boring. Horrified and furious Sally was admonished several times over by her brother and me, whilst my daughter-in-law to her eternal credit pointed out that nothing untoward had happened to the precious infant. In the end, learning difficulties and the inability to think through consequences are far more of a problem than the inability to spell long words or do algebra.

Sally was lodging away from home in a nearby town and was reasonably happy. She was being trained at a special café. She certainly liked it much more than her Independence course at the local tech. There she regularly refused to get out of the car in the morning until a member of staff came to persuade her. Even when she had been wheedled into the institution she often made her escape to Tesco's loos as soon as possible where she spent the rest of the day.

One day we got a phone call to say Sally and her friend were missing. All attempts to get her to answer her mobile phone failed. The police were notified and since they were vulnerable young people they took the disappearance seriously. Sally and her mate were missing all night long. The police then suggested that if she had been using ATMs the bank could track her whereabouts. Through this we learned that Sally had spent the night in a luxury hotel and had withdrawn money in the city centre. Our son who worked there was out scouring the streets and finally spotted them (Sally should not choose tall friends with red hair). They were brought back home not entirely repentant. Sadly, later attempts to enjoy some of the delights of 'normal' youthful independence, resulted in Sally being banned by social workers and the other lass's parents from ever seeing her friend again.

PAT AND CLAIRE

1986

We arrive at the Child Development Centre in good time for my daughter Claire's appointment for a brain scan. She is about 4 years old and is undergoing investigation for general delayed development. She does not understand what is happening, or what is expected of her, so is given a sedative in a drink form comprising an orange flavoured liquid. Shortly after drinking it, she becomes very distressed and begins crying, screaming and fighting us. Shaken, we are taken into a side room, as her screaming is distressing to other children and parents attending the Centre. Time is passing and after almost two hours the sedative still seems to be having the opposite effect on her and the procedure has to be cancelled. Frustrated and exhausted physically and mentally, my husband and I leave the hospital in a daze with our screaming bundle, and drive the short distance home. As the car pulls into the drive we turn to see her completely comatose, at last, and slumped over in her booster seat. The sedative has at last kicked in. We look at each other and hysterically both burst out crying and laughing at the same time.

September 2001

We are at Sheffield Hospital with Claire, now almost 19, waiting to be seen by a professor who is an autism specialist. After years of being diagnosed with speech and language development delay there is a suspicion that she might be on the autism spectrum. We have had to fight to get this referral on the NHS via the local PCT because the professor works for Sheffield Hospital. With the support of our GP and a consultant working with adults with learning disabilities in York, we find ourselves here after nine long months of fighting. The day is long and we are all seen together, then our daughter alone, and then just ourselves with the specialist. At the end of the day, he calls us in together and tells us that he is satisfied that Claire is on the spectrum with Asperger's Syndrome. We drive home in a daze. A double-edged sword; at last a reason – a diagnosis for all those years of wondering and worrying; but also tinged with a great sadness in the knowledge finally that our beloved daughter will not have the opportunities in life we had hoped for her, and will need support for the rest of her life. On our own, away from Claire's eyes, we grieve and weep together.

April 2005

The surgeon calls me over to look at the x-rays. Claire has been admitted to hospital as an emergency patient. She is 24. Following a diagnosis five months earlier of ulcerative colitis (an autoimmune disease which affects the large bowel) and a prolonged recent stay in hospital when she was pumped full of drugs to try and control the intensity of the disease, she had been allowed to come home. However, a relapse followed after a few weeks and here we are. The surgeon explains that her bowel is possibly on the point of perforating and that there is no further option other than major surgery to remove all or part of her bowel. None of the drugs had worked. This will leave her with an ileostomy for the rest of her life. We knew this might be a possibility but the enormity of what it will leave her with is too horrible to think about. We are stunned. This can't be happening. My husband goes off to speak to one of the consultants. I later learn that he needed reassurance that nothing else could be done for her to spare her the surgery. I lie with her on the hospital bed. She is in a lot of pain. The surgery has to be done. The following morning, she is taken down to the operating theatre. We go home to wait. It will be a 6 to 8 hour surgery. We are totally drained and devastated. The injustice of it all stabs like a knife through our hearts. Surely she has enough to contend with in life already? Once again at home, away from the eyes of the world, we weep and grieve for our beloved daughter.

LINDA AND ANDREW

May 1996

A midwife woke me at 6am to tell me Andrew has been taken ill during the night and is showing signs of infection. He is one week old and in SCBU due to his prematurity. I hastily grab my dressing gown and rush to the baby unit, to find that he has had a lumbar puncture, numerous blood tests and swabs from every orifice. "Why didn't you wake me?" I ask, devastated that my son has been put through all that without my knowledge. "We didn't want to disturb your sleep" is the reply. It's not that I wouldn't have wanted them to do all this to him, but I feel I have let him down because I wasn't there.

January 1997

Andrew is 8 months old and is in hospital with bronchiolitis. He was admitted on New Year's Eve and his condition deteriorates on 4th January. He has a lumbar puncture and they take lots of blood samples. Andrew is moved to a side ward and John and I are advised to stay overnight. On the morning of 5th January, we are woken by a nurse to be told that he is very unwell and that he will need to be ventilated. We rush to the side room and Andrew turns to me with a look of sheer terror in his eyes as he fights to breathe. I am devastated that I had not been with him during the night. We have to leave the room while they put him on the ventilator.

Andrew is in the Paediatric Intensive Care Unit at St James's Hospital in Leeds, where he was transferred on 5th January, critically ill with bronchiolitis. I spend my days sitting by his bedside reading, cross-stitching, doing puzzles – anything to occupy my mind. I am reluctant to leave him apart from mealtimes and overnight. The staff urge me to take a break and go home. I cannot even contemplate leaving the hospital, let alone Leeds. We have a room in the corridor just outside the unit, and I occasionally go there for a rest. He has been here a week and is no longer on the critical list, but he is not out of the woods by any means. I pluck up the courage to go into Leeds. We are only away a couple of hours. Everywhere we go I am acutely aware of families with babies in prams, of shops displaying baby clothes and toys, and of giant posters of happy, healthy children. I feel an urgent need to get back to the hospital. On our return, I can tell from the nurse's face that she has bad news for me. Andrew has taken a turn for the worse and he is back on the critical list. I feel so guilty. Is it because I went away and left him?

Threading through these snapshots is my feeling of being disempowered, guilty and helpless. My underlying fear is that something bad will happen to Andrew if I am not with him.

PAULINE AND ALISON

Changing Places
25th October 2001

I got a call from Alison's care manager this afternoon. She told me John (Alison's partner of six years) had left Alison and wouldn't be coming back and that Alison was very upset and could I possibly come round to Navigation Road for a crisis meeting. I wonder if she's told Alison's Dad the news – I bet she hasn't! I'm actually delighted to hear this news, but I know just how devastated Alison will be. This has been on the cards for a long time, but as usual no one wanted to intervene, even though that might have averted the crisis which has now finally happened. Alison won't be able to cope on her own and I can't see her wanting to share a home with anyone else. God knows what happens now!

Adult Placement Provision 6th July 2003

I took Alison home this morning as Liz (Adult Placement Provider) was back from her holiday in Italy. We were both pleased to see her, but what she had to say was a bombshell! I'd had my doubts when I learned that Alison's new adult placement scheme carer was a Jehovah's Witness, but had decided to give her a fair chance; would that she could have done the same for us. She has come back to tell us she's going to move to Cyprus and become a missionary – and that she'll be moving in six weeks time. Just when I thought Alison was happily settled into what seemed to be long-term, settled, secure accommodation. I'm shattered by this, I feel as if I'm back at the bottom of the snake, with no ladder in sight.

Shared Bungalow 21st March 2006

It was Alison's annual review today. What a shambles! Alison had been so upset that the support worker had been in her room and thrown some of her things away without her being there. I had to bring the subject up. The support worker fled the room in tears, followed by her manager; and left the care manager and I just sitting there, gob-smacked at such unprofessional behaviour. Once again the writing's on the wall. Alison's been very unhappy here for long enough and this has been the last straw. I've been so worried about Alison's mental health that I've been taking her for Indian head massage just to try and relieve some of the tension.

The thread which links all three of these snapshots of Alison's life is the lack of choice and control over where people with learning difficulties live and the staff who support them. For me this has been the most difficult aspect of Alison's life I have had to support her with. Since Alison first left home at the age of sixteen she has lived in nine different places in many different kinds of accommodation. These ranged from full residential care, through the adult placement scheme, shared houses with support, and independent supported living. Rarely has she been able to choose where she was to live, and often, has had to move whether she wanted to or not; conversely she has had to stay for long periods of time in places where she was very unhappy. This in turn has generated a constant never-ending stream of new support workers or care workers. Some of these she loved and grieved for long after they had left – some she was happy and relieved to see go. And all this for someone who finds any kind of change incredibly difficult to deal with and which affects her very adversely.

I'm happy to say that finally we do seem to have got it right for Alison. I just hope and pray that the government's attacks on disabled people's welfare benefits don't ever mean that Alison will have to move again. It would just about kill her and me as well.

ANNIE AND MAX

These snapshots relate to some bad experiences we've had with people and authorities.

The first was a problem with a teacher. When children have limited language with their disability, it should be obvious that they do not express themselves with as much clarity as others. When Max was 6, and I asked him to stop doing something, for example, to stop watching tele to come for dinner, he would say 'No! No! No tele!' He would cry this emphatically, whilst banging his head with his fist. I would calmly say, 'Ok. There's no need to do your nut. It's time for dinner.'

One day, around this time, his teacher at school asked him to put away his book. 'No! No! No book!' he screeched in a distressed voice. She concluded wrongly that he was being defiant. She got level with his face, waved a finger at him and yelled angrily, 'Max McLaren! Don't you EVER say "No" to me again!'

After this incident he trembled with fear violently every morning when I dropped him at the classroom door. His Teaching Assistant had related all this to me and we both knew he was now fearful of the teacher, but we felt powerless to do anything. The TA had explained to her that she had misunderstood what he was saying, but the damage had been done. Her anger had caused him to react towards her with fear, in the same way he does even now to a barking dog, an over-revving engine, or a raised voice. I did not want Max to move class, away from his few friends. As the incident was past and the TA had explained about what Max had really meant, I didn't want to antagonise the teacher over it. I wanted him to get over it himself and become more hardened, but he never did that whole long year. I also didn't want him to conclude that I would pander to his every need if he was upset as this might give him the wrong message. It's difficult with raising disabled children to know the difference between pandering and advocating, sometimes. I don't know if I got this right, even now. Teachers should take some time to think, before making assumptions about what pupils with limited powers of expression mean, when they speak. They should never use anger in the approach to a child with autism as it doesn't work, and only serves to alienate relationships catastrophically.

Another snapshot happened on a plane journey. After taking Max to the toilet, our way back to our seats was blocked by the drinks trolley. The two air hostesses were very assertive. They ordered me to 'Stand in there!' and indicated this minute space adjacent to a man's knees. They screeched at Max to 'Stand in there!' pointing to a similar virtual refuge in the row behind. He had no idea what they wanted him to do, and, in panic made a lunge to get past the side of the trolley. The frenzied hostesses started to physically ram him into the imagined area and this, they began to realise, was a mistake. By this time he had frozen, and nothing was getting through to him. His face had melted down into a disconnected mask. They finally realised something was up, but they had no idea what. They said seemingly helpfully, 'What seat are you in?' but instead of backing the contraption a few rows to allow us access, they created a sliver of a gap to the side of the wretched trolley. I breathed in and with difficulty, stood on tiptoe to squeeze my upper legs through the tiny gap. Max then made a bolt for the small space grabbing my hand desperately, like a boy drowning. They all looked on while it unravelled. We made it through. I wonder what they concluded. I don't care. Air hostesses should have awareness training that some people who may look completely normal, may need some extra care, time and understanding. They should be less authoritative, less physical and kinder.

This last snapshot relates to our difficulty with secondary school and their inflexibility. When Max was three we used a method called applied behavioural analysis, or ABA, to try to help bring him on. We engaged a team of students and friends who were taught the methods of ABA. We were all shown exactly what to train Max in and exactly how to do it. We had regular meetings and advice from a team who came from America, initially. His learning goals were broken into small parts and each part was taught and mastered by the child through repetitive exercises. He learnt to concentrate without as much flapping or running off. He practised colours, numbers, and how to ask questions back in a conversation. He had to describe something using descriptive language. He copied brick towers and shapes. He learnt to obey simple commands. Gross motor and fine motor skills were practised. Praise and rewards were given for getting it right and these were the motivators.

When he went to school, one of the team, who was a friend of mine, became his TA. She used this approach to help him progress through primary school and he did very well there. It all stopped at secondary, as schools in our area do not use these methods. We were made to feel quirky when we suggested that the learning support department, or even just his new TA, could have some training in this technique. We were willing to provide training at our expense. They were against it. He had to adapt to a different approach. All the secondary teachers and TA's wanted was for him to motivate himself. We were brick walled. No flexibility, they were going to do things as they always had. He just has to cope as best he can now. In America there is full government support for behavioural method schooling for autistic children and the outcomes are impressive. ABA for Max uses similar motivation methods to companies who award bonuses to their employees for good work done. It's just that Max was rewarded with Pringles and spinning tops instead of money. If an autistic child doesn't understand why he's doing something, then he will not do it, or he will only do it after major nagging. The best motivator is usually an immediate reward; even verbal praise can work with some more advanced children. He has not done so well in secondary school. They all remark that he is polite, and chatty, but his progress with most things has stagnated.

Every day he is only too content to tread water and they don't care. We now accept that he will learn what he is interested in and the rest can take its chances. I wish schools would realise that autistic people are motivated differently to neuro-typical children and adapt accordingly to help them. I wish schools would be more flexible. I wish schools would listen to us, the parents.

GRAFFITI WALL

He doesn't look like either of you.

He'll never grow very tall.

Where does all this autism come from?

My son couldn't possibly be handicapped.

It's not from our side of the family.

He needs to change his behaviour to fit in.

Is there any medicine for it?

How long has she had it?

I feel uneasy with them.

You won't get the same support when he's an adult.

They only want him to go to college because they can't cope at home.

Do they get autism in Africa?

It must be something you ate when you were pregnant.

She is a little peculiar isn't she?

Well what's wrong with him?

She can be quite rude!

She's very lazy.

Well, you're a middle class professional and a single parent. What do you expect?

She doesn't talk much does she?

How did she get it?

Will she grow out of it?

Which side of the family does it come from?

She'll never have babies or get married.

She'll never be brilliant.

He sticks out like a sore thumb.

Poor you. How do you cope?

SIBLINGS

SUSAN AND KAREN

Note: This has been written as if through the eyes of Karen's brother Steven

I can't remember when I became aware that Karen was different but I have a clear memory of her pushing me down the stairs and standing at the top laughing loudly as I bounced down. She has always enjoyed slapstick comedy. I was about three years old and Karen was five. Luckily, I wasn't badly hurt, just one or two bruises but mum was furious. "He could have broken some bones", she shouted. Sometimes, Karen broke my toys and she wasn't very nice to her dolls, she would sometimes pull their legs or arms off. She would scribble in books too or sometimes tear pages out. I would be cross if it was one of my books and mum would be upset if it was a book she had been given as a child.

When I grew older, my sister would annoy me by hanging round me and my friends. Sometimes she would stand too close to me and make what I thought were silly noises. She did not always speak clearly and would speak in short phrases rather than sentences but I could usually understand what she was saying even if others couldn't. She would repeat herself a lot and tell you something over and over again. Several weeks before her birthday, she would keep asking, "How long to my birthday?" Sometimes, she would talk really loudly and get very excited and people would turn and stare at her. I found this embarrassing but Mum said "Just ignore them".

When I was ten or eleven, I went to see the film "Grease" with some friends. Mum asked if Karen could go with us; "She'll enjoy it" she said. I agreed reluctantly because I didn't want her to show me up in front of my friends with her loud comments and raucous laughter. When Olivia Newton John started singing "You're the one that I want", Karen joined in with loud enthusiasm but her singing voice was not very tuneful, in fact she was a bit of a growler. I wanted to crawl under the seat but my friends were not too bothered about this and actually found it quite amusing. When I later complained to mum about Karen embarrassing me, she just laughed and was pleased that Karen had had a nice time.

Our grandparents lived near a park and we would often be taken there to feed the ducks and play on the swings. Karen loved seeing the ducks, they made her laugh when they quacked and waddled. She has always liked animals and enjoyed taking the dog a walk with our grandad. We would walk through the park and along the riverside. One summer day, we were in the park with Joy, a teenage girl who was looking after us during the summer holidays whilst mum was at work. Karen's balance was not terribly good and she fell into the lake. I think she was looking at the ducks rather than where she was walking. Joy managed to haul Karen out; she was not hurt but was dripping wet and she was laughing. I was glad that none of my friends were around to see what had happened. Our grandparents lived nearby, and we all went there. Luckily, Nana was at home and not out shopping so she was able to dry Karen off and find some spare clothes for her.

When I was eleven, we were given a kitten. Mum and Dad suggested names and both Karen and I liked the name 'Sophie'. Sophie was quite timid at first but soon got used to Karen chasing her round, shouting 'Sophie' and picking her up. Sophie did not always appreciate being picked up and cuddled and Karen got scratched a few times.

During my early and mid teens, I was not very tolerant and understanding with Karen but became more accepting as I grew older and more appreciative of her sense of humour and ability to see the funny side of things.

LIZ AND SALLY

The social workers were dubious: could the youngest child with learning difficulties cope with an adopted sibling? This child would be female and the youngest, thus usurping Sally's protected place in the family, and a possible rival in the extended family where Sally enjoyed the privilege of being the only girl amidst several boy cousins. The whole adoption process took forever because of course there were also fears as to how the newly adopted child would cope with Sally's problems.

In our family there have been many unanticipated complications and issues, but all the professionals' many justifiable anxieties about the advent of Rose turned out to be groundless. From the very first weekend visit Sally was enchanted with her new sister and Rose always seemed to understand and deal with Sally's fears and idiosyncracies.

What none of us expected was that Sally would become a fierce advocate for her sister in those early months. The social workers insisted that the girls shared a bedroom and this meant that safe in their attic, Rose could share her anxieties with Sally. So it was that Sally filled us in with the likes and dislikes that Rose was too scared or too polite to voice. 'Rose really hates that dress you made her wear'. 'Rose really dislikes Jim, he always stands in front of the telly when she wants to watch it'. 'Rose doesn't know her tables'.

The good relationship seems to have continued into their adult lives. Rose has nearly always lived close by and Sally has been a loving aunt to Rose's four children. She loved them as babies and was somewhat disconcerted when later they could do things she could not. But most of the time, as the children grow older, they cope with her very well and indeed any child in their class with learning difficulties. I am sure that at times Rose has found Sally a bit of a pain. Sally's admiration for her sister knew no bounds and at times she would irritate Rose by slavishly copying her clothes. She would sometimes buy something exactly the same. She also developed an inappropriate liking for Rose's husband and would inundate the guy with endless texts until she was stopped.

As parents we are immensely grateful to Rose She provides the companionship of someone of a similar age to Sally. Sally so much prefers her company to that of her mother; Rose is much, much more cool. So Rose finds time between her kids and her husband and her psychiatric patients to take Sally for a swim or to the shops. Perhaps she too is grateful for the support her sister gave her many years ago.

GILLIAN AND WILLIAM

When my twins arrived, they completed the family, but life became extremely busy, as I had produced three children in twenty-two months. Because I had no family living nearby, Social Services offered a mother's help, who appeared every morning for two hours for two weeks, which gave me some breathing space. Michael loved "Scarborough," and followed her around. When she left, he was sad, but tried to help me like she had. He loved to have "story time" while I fed the babies. He had to hold the books and turn pages, as it was impossible for me – my hands were somewhat occupied in balancing the new-borns on pillows as I learned to breastfeed them together. Not to be outdone, Michael would fetch his favourite teddy and lamb, and "feed" them.

I decided that it would be a good idea to use the unexpected extra child benefit to employ a young girl to spend time minding the twins so that Michael could have some uninterrupted time with me. He was still mourning "Scarborough" (he was convinced that was her name!) and Anna filled the gap, being happy to play with him or look after William and Margaret. When William was in hospital, she was a boon, as Michael was relaxed and happy in her company. Margaret spent the days with William and me in a borrowed camping cot at the hospital – there were no spare cots.

Transporting the children was an interesting exercise. We only ever had a single pram, so the babies lay on their sides, and Michael sat proudly aloft on his pram seat, showing off "his" twins. He didn't seem to mind that passers-by would coo at the other two, ignoring him.

At playgroup, William and Margaret attended one joint session, and one each on their own because I felt that this would create an opportunity for them to have time to develop friendships individually. The local school offered William three sessions a week at nursery the term before he officially started, as the teacher felt he would find it hard to settle.

This worked well, and Margaret enjoyed her solo time at playgroup, although she was worried about how William would cope without her. She was four, and already picking up that she was William's protector. This role continued at school, even though after spending three terms together at nursery and in the reception class, the head teacher suggested that it might be beneficial to separate them. I was pleased about this, but Margaret only told me when she was an adult that whenever William had a meltdown at school, she was asked to go and calm him down. This resulted in her accepting a load of responsibility and missing lessons, and in me feeling guilty that she had never mentioned what was going on. William's older brother was at the same school but it seems that he was never summoned. No wonder Margaret refused to go to the same secondary school as William.

William was aggressive towards Michael and me, pinching and scratching us when he was stressed, but rarely hurt Margaret. He was, and is, proud of being a twin, and feels that they should have a special relationship. His sister continues to monitor how things are going for him, but he can be rather intrusive, and often embarrassing. She seems to take this in her stride, and her daughters think he is wonderful. He joins in their play with no inhibitions! However she is not happy that William would prefer her to be the official contact for his support service rather than me.

Michael lives abroad, but contacts William regularly on Skype, and always arranges to spend a day out with him when he is back home on leave. Michael was the target for a lot of William's destructive meltdowns, but they get on well now. Maybe distance is an advantage – and William's maturity is continuing to develop, which no doubt helps.

Life with William was always stressful as he just kept on going, and creating turmoil; which I guess fits in with his ADHD. His tendency to take things literally could leaven situations, and his enthusiasm could be excessive, but his siblings survived, and now both get on well with him, and enjoy his company now it is in moderation.

PAT AND CLAIRE

My son was my first-born child. For three and a half years, he was our only child. He was a good baby, and fed very well. He arrived a week early, and weighed a rather surprising 8lb 5oz. He was always eager to feed and was a happy contented little soul as long as he got his feeds on time. He slept through the night from 9 weeks old, and was adorable and cute in every way, and very healthy. I remembered thinking that motherhood was relatively easy and straightforward and couldn't understand what all the fuss was about! Anyway, he had his moments – terrible two's tantrums and broken nights sleep with night frights – developing and growing into a mischievous but lovable toddler. He walked, talked and was potty trained according to all the guidelines. We moved after he was born to a different area of the country and, for a while, spent time settling into two different homes. Before we could blink, he was coming on for three. We didn't want to have just one child, as we perceived that 'only' children could sometimes find it hard to learn to share in some aspects of their lives.

Three and a half years after my son was born, my daughter Claire arrived. She was a good weight, 7lb 6oz, but from the start struggled to feed and was diagnosed with having colic. For the first few months of her life I seemed to be constantly feeding her, changing her after she was sick, and then trying to feed her again. It was non-stop, day and night. I took up residence in the spare bedroom so that my husband could get some sleep during the week whilst he was working. I don't remember much about my son around that time, as all my time and attention was spent on my daughter. How must he have felt? He never showed any animosity towards his sister although it must have been a real ordeal for him – all the crying and night disturbance; a shattered and emotionally drained mother who had very little patience.

After developing ear infections, Claire's persistent crying, especially at night, became even worse. I was eventually diagnosed with postnatal depression when she was around 9 months old. I was put on the road to recovery after moving back to York, where we had originally lived, after 4 years away. Medication and a psychologist helped me to regain some of my self back. It was indeed a dark time, and I feel I must have been a terrible mother to him around that time.

Life improved once we were back in York, and Claire was referred to the Child Development Centre. My son settled into the local primary school and my daughter was found a place for 3 days a week at a day nursery. Putting some distance between her and me enabled us to develop a better relationship. Her delayed speech and general development continued to be a worrying problem, and so the next 10 to 15 years continued along the same lines. When I think about how my son must have suffered from lack of attention, it hurts me. He was such a good little boy and was never any problem to us. He never questioned us or complained about anything, such as the amount of time we had to spend helping Claire with all aspects of her physical and mental needs, although I'm sure he must have felt it. I know his circle of friends teased him a lot at school, both at primary and secondary stage, about his rather 'strange' little sister. Fortunately, he was perceived as very bright at school and achieved good GCSE and 'A' level results. He never seemed to have to try too hard at anything he put his mind to. He played tennis well and won cups in competitions; he learnt to play musical instruments – self taught guitar and piano and was in bands at various periods at school and after university. It's almost as if he was given all of life's lucky genes.

Since going to university at 18, he has never lived at home, only visiting, and always coming back to support us during the difficult times when Claire's physical health deteriorated in recent years. He had a kind of rebellion when he went to university initially and behaved recklessly when it came to money matters. I spent many nights taking one am telephone calls from him, reassuring and talking to him when he rang me for comfort and advice at a time when he was struggling to maintain the impetus to complete his degree. (This was at a time when I was also working full-time in a demanding and responsible job.) However, he finished his degree course with a 2.1. BA, despite all our concerns.

I always tried to support him throughout his difficult years at university and beyond, and we are good friends. He has always turned to me, rather than his father, for emotional support. He has turned out to be a kind, loving and generous person who thinks the world of his little sister. Now in his thirties, soon to be married, still living away in London, I often wonder what memories he has of those earlier years. He certainly got our attention for a while when he went off to university so I know that was his way of saying "I'm here – don't forget me – I need you too!" There are occasions even now, when he comes home to stay for a few days that my daughter becomes very possessive if I am having a chat or a cuddle with her brother. She tries to intervene and he becomes quite frustrated with her. "You have mum all the time. It's my time with her now". I have to be very firm with her at these times – not easy to negotiate sometimes with someone with Asperger's Syndrome.

I often wish I could turn the clock back and do it all again – only this time I like to think I would be more aware, and cope a lot better. However, we all know that we have to learn our lessons in life by living through the hard and difficult times. That is, I believe, what shapes us and makes us who we are. Most of us as parents aspire to be the best we can be, but parenthood, although rewarding in many ways, can be tinged with guilt and feelings that we could have, should have, been better. I have often asked him about how he felt when he was growing up as the sibling of a younger child with a learning disability. He doesn't say much and he has never shown any resentment towards his sister or us, his parents. What he really felt inside is something I will perhaps never know and perhaps the raw truth from him would be more than I could bear.

ANNIE AND MAX (Written by Sophie)

'What a smiley baby' everyone remarked as we knelt on the sitting room floor with Max on a sheepskin rug in the middle. Max lay on his back, arms and legs flopping out to each side not moving much. 'Look' I proudly said as I put my head near him and he started to smile again. Max was four months old and should have been starting to hold his head up but for some reason he was still just lying and a bit floppy. Sometimes if I moved my finger in front of his eyes he wouldn't really blink but he always recognized a face in front of him.

Being ten at the time, it was difficult for me to bond with a baby who didn't really do much, but this party trick was my piece de resistance. Since my Mum and Dad had told me they were having a baby, I had felt quite numb. I didn't really know how it would affect me. People were saying he would be fun to play with but so far he didn't really seem to be.

We found out later that he had delayed visual maturation and some element of dyspraxia. He couldn't see much until ten months old, and when he started walking it was late and with some difficulty. When we got the diagnosis of autism we all trained so that we could teach him to deal with some normal situations that most children learn by copying. At the age of 13 I was qualified to teach him using the methods of behavioural therapy we had all been taught.

'What are you doing on Sunday, Sophie?' my friends asked.

'Oh, looking after Max.'

'Ahhh. That will be so much fun.'

But it wasn't. Building wooden blocks in different formations and getting Max to copy while he tried to leave the table, banged his head and shouted 'No, no, no.' Not any fun at all. We would have a break by walking to the park and playing on the swings. This was the fun we both looked forward to and I loved talking to Max absent mindedly, sometimes to teach him about social communication skills, at other times chatting about children's TV programmes and singing his favourite songs. As time went by these breaks became a little longer and the 'boring stuff' a little shorter- something I would under-emphasize when telling Mum and Dad about what we had got up to!

Now Max has mastered the things we taught him, all of our time together is leisure time. We chat about his school friends and play our favourite 'guess the song' game. He and my boyfriend are very close and as they walk along together deep in conversation, the same height, they look more like friends. I walk happily behind remembering the little child who couldn't do anything for himself. Look at what we have taught him, look at what he has taught himself and look at what he is capable of now- what a brilliant feeling! In the early days I never thought that I would have a relationship with this person who wasn't moving fast enough or speaking well enough for my impatient self, but I love Max with all my heart and when we are together chatting about nothing in particular it makes my heart sing.

SPECIAL OCCASIONS

SUSAN AND KAREN

A Perfect Birthday

In 2010, Karens's birthday was due to fall on a Sunday; she would be forty five. "Great, we can have all day to enjoy it" I said to Tom. The plan was that we would take Karen to Fairburn Ings for some bird watching and a picnic lunch. She is very interested in birds; she had visited Fairburn a few times with her Social Club and had thoroughly enjoyed it. Later, we would have a meal in a small restaurant in Castlegate followed by a show at The Grand Opera House. It would be a day full of wonderful surprises for Karen.

It did not start well. When we went to collect Karen from "The Rowans", her residential home, that morning, she was tearful. This was because one of her twin nephews had not sent her a birthday card. One of Karen's autistic traits is to notice what is missing. "Teenage boys are not always good at remembering birthdays" I said. I explained that because A lives with his mother, whilst J lives his father, (Karen's brother Steven), it was possible that no-one had thought to remind A. "You have some lovely cards and presents and we have some lovely surprises for you today", I added.

We set off for Fairburn Ings with a subdued Karen sitting in the back of the car. The previous day, she had been on a trip to Newcastle, to see "Disney on Ice". Usually after something like this, she would excitedly tell people all about it but when I asked her whether she had enjoyed the show or whether there were characters such as Micky Mouse, Goofy or Snow White, she answered in monosyllables in a voice that was barely audible. She sat quietly in the car with me trying to engage her in conversation. When she saw a road sign for Fairburn Ings, she started shouting "I don't want to come here, I don't want to come with you, I go here with the Social Club". At that point, it might have been sensible to abandon Fairburn Ings and go elsewhere, perhaps Lotherton Hall or Temple Newsam. However, we drove into the car park and Tom went to buy coffees from the café whilst I asked Karen why she was angry. "Is it because A didn't send you a card?" I asked. She burst into tears, and after a good cry, calmed down although she was still subdued. "I don't want to see no stupid birds" she muttered. We ate the picnic and then Karen agreed to walk round the site. She was delighted to see a flock of lapwings and was fascinated by a hairy caterpillar she spotted on the path. "Better not touch it, they can give you a rash", I said. She stroked it as if to challenge me and then grinned at me. We continued our walk and all seemed well.

When we returned to our car, Tom opened the boot and Karen saw her dress that I had sneaked in earlier. The reason I had done this was because sometimes Karen cannot cope with the anticipation of going to an event that is not part of her routine. She may become stressed and then have an outburst. An element of surprise and seeming spontaneity usually works well as there is no time for anxiety to build up. When Karen saw the dress, she started shouting "I want to go home, I don't want to be here". I tried explaining about the meal and the theatre but she wasn't having any of it. "I want to go home. I have my dinner at The Rowans at teatime on Sundays. I want to go home". "Right, you're going home", said Tom who was feeling fed up by this time; he finds her rages more difficult to deal with than I do. There was nothing I could say to ease the situation or lighten her mood. She didn't want to listen and I felt as if I was running out of steam; things looked hopeless.

We took Karen home, there seemed no other option. When I accompanied her into the house, two staff members greeted us and Karen started crying, "I didn't get a card from A" she said. I started crying too. We hugged each other and then I said goodbye and left. I felt drained, I'd had such high expectations and the day now seemed like a dismal failure. "I suppose I'd better cancel the restaurant" I said to Tom when I got back into the car. "No don't do that. I need cheering up" he said. So Tom and I went to the restaurant and we saw the show which featured a band singing ELO songs in the first half and Queen songs in the second. It was excellent, Karen would have enjoyed it.

I learned some valuable lessons that day. Firstly, to try to ensure, as far as possible, that all family members remember Karen's birthday. Secondly, to keep things simple so that Karen does not feel overwhelmed and thirdly, to involve Karen in deciding how to celebrate. Maybe asking her, on the day itself, if necessary, what she would like to do, for example lunch at a café or afternoon tea. I am still learning.

LIZ AND SALLY

There is much to annoy grumpy elderly people about the modern Christmas. It starts with the Christmas cards in September, and then 'Silent Night' (!) belted out in the supermarket long before Advent has arrived. Then there are the months of debt-inducing adverts culminating in the hideous Boxing Day sales. Even Midnight Mass doesn't take place at midnight any more but at eight o'clock with over tired kids in attendance. Despite this, I have always thrown myself into all the preparations and enjoyed it. I have done stockings and sprouts; baubles and candles galore; studied Delia and Mary Berry and stood in endless queues in the Post Office. This year was no exception.

But of course, the season of good cheer is also the season of bugs and germs and for us, as for many, the seasonal delights have included a visit to the GP, another to the out-of-hours clinic and a lengthy conversation with 111. Sleeplessness was induced not by an excited wait for Santa but by some nasty germ. We had our Christmas dinner alone, waiting for food to be delivered from our son. All that effort and we're waiting for meals on wheels with not a candle in sight.

And yet. A few days later….the card table sits in front of the fire, containing all that has been the best and the worst of this year's celebration. A half-finished jigsaw waiting for my daughter to return, as she is the only one who can manage to make the fine distinctions between the bits of leaf and shadow that are required to complete it. Two half eaten boxes of chocolates symbolise all the indulgences of the season. A box of antibiotics nestles unsafely between a cribbage board and a pack of cards. There is a long family tradition of this game into which all grandchildren and in-laws are inducted. It is only played on high days and holidays when the children can be wrested from their electronic devices and the grandparents from their dozing or their busyness. An hour or two of harmony combines with a strong competitive spirit. A burning log, a supine dog, ginger creams and of course, winning. Christmas is still THE special occasion.

GILLIAN AND WILLIAM

William gets very excited as his birthday approaches, and always tries to organise an outing for his friends and himself. This plan does not always come to fruition, as he forgets to ask people he invites to confirm whether or not they actually intend to come on the night. When extending invitations he tends to be very enthusiastic, and friends and acquaintances agree that it sounds like a good night out. William then makes a provisional booking, which needs to be amended once he has finally discovered who is definitely joining him. My role in this seems to be to fill in for his missing peers by having a meal out with those who have stayed the course.

One year he and three friends had a very successful day out at Go Ape, a high wire adventure in Dalby Forest. I refused to consider attempting this activity, but William and his friends had a wonderful day out! Last year he went skiing in Switzerland with an organisation that arranged group holidays. He considered this to be his birthday treat, as he got home on his birthday, so had spent the whole week celebrating. He was triumphant that he had gone down the black run featured in a James Bond film. I'm glad I was not aware of that aspiration in advance. I am proud that William made all the arrangements for himself, remembering the process his friend and I had supported him through the previous year. This time he checked each stage with me as he sorted out the details. The last time, William suddenly announced that contrary to our advice he had agreed to join the party at the Kent base, and that he would need a lift to Sevenoaks from me, an opportunity in which I declined to participate. This necessitated a quick dash to York to help him to buy a disabled person's coach card, and book a ticket to Victoria, where other members of the trip were being collected on their way to Sevenoaks. None of this was good for my blood pressure, but William sailed through my anxiety with no obvious ill effects! At least he learned from this experience how to plan better the next time.

For another year's birthday outing a group of friends went out to a pub for drinks. I had taken William for dinner beforehand so that he started out on a full stomach. Most of the group were sensible, but one was sufficiently drunk that he was unable to get home on the bus under his own steam, and William had to take him back to his own flat. Unfortunately his friend managed to block the toilet by trying to flush a complete toilet roll, and the landlord was not best pleased. Oh dear! All was forgiven in the end, although William was out of pocket by the time the repair was done. He does now make sure he has eaten before a visit to the pub, so I guess the experiential learning curve is progressing successfully.

Whatever else happens on William's special day, my job is to take him out for a meal, and to produce a present. I have learned that he is uneasy about receiving presents, commenting that he does not like surprises. He is reluctant to open anything unexpected when it is given, a response shared by my friend from Singapore, for whom it is culturally inappropriate to open a gift in the presence of the giver. My most successful presents for William have been bought weeks in advance. This means that items can be left around my house in a variety of partially hidden corners. William has always enjoyed rummaging through other people's belongings, and can often tell me where something I have lost is located. I'm never sure if he has hidden it, or whether it has been absorbed into the general chaos. He even found a Gameboy I had confiscated from the children ten years after I had had to replace it. I'm still not sure if I had found a particularly secure hiding place, or if the toy had been moved by "Mr. Nobody".

William will comment on what he has discovered – his detective skills are finely honed – and I put the object he has mentioned most often into a shoebox. I used to decorate this with stickers related to his particular interests, but this no longer seems to be needed. Part of his script for receiving presents is changing, but he always expresses amazement and delight, a longstanding part of his strategy for dealing with presents.

PAT AND CLAIRE

The day had at last arrived. This would prove to be a most significant day in our daughter Claire's life and one in which she more than rose to the occasion. It was September 2010, and my husband's goddaughter was getting married. It was a bright sunny morning, and my daughter was full of excitement as I woke her early. It wasn't just the bride's special day – my daughter was going to be a bridesmaid, for the first time and she was so thrilled. We had known the bride's parents since before we had our children, and the four children of both our families had grown up together.

It was to be a big wedding. There were four adult bridesmaids and two little pageboys. The venue was one of the biggest in the city, with more than one hundred guests during the day, increasing to 150 for the evening. It was to be a lavish event with no expense spared. Claire was a young woman of 27 at the time and we weren't really sure how she would cope with the day. Being Asperger's was a challenge in itself, as social skills and interaction with others can sometimes be confusing and difficult. However, the bride had pleasantly surprised us all by asking her to share her 'big' day, and it had been in the planning for at least two years. She had known the other bridesmaids as friends of the bride for many years and the chief bridesmaid was also a hairdresser who had been doing our hair for some years.

After showering and with her hair washed and wet, she was duly dispatched to the bride's home nearby, where all the girls would be getting ready. Priority, of course, was the bride. The next time we would see Claire would be at the church. It was a relief to me that someone else would be getting her ready. She has never enjoyed me fussing over her long hair, and has resolutely refused to wear any kind of make-up. She had been told firmly by the bride to be that she would have to wear make up and have her hair styled along with the other girls. She had accepted this without question. A few days before she had had her long hair highlighted with blonde tones.

We got to the Church in time to see the wedding party arrive. The bridesmaids came in their car first, and out stepped four stunning young women. They all looked so pretty in their gorgeous long wine coloured dresses. They all had their long highlighted hair in similar styles. I couldn't help but get a huge lump in my throat when I saw her and had to bite back the tears. She looked so lovely. It broke my heart to think she would be unlikely to ever have a wedding of her own. Her make-up was subtle but really made a difference and enhanced her pretty face. She was very much part of the 'group' – something she doesn't experience very often.

She was a little overcome with tears as she followed the beautiful bride down the aisle; the bride's father was also choking back the tears so we could forgive her for that. I was also trying very hard not to let her see how emotional I was feeling, but was so proud of her. I had deliberately positioned myself away from the aisle so that she would not see me if I started crying. Her father, who was next to me, shielded me from her eye line and was tasked with taking photographs as the wedding party moved down the aisle. We had been very careful to stress to her that it was not all about HER on the day, but the bride, and under no circumstances was she to deflect attention. Sufferers of Asperger's can be very self-centred unfortunately and can have difficulty suppressing their emotions.

The day was one that we will remember for a long time. We felt immensely proud of our daughter for the way in which she conducted herself throughout the day and evening with such dignity, and anyone not knowing Claire would not have guessed she was autistic. The bride's father, during his speech paid tribute to all the bridesmaids, and gave her a special mention, which moved me to tears. We will always be so grateful that someone gave her the opportunity to experience being part of such a special day. She may never experience her own wedding but this was the next best thing. It was indeed a most significant day for us all.

PAULINE AND ALISON

A few years ago, I attended a workshop given by John O'Brien, a leading advocate for people with learning disabilities from America. It was a very interesting, but very interactive day, with the audience contributing as much as the workshop leaders. I was sitting next to a friend I hadn't seen for a number of years and had been off-loading my anger and frustration at social services' inability to find suitable living accommodation for Alison and how depressed she was becoming. Towards the end of the workshop, one of the workshop leaders asked for four people from the audience who had a problem to come to the front of the room. My feet seemed rooted to the floor; even though part of me wanted to take this opportunity, my inherent fear of being the centre of attention took over, and I remained firmly in my seat. I felt an elbow nudge me in the ribs, and my friend said "Go on, you've got a problem!" Still I couldn't move – another nudge, this time firmer – another louder encouragement to go forward. Now people were starting to look over at us. Well, I thought, if people are looking anyhow, what have I got to lose, but still rather reluctantly, I got to my feet.

The rest of the audience were divided into four groups, each group attached to one of the people with the problem. I had to describe my problem to the group and they had to come up with ideas of how the problem could be solved. The conclusion the group came to was that I couldn't do this on my own any longer and that Alison needed a circle of friends who would support her in trying to achieve the kind of life she wanted.

How glad I am that I finally got up my nerve that day about four years ago, and that I overcame my initial reservations. I started asking people if they would be interested in supporting Alison, and without exception every person I asked was willing to give whatever they could to the circle. Her life has been enriched beyond measure by having this group of people in her life. At first the circle meetings, which happen four or five times a year, were led by the friend who'd encouraged me at the workshop, but gradually it became evident that Alison wanted to lead it herself and as her confidence grew, and with help she is now totally in charge. She sets the agenda and we listen to all she has achieved between each get-together, what has gone well and what isn't going well. Everyone encourages her and gives her lots of positive feedback. One circle member goes to a card-making class with her once a month. Another invites her out for the day, and they have a meal together. Another one invites her to stay with her in Scarborough for a weekend every now and again. As the circle has grown, everyone has become friends and they all say their lives have also been enriched in the process.

Alison has always loved having parties, and her birthday and Christmas have been the highlights of her year. Now she has the circle of support, she has an excuse for a party at least four extra times a year, and we often end the meeting with pizzas all round.

LINDA AND ANDREW

It is my son's first birthday, and we are having a small party with family and close friends. Just like his first Christmas, this is an occasion we have been looking forward to with great anticipation. Andrew's first Christmas had not been a happy one as he was clearly unwell. I try not to think about it, but the memories come flooding back as I am opening his birthday presents. On Christmas Day, he had been listless and disinterested in the decorations, the tree, and his presents which we had to open for him while he sat gazing into space. We didn't know at the time, but he had bronchiolitis, which became gradually worse between Christmas and New Year and nearly took him from us at the age of 8 months. He was left very weak and unable to eat enough food to maintain his weight, and came home from hospital on oxygen therapy and with a nasogastric tube through which we have to give him a formula feed twice a day and continuously through the night.

Today is going to be different. Today we have removed the nasogastric tube, partly for the photographs but more importantly to give Andrew a break from the discomfort of a tube in his nose and throat. There are lots of presents, and Andrew is in a giggly mood and looks the picture of health. I bring the birthday cake through from the kitchen, walking slowly so as not to cause a draught and blow out the candle. As soon as we start singing "Happy Birthday" to Andrew, his bottom lip quivers and two fat tears roll down his cheeks. By the time we have finished, he is sobbing, and has buried his head between his feet. After lots of cuddles and soothing words, his sobs gradually subside and he gives us a watery smile.

He laughs and claps his hands repeatedly as we ceremoniously open his presents one at a time. He is not interested in the contents, only the sound of the paper which we rip off and crumple up when we see how much he is enjoying it. Once the presents are all unwrapped, we put him on the floor to explore his birthday gifts. Ignoring them all without exception, he starts to throw the crumpled up balls of wrapping paper around the room and is soon conducting a game whereby he is sitting in the centre of the room while we run around picking up the paper balls and throwing them back at him.

The party is over and the guests have gone home. The dreaded nasogastric tube must be re-inserted. I swaddle Andrew tightly in a sheet and John holds his head still while I push the tube up Andrew's nostril, slightly changing the angle of the tube as it hits the back of his nose. My son is wide eyed with terror. He turns pale and clammy, tears stream out of his eyes and he gags as the tube snakes down his throat and into his stomach. He knows the drill. This happens on a daily basis and sometimes more, as he frequently pulls the offending tube out of his nose. At the age of 12 months, he understands that if he keeps his head still and doesn't fight, the ordeal will be over more quickly. Once the tube is in place, I tape it to his face. Andrew's body relaxes and the birthday boy gives us a beaming smile.

ANNIE AND MAX

Gus and I always try to give good parties. When Sophie, our daughter was little she had brilliant parties, in the garden, which involved fantastically imaginative assault courses for the teams of kids. There was a large horizontal pole to sit astride, covered with old carpet to make it comfortable. Two children had to beat each other with pillows, till one fell off onto the soft mattress placed underneath for the purpose of catching the vanquished. There was also the jousting game where one child was put in a wheelbarrow and covered to the chin with a black bin-bag. Another child pushed the barrow fast towards a vertical board, suspended up high, with a hole in the middle. The child in the barrow was simply required to thrust a joisting pole she was carrying through the hole and all would be well. If, however the pole hit the board instead of the hole, as all too often happened, the board would tilt and a bucket of water would drench the wretched child, hence the bin bag for waterproofing. It was all great fun for children. I would, of course, make a homemade cake, which I saw as a token of love. These were in the shape of the moment for Sophie: now ballet stage with plastic dancers, now violin with liquorice strings so real you could almost play it, and latterly, a Barbie style fashionista cake. The worst incident was Amy weeping and shivering uncontrollably, after she had been pushed into the pond by Charlie. It was all such fun that I inevitably contracted a migraine afterwards, the sign of having hosted a brilliant party and having survived another year.

When Max came to the party years at school, we decided on a Halloween theme, as his birthday is October 20th. We felt especially bound to give a good show as Max was a disabled child in a mainstream school. The invitations were a work of art: black card, spooky gold writing, and the special touch, a stuck-on scrunch of orange tissue paper which put you in mind of bonfires, or fireworks. A year is a long time in the life of a child of a certain age, and these things are irresistible to them. Coming up to October/November, they are desperately looking forward to the sights and sounds of Halloween and bonfire night for another year.

We would ask everyone to dress in theme and parade them all up our road to kindly neighbours and friends, for prearranged visits. They would stuff themselves, as expected, with sweets. The bravest, or most foolish, would sing a song tunelessly or tell an unfunny joke. The adults would clap and laugh and say,

'Here, have some more sweets, you've earned them.'

Clutching handfuls of sugary snacks, the bedraggled, straggling line of Harry Potters, ghouls, witches, Goths and skeletons were marched home. There, a blazing log fire was waiting for them in the old summerhouse for the purposes of cosy ghost story telling, and games. These consisted of ducking for apples, eating a sticky treacle bun from a dangling rope without using hands, and a treasure hunt in the garden. They would be given hot dogs and toffee apples for tea. The themed cake was invariably a ghost train. They were each provided with spooky headbands supporting lit up skulls or pumpkins bouncing about on springs. Now it was dark, they were encouraged to run wildly around the field making weird noises. Gus lit a lovely bonfire and later, we had fireworks. Everyone would help comfort Max, who would be a bit phased by now. We would avoid loud rockets, as he was petrified of them, and concentrate on roman candles and sparklers. The picking-up parents would be treated to wine in the summerhouse and children would start crying as they didn't want to leave. It was all very gratifying, as parties went.

FOOD AND EATING

SUSAN AND KAREN

When Karen was in her teens, she enjoyed making Victoria sponge cakes. At first I would help her to weigh the ingredients out and tell her what to do. Then I had the idea of writing a recipe card out for her. I listed the ingredients at the top and broke the process down into easy stages that she could follow:

Victoria Sandwich Cake

4 ounces margarine

4 ounces sugar

2 large eggs

4 ounces self-raising flour

1 level teaspoon baking powder

1. Grease the cake tin.

2. Sieve flour and baking powder.

3. Cream margarine and sugar together with a wooden spoon until light and fluffy.

4. Beat in eggs, one at a time. Add some flour with the second egg.

5. Fold in the rest of the flour with a metal spoon.

6. Beat with wooden spoon until well mixed.

7. Put cake mixture in cake tin.

8. Bake in oven at Gas Mark 5 for 40 minutes.

Karen soon learned to weigh out the ingredients on the kitchen scales by herself and before long could follow the recipe without help. She loved beating the mixture vigorously. "You've got really strong wrist action, much better than your Mum's" said Tom. Karen giggled at this. "I can do this better than you", she laughed. She made very good Yorkshire puddings too, they were always light and fluffy; the secret of course was in the wrist action. Karen also enjoyed making scones. My scones never rose, Karen's and Tom's always did. "Nice biscuits", Tom would commented after eating one of my scones or "These would be good for filling in holes in the pavement". Karen found this hilarious.

Although Karen was conversant with numbers and could count, she was unable to calculate the time that the cake needed to be taken out of the oven. However, she was very competent at setting the timer for forty minutes, once the cake was ready for baking. After the timer rang, she would carefully take the cake out of the oven using oven gloves. She has always been very good at following health and safety instructions and will remind others about them too.

Whilst the cake was cooling, she would make the butter cream icing using Stork soft margarine and icing sugar. I would cut the cake in two and Karen would spoon half of the butter cream onto the top of the bottom half of the cake. After putting the two halves back together, she would spread the remainder on the top of the cake and then make swirly patterns with a knife. She would proudly bring it to the table at teatime, saying "Look what I've made". "That looks fantastic", Tom would say, "I can't wait to try a piece". Steven, Karen's younger brother usually did not comment but would wolf his cake down and ask for another piece.

LINDA AND ANDREW

25th January 2013

Andrew came home from school today with a certificate of achievement:

STAR OF THE WEEK

This certificate is awarded to Andrew

For eating all his school dinner (even his pudding)

This is a phenomenal achievement for Andrew, and something we thought might never happen.

Andrew has always had a complex relationship with food. Due to his prematurity, he was fed via nasogastric tube for the first six weeks of his life in SCBU. Once we were home he struggled to gain weight despite the fact he was a keen and frequent breast-feeder. We tried to give him complementary bottle feeds but he would spit the teat out in disgust. We discovered months later that he had a cow's milk intolerance.

Andrew's critical illness at the age of 8 months left him unable to take enough nutrition orally, and he was discharged home with a nasogastric tube in place. Just after his second birthday, Andrew had an operation to site a gastrostomy. The gastrostomy was only ever going to be a temporary measure as far as we were aware, and Andrew continued to enjoy eating. He had a continuous gastrostomy feed through the night, and would have a top up feed during the day depending on how much food he ate.

He would not eat in public, and this presented a problem when he started reception class. Andrew's teacher initially gave him his lunch in the classroom while the rest of the class went to the dining room. She gradually "de-sensitised" him to the presence of other children in the room while he was eating, and within a year he was eating his lunch in the hall with the rest of the school. By the time he was 8, he could pick up a beaker and give himself a drink, and would hold the spoon which had been loaded with food for him, and lift it to his mouth with only a gentle nudge of his elbow to prompt him. The next step was for him to load the spoon himself.

And then he stopped eating.

We took him to the GP and to the dentist to see if there was a physical reason, but they could not find anything untoward. I asked if anything had happened at school that might have affected Andrew, but this also drew a blank. Andrew was purely gastrostomy fed from then on. In a chance conversation almost a year later, I learned from another parent that the lunchtime routine had changed around the time Andrew stopped eating. The children used to sit around a table with their classmates, and a familiar member of staff assisted those children who needed help with feeding. She told me that the children were now sitting in long rows and those who needed help were fed by whoever was available, and not necessarily by the same person each day. We went into school to ask them if there had been a change in the lunchtime routine, and if so when it had happened. We were told that the lunchtime routine had only just changed, which I asked them to put in writing. I have a very large folder full of correspondence between me and the school, but they steadfastly refused to confirm in writing when the changes took place. This made it very hard not to draw the conclusion that the other parent was telling me the truth and that Andrew had put the shutters down because he was not receiving the consistency of support he had enjoyed for the previous 5 years. The school is under new management and we have had to accept that we will probably never know why Andrew so dramatically stopped eating, but the seeds of distrust had been sown.

When Andrew transferred to a special secondary school, his feeding issues were put on the back burner to give him the opportunity to settle into the new routine without putting any pressure on him. Over the next few years, despite everyone's best efforts, Andrew continued to resist taking anything orally. I requested a meeting with the Educational Psychologist and school staff, and asked "What would happen if a child who did not have learning disabilities suddenly stopped eating at the age of eight? Would you just assume that they didn't want to eat any more?" Andrew's teacher listened intently as I related how much Andrew used to love eating. She made it a priority to help Andrew overcome his oral defensiveness, and gradually, painstakingly, she gained his confidence and he started to open his mouth to accept a spoonful of food. Within a year, he was eating a full pot of my home made puree in the dining room.

Andrew fully deserves his Star of The Week award, but he would never have received it if his teacher had not listened to me and helped Andrew overcome the psychological barrier that was stopping him from enjoying food. He loves going to after school cookery club and is a willing participant in making food which is then pureed for him to enjoy the next day at lunchtime. Ten years since he stopped eating, Andrew is back to lifting a loaded spoon to his mouth and is truly enjoying food. We are now hopeful that he will, after all, get rid of the gastrostomy one day.

GILLIAN AND WILLIAM

William failed to thrive as a baby and lost weight when he had a virus just after his first birthday. At thirteen months – and twelve pounds – he was seen by a paediatrician, who checked heart, lungs, kidneys, and then referred William to a gastroenterologist, as tests indicated that he might have coeliac disease. William spent four days in hospital, being checked for cystic fibrosis and food allergies as well as having a stomach biopsy, and was then referred to a dietician. She declared that he was probably intolerant of several foods, but decided that he did not need to be put on an exclusion diet. This naturally meant that I researched this and tried to identify the guilty foods at home.

Food colourings seemed to be culprits. In those days tartrazine gave fish fingers a bright yellow hue. We had always joked that if William ate more than one, he became irritable. Orange squash led to screeching and increased activity, and raw tomatoes (William's favourite, regularly stolen from the fridge) resulted in a maelstrom of destruction. I avoided foods that affected him, wondering if I was jumping on the middle class bandwagon of blaming bad behaviour on food allergies. However, I broke my ankle when the twins were three, and my husband brought home convenience foods, which led to a considerable deterioration in William's conduct. After a week we all rebelled against our new diet, and normal eating patterns resumed. William was immediately more settled. My initial assumption had been that he was reacting to the changes in me by running away with my crutches and attacking his poor siblings, but I came to believe that this extreme behaviour was related to the dietary changes.

We had a family ban on sweets as William responded adversely to chocolate (recommended by the dietician), sugar and food colouring. All three children enjoyed snacks of fruit, raw vegetables and breadsticks, so this was easy to implement. My mother once gave each of the children a packet of Smarties for a train journey because she felt that they were being deprived of treats. William spent the subsequent five hours literally swinging from the luggage racks whenever I was not restraining him. I never tried it, but was sorely tempted to feed him Smarties just before Mum was due to babysit.

At nursery William's teacher commented that he never concentrated after he had been outside in the play area. Investigation showed that one of his brother's friends had been slipping him Smarties through the fence at playtime because she thought he was cute! I had to explain to this kind child that this was a bad idea. She was always protective of William, and when he was seven, asked me if he was handicapped after observing his poor coordination at a gymnastics class they both attended.

My favourite episode was when another mother told me off for making William go to swimming lessons, as he had informed her proudly that he was allergic to water. I had to explain that I had told him this in the context of his reluctance to wash, and that swimming club was the highlight of his week! He had obviously taken my joke literally.

William now has a varied diet, with a preference for fruit and vegetables. However he also has a penchant for burgers, possibly because they are consistent and he can anticipate what he will be eating. Over time I have realised that he uses car journeys to discuss problems and concerns. When his anxiety decreases William announces that he is hungry. "Mum, can we go for a Happy Meal?" Is this taking the "happy" literally? It certainly seems to be his way of indicating that he is feeling better and that the debriefing has been satisfactory. William has a variety of scripts for such situations. When he asks if we can spend some quality time together, my immediate unvoiced reaction is "Oh no, what's wrong this time?" However this phrase is used for anything from a desire to procrastinate starting a task to major distress. If William wants to go out in the car, it is a useful clue that there is a real problem, especially when his target is a town with the "golden arches."

Does this mean that food is part of William's strategy for expressing his feelings?

PAT AND CLAIRE

From the day my daughter was born she has had problems with food. Not so much the food itself, but more her body's ability to process it. This was evident from birth when she was constantly being sick, and having diarrhoea. She had colic for quite a long time after she was born. During the early days of feeding she could only take very small amounts of milk before being sick, and then trying again. Then, between the ages of 9 months old to around 2 years old she developed one ear infection after another. The doctors' solution to this was to prescribe antibiotics. She developed a bad reaction to some of them, septrin in particular, which resulted in a bad rash around her bottom area, which then spread all over her body. We were referred to a skin specialist at the time, and it was he who came to the conclusion that it was caused by the antibiotic, septrin. I also now believe that the damage caused internally to her already fragile digestive system by this constant onslaught of antibiotics resulted in her ongoing battle into adult life with digesting and processing food, and ultimately a diagnosis of ulcerative colitis in her early to mid twenties. This in turn led to recent years of major surgery, a permanent ileostomy, and severe inflammatory bowel disease with her remaining digestive system struggling to deal with a daily intake of food. I wish I had had more knowledge about the long-term effects of the overuse of antibiotics, which is now more acknowledged.

She really does enjoy her food and when she's having a rare good spell, her stomach allows her to eat a varied diet. She will often over-eat at these times if not watched carefully, as she doesn't seem to register when she is full, thus setting off the cycle of discomfort. She enjoys eating out in restaurants when she is well, and can appreciate the pleasure of food, despite the effect that eating can have on her body.

Her favourite foods include bread, cheese, pasta and pizza, all of which are not the best to eat with a delicate stomach, although gluten free varieties are more available now. Frequent spells of discomfort can involve pain in her upper stomach on eating, constant nausea most days, sometimes retching and bouts of diarrhoea; all make it difficult to help her to maintain a healthy weight and it is a constant battle for us all.

Despite medication to help with the nausea, and tablets taken before she eats and at intervals throughout the day during a bad spell, she loses her appetite and consequently, weight loss occurs. Because of this, in the times when she feels well we tend to let her eat more of what she actually really enjoys.

We have tried all sorts of restricted food diets to try and alleviate her struggles but nothing seems to improve it. She has recently been tested again for coeliac disease and Crohn's, but (fortunately) all have come back negative. I often think my daughter would fare better in a world in the future, when we all get to the stage where we just take a couple of pills each day to sustain us!

Through my daughter's ill health over the years I have become more aware of food and the effects it can have on our bodies. For many years I have practised preparing and cooking food which is intended to be a healthy all round diet for the rest of the family. Food is one of life's real pleasures, providing it is not abused. Even though excess and over processed foods can make us quite ill in one way or another, and is recognised as responsible for causing a raft of modern day food related illnesses, we can celebrate with food, and also console ourselves with it. The saying "a little of what you fancy does you good" is so true. Although food is a major part of our lives, Eat to Live not Live to Eat, is a mantra well worth remembering.

LINDA AND ANDREW (UPDATE)

Today has been just about the best day I can remember in a long time. It started off pretty much as usual, making breakfast for the guests – a group of three young women from Brazil and a family of four from Canada. The family comprised mum, dad, daughter and son in law. Dad and the daughter went out for a run at 7.15am, which kind of gave me a clue that they wouldn't be going for a full English! True enough, Dad wanted two boiled eggs, boiled for exactly five minutes – no more and no less. No pressure there. Mum and daughter opted for scrambled eggs on wholemeal toast. Son-in-law went for three hash browns and two croissants, prompting his father-in-law to ask "Is that a healthy breakfast?" He didn't answer, but I very pointedly directed my comment "Enjoy your breakfast" to son-in-law.

In the afternoon I got Andrew's bag packed as he is staying at the Short Breaks home overnight. I picked him up from the after school sports club at 4.30pm as usual. He has started having a chocolate mousse as a teatime treat, but I hadn't got any in the house so I called in at the Spar opposite the school. When Andrew saw what I was buying, his eyes lit up and he shouted "Urgh Urgh" which is "I want that chocolate mousse now!" in Andrew-speak. I put the chocolate mousse on the back seat of the car and turned to Andrew who was sitting in the front. "I haven't got a spoon but you will be able to eat your mousse when we get there". Throughout the journey he kept hitting me on the arm, swivelling round in his seat and eyeing the mousse longingly. After refusing to eat for eight long years, I can't find the words to describe the joy I feel seeing him so excited about food.

ANNIE AND MAX

From the start, Max has had difficulties with food. He posseted as a baby and frequently vomited as well. As soon as he started solids, he developed intractable diarrhoea. He had severe gastroenteritis when we were on holiday in Puerto Rico when he was only five months old. He was admitted to hospital over there on two appallingly memorable occasions. He was dehydrated and put on a drip both times. One night at the hospital, my white t-shirt became covered in his vomit. I turned it back to front to pretend it was clean, which must have been confusing and disgusting for the people standing behind me in the coffee queue at the hospital canteen. I was at rock bottom and desperate to get back to England, with my ill baby. I was awake all night breast feeding him, whilst the others slept. His breathing was erratic with long pauses between breaths and I thought he would die. I remember on repeated occasions, lifting him out of the cot, gently shaking him to elicit breathing again and whispering to him,

'Don't die, don't leave me.'

Later, he would have toileting accidents all the time, sometimes several times daily. This became a recurrent theme when he was being looked after, babysat, or out at someone's house to play. It happened more in these circumstances because he was nervous. It became a heart sink situation, when we picked him up; the same old story.

'He was fine. He just had a toileting accident that's all. I've put him in spare jogging bottoms.'

They all made it sound like nothing but it was an awful situation for them to deal with. This is one reason we had to stop employing young people as babysitters in case the worst happened. He was fairly normal about going to the toilet for a wee, but just couldn't manage his bowels. His stool was mostly watery, and we felt that he couldn't understand the messages his body was giving him.

We must have a thing against 'fancy diets', because it wasn't till he was eight years old that we decided to try a gluten free diet. The next day, he had improved. Buoyed up by this we decided to go dairy- free as well. Things improved further and he was soon continent for the first time. We have noticed that if he has gluten-containing foods, his tummy will swell and his behaviour become vague. He also now complains of tummy pain, and this will be followed by diarrhoea. When he eats dairy containing foods, the effect is not as bad. It may be the milk protein, casein, which is the problem for him with these, we are not sure. All these dietary things are trial and error, really.

It is now thought that 70% of autistic people have bowel disorders, similar to colitis. The inflammation has shown up in the appearance of biopsies, where these have been taken in autistic people. These bowel problems are thought to lead to a condition called the 'leaky gut syndrome,' which is as yet unproven. It is thought that gluten and casein proteins leak into the blood stream through the inflamed, and as a result, 'leaky' gut wall. These large, undigested proteins circulate in the bloodstream, cross the blood–brain barrier and result in morphine–like effects on the brain. In other words, eating these substances results in the autistic person becoming zombified, and 'away with the fairies.' It's as if they are on drugs. There is extensive evidence for inflammatory changes on biopsies, but the possible mechanism for the behavioural effects is mostly conjecture. All we know is that the diet works for us, and we dare not relax it too much.

The autism expert we sometimes see, who is a child psychiatrist, is against gluten and casein-free diets, because of lack of scientific evidence that they work. I suspect the evidence will appear years down the line. It will lag, as it so often does, behind anecdotal stories of the efficacy of diets for which there is no absolute scientific proof. No proof as yet, anyway. As in many things 'Absence of evidence is not evidence of absence.' Scientists would do well to listen to parents more and not just think we are all hysterical nuts.

A JOURNEY

LIZ AND SALLY

Four days a week Sally leaves home and walks to work at 8 o'clock in the morning as many people do. This journey takes about twenty minutes. She has been doing this for nearly three years and although it would seem unremarkable to most people, for us this journey is a triumph. When she gets to work she has to open up the restaurant where she works and then spend a couple of hours cleaning before walking home again. Although she sometimes stoutly declares she doesn't want to be a cleaner all her life, nevertheless she is proud to be working for a wage.

When Sally first got her job we would not have expected her to be doing it three years later. We also did not expect her to get herself up and out without any prompting or early morning calls. We thought one or other of us would be involved in cajoling her out of bed, giving one of our oft rehearsed lectures about people relying on you etc., followed by a lift into town. To our amazement she has never lingered in bed and heads off willingly every morning. Even on miserable half-dark January mornings she trudges off, rarely wearing gloves or any of the woolly hats and scarves provided by her ever loving mother.

We have been very grateful to the restaurant owners who gave Sally this chance of employment, which has greatly increased her self-esteem and confidence. There have been a few ups and downs and Sally has got very agitated with one of the chefs who she claims would not let her fill her bucket. She has also, quite rightly, got into trouble for swearing at her bosses on her mobile phone. The finer nuances of the work 'protocol' elude her. She doesn't get that you can't swear at your boss if you want to keep your job. She also thinks that when people are friendly, they are friends so would leave a lot of notes for her employers about her loneliness and other problems she had, which were not work related. Gradually she has learnt what is more appropriate and she complains less about bullying chefs and the inadequate cleaning standards of the lad who is also disabled, who cleans on the other days.

For us, Sally being in employment has given us a few dilemmas. As parents we would not normally be involved at all in our children's jobs. Yet because of Sally's learning disabilities we sometimes have to be. There have been times when she has been ill and we have to ring up for her. This is a problem for her employers as restaurants must be cleaned and sometimes they seem rather unsympathetic and press for Sally to go in later. They now seem to have contingency arrangements for illness and holidays. The Benefit Office sometimes requires paper work and it is usually our task to sort this out with Sally's bosses, feeling apologetic and indignant at the same time when we have to occasionally press for things like wage slips. Sally can imagine difficulties where none exist and luckily we have learned to take her statements with a pinch of salt before wading in to protect her. We hope her colleagues have learned to do the same.

Like Sally we would not necessarily want her to be a cleaner all her life, but this journey is of great significance for her and for us and when I receive a text telling me she is at work, I am proud.

GILLIAN AND WILLIAM

Each time I visit my son Michael at Crossroads in Hong Kong, I try to find a different route. One year I flew from Heathrow, having carefully researched an itinerary that would avoid London Underground's long passages and steep stairs and escalators. Having booked tickets accordingly, I awarded myself Brownie points for enterprise.

I stayed overnight with a friend who lived near the bus station, and my younger son, William, accompanied me to York. He insisted on dealing with the heavy holdall, which contained mostly presents and books. There were also boxes of Yorkshire tea, requested by Australian friends. At York station William vanished to get me a cup of tea, and on his return produced an A4 sized card and a large box of chocolates. I had completely forgotten that the next day was Mothering Sunday, but managed with some difficulty to cram my gifts into my haversack and to repack my picnic lunch in a carrier bag. William had absolutely no awareness that he had presented me with a dilemma.

William jogged along beside the train as it pulled out of the station, and returned to his house, dutifully phoning to report his safe arrival, and requesting me to confirm my safe arrival in London. I very much appreciate his rare moments in parental mode, and I had just experienced almost two hours of care and helpfulness.

At Kings Cross, I loaded a trolley and limped across to St. Pancras. I eventually located the SouthEast Trains entrance point, which was deserted, with shutters barring entry. There was a notice stating that this terminus was closed every weekend in March. As it was Saturday March 1st, I was out of luck, and distinctly irate. This closure had not been advertised earlier that week when I had checked details of weekend engineering disruptions and booked my tickets. No details of alternative arrangements were posted and Eurostar and ScotRail staff seemed to have no knowledge of local services. When I burst into tears a porter investigated possible solutions, reappearing ten minutes later to report that a replacement coach service to London Bridge had been laid on.

When I was safely installed on the coach, I chatted to the only other passenger, an air stewardess on her way to Heathrow from Stansted airport. She too had been unaware of the station closure. At London Bridge we left the coach. This was not a very accessible station – there were no trolleys, and I was faced with a fairly steep slope to climb. I reached the platform just in time to catch the train, and my bags and I were hoisted aboard. Phew!

I descended at Heathrow station, only to find that the lift was out of order, so I would have to use the stairs. The air stewardess popped up again and produced a porter (my hero!) who hauled my luggage upstairs for me. By the time I had crawled up the stairs to the summit he had acquired a trolley, paid for with a Euro coin received as a tip from another grateful customer, and had loaded my belongings.

Much to my surprise and relief, once I had phoned William as required, all went well, including the assisted wheelchair service I had requested. The airport porter who was taking me to the departure lounge even bought me a cup of tea on the way, proudly announcing that he had used his staff discount for the transaction to save me money. The rest of my journey was as relaxing and uneventful as possible for a fourteen hour flight. However I have avoided London on all subsequent trips!

PAT AND CLAIRE

On reflection I should have taken the events of the last weeks as some sort of omen. Back in the mid 1990's we had planned and booked a holiday to The Gambia, in West Africa. It was just beginning to emerge as a popular affordable holiday destination, and after all, husband and I had experienced living in East Africa during the 1970's, and had a yearning to see and explore further African states. The west coast sounded ideal. Holiday booked, cases packed, anti malaria tablets and jabs all in order, we were one week away from going. Then…disaster. A military coup had taken place overnight, and the Foreign Office was advising all holidays to The Gambia be cancelled with immediate effect.

After much struggling at the travel agents over the next few days we eventually settled on a comparable holiday to Mombasa, Kenya. We were quite surprised as at that time holidays to Kenya were more expensive, but were very pleased at the outcome.

The day of travelling arrived. We set off by car from York for Manchester airport in good time. We had arranged to leave the car at a car park in Stockport, and be transported to the airport by mini bus. As we drove on to the M62 towards Manchester, we hit a solid queue of traffic across all the motorway lanes. It just wasn't moving. What had happened? We tried to get information on the car radio but none was forthcoming. As we waited and waited our anxiety grew.

To cut a long story short, we eventually took a road off the M62 around Huddersfield, and ended up on a B road that looked as if it might bring us out somewhere in Manchester – but we also met a long queue of traffic from those annoying people who had also had the same devious plan to beat the queues.

At some point along this B road, my husband seemed to break, and became very emotional, declaring that we were never going to get to the airport on time. Our two children in the back seat obviously picked up on the panic, and also started to crumble and cry. I was a bit stunned and realised that I wasn't going to be allowed to have a mini breakdown myself (bit annoying really!). Anyway, I suggested we turn the car round and take the first road off and just go for it. We duly did, and goodness knows how, but we eventually came out near Stockport and made the car park.

We got to the airport on time and went through to wait for boarding – only to be informed that the flight was being held up due to a fire on the M62 and several passengers still trying to get to the airport. How inconsiderate, I thought!

We eventually boarded, and took off – for Gatwick! (That wasn't mentioned in the itinerary). We arrived at Gatwick only to be informed of yet another delay. There had been a bomb scare (IRA) and the airport locked down. We had to wait a further hour before the Gatwick passengers boarded. This was turning into a nightmare. We had already been on board for three hours. The seat pitch on the plane was disgusting (remember Monarch in the early days!) and we were so squashed and uncomfortable at this stage – and we hadn't even left the UK.

Round about this time, my stress levels must have reached warp 9. On a visit to the loo I discovered that I had an unexpected full on visitation from my monthly 'friend'. I was smack bang in the middle of my cycle, normally as regular as clockwork, and this should not have been happening. Needless to say, I was not prepared at all, and had to ask the stewardess for help – any help. I couldn't believe it when she said they didn't have any supplies on board! Luckily, a very kind lady who was sat near the loo and had heard my plight offered me help. I was so thankful for that lady.

By this time I was feeling really awful with stomach cramps etc. It wasn't helped by the fact that we had to stop en route to re-fuel – yet another wasted hour! My stomach turned, and I started to make frequent trips to the toilet. I was quite ill, and can only think that this was the stress coming out of me – instead of blowing my top earlier I had kept it all in. Was this the price to pay?

We finally arrived at Mombasa airport, which then consisted of a couple of huts, no air conditioning and definitely no European toilets – much to my horror! By this time we had been on the plane for nearly fifteen hours.

As we trundled through the poverty stricken villages on the way to our luxury hotel, almost at the end of our horrendous journey, all I could think about was getting to a decent loo. I was convinced that the holiday was going to be a total disaster and I had plans in place to divorce my husband and leave my children by way of revenge for what I had been through! However, on arrival we were transported to a paradise, which was actually obscene by comparison to what we had seen on the way to the hotel – but that's a story for another day.

LINDA AND ANDREW

27ᵗʰ September 2009

Andrew is sitting on his custom built tricycle, an impressive piece of workmanship painted in a cheery yellow. It has support bars which fit around his hips, and a seat belt. His feet are strapped to the pedals and he looks very comfortable and secure as we gaze out across the vast expanse of the Humber Bridge. We are standing on the footpath at the approach to the north side. There is not a cloud in sight, the sky is blue and the far side of the bridge is shrouded in a heat haze. I am relieved it is such a beautiful day as I did not want to call off this very special event in my son's life.

As we leave the security of a path on firm ground and start to cross over water, I grip the steering handle fitted to the rear of the trike and try not to look down at the fast flowing brown water of the Humber. My own anxieties are soon overridden by a sense of pride in my son. He is fearlessly pedalling onwards, oblivious to the fact that we are hundreds of feet above water and have one and a half miles to go before reaching firm land again. We are accompanied by a group of family and friends who are supporting Andrew in his attempt to cycle across the Humber Bridge – and back – in order to raise money for his school. One of the people accompanying us is Dawn, a fundraising co-ordinator for our local branch of one of the big supermarket chains. Dawn had approached us in the store earlier in the year. She had been set the task of raising money to buy something for a local person which would make a positive difference to their life. We had been saving up to buy a custom built trike for Andrew, but we were a long way off affording the £1200 it would cost. Within a few weeks, Dawn and her colleagues had raised the money, and Andrew received his new trike a couple of months later. He took to riding it straight away and clearly loved the feeling of independence it gave him compared to being in his wheelchair. We were overwhelmed at the generosity of people who donated towards the cost of Andrew's trike, and we felt we now had to do something to help others. Andrew has already been sponsored to the tune of £1000 for today, and that is now playing in my mind as I worry whether this is too ambitious for him. We are also pushing his wheelchair across the bridge, just in case he gets too tired.

As we reach the halfway point, Andrew is still pedalling happily, with an occasional push from behind. There are lots of other people crossing the bridge for charity today. There are families with babies and toddlers in prams and pushchairs; some people are walking their dogs across; one or two are in fancy dress. One elderly man is jogging across, but he slows down to Andrew's pace and admires the trike. Andrew visibly swells with pride and gives him a great big smile. This gentleman is 82 and is attempting to break his previous year's record by doing six laps – one lap being from the north side to south and back again – a total of 24 miles! He is very interested in the story about the trike, and he wishes Andrew good luck as he breaks into a jog again.

Half an hour later, we reach the south side of the river and we stop for a drink and a breather. Andrew is very reluctant to get off his trike, and looks disgruntled when we sit him down on the grass and stretch his legs. His gaze is firmly fixed on his trike, and he claps with glee when we strap him back in twenty minutes later.

On the journey back to the north side, I reflect on the difference this trike has made to Andrew. His leg muscles have visibly developed and he is walking more confidently, albeit with support. He has a newfound air of confidence and he sits up straight, head held high whenever he is riding the trike. It is almost like he is saying "Look at me". We reach the north side again with the wheelchair remaining redundant and Andrew looking exhilarated and not in the least bit tired. We all clap and cheer. He did it!

PAULINE AND ALISON

Dilston Hall

September 14th, 1980. A day I shall never forget. My beautiful, endearing, loving, funny, exasperating, sometimes difficult daughter is leaving home. Alison is just 16 years old, young for this in the normal course of events, but Alison was born with learning disabilities (mental handicap/special needs back in the 80's), and in many facets of her personality and abilities she is much younger. I've worked very hard to make this day happen.

Since Alison was born there have been two things that I instinctively knew I needed to do. Firstly, I felt it was my God-given duty to try to support and encourage her to reach as much of her potential as she could. Secondly, in view of my mortality, I had to ensure that she became as independent as possible. This has been at times an exciting, always interesting and fulfilling journey, but also at times frustrating, worrying, physically tiring and emotionally draining. As parents and carers we have to battle the social care system to achieve what all parents want – the best for their sons and daughters.

Our destination today is Dilston Hall, near Corbridge, in Northumberland. Corbridge is a small town on the old Roman road, on the direct route from York to Scotland. Dilston Hall is a country mansion, once owned by the Earls of Derwentwater and now a residential advanced social training centre, run by Mencap for young people between the ages of 16-18 who have a mental handicap.

As a parent governor of Fulford Cross Special School I was well aware that there was no further education provision in York for anyone leaving that school and felt very lucky to have found out about Dilston Hall.

As we load up the car, I am in turmoil. One part of me, and at the moment not a very big part, knows that I am doing the best possible thing for Alison and ultimately for myself. Lots of other parts of me are screaming, "You must be mad. How can you possibly do this? Nobody will ever know and understand Alison like you do." All the while, I try very hard to present a calm, unruffled face to the world. The last thing I want to do is to let Alison see my doubts and fears. She is excited, but apprehensive and will need all my encouragement and support on this very important step on our journey together.

Only I know how symbiotic the relationship between Alison and me is. How will either of us survive without the physical aspects of the unconditional love we have for each other? I have to acknowledge my own dependence on our relationship, which at certain points in my life has been the only thing that has kept me going. I believe there is something mystical about the relationship between handicapped children and their parents, especially mothers. The dedication and commitment necessary to nurture these children is immense and often lasts for a lifetime. Guidance for me has seemed to come from some inner source or intuition and has enabled me to surmount obstacles on Alison's behalf, which I would never have dreamed of even attempting for myself.

We drive through the familiar territory of my childhood on the A19. I remember Easingwold, where I went to school, Thirsk, where I played hockey and tennis for my school, passing signs for Bedale, Leyburn and Northallerton. After Scotch Corner, on the A1 the signs are less familiar – Darlington, Middlesbrough and Durham. My inner anxiety and fear is increasing it seems, in direct proportion to the decreasing miles to our destination. Alison and I are singing loudly and discordantly the Bay City Rollers old hit single "Bye Bye Baby, Baby Goodbye" – her favourite group and the song of the moment. The poignancy of the words hits me and my voice trembles, the pain in my chest is making me breathless, so I quickly turn on the radio to distract her. I register very little of the countryside. All my energy and attention is focussed first on the road, and then on trying to hold myself together. Gateshead, Newcastle, Hexham, then off the motorway on to local roads. We are here.

My actual recollection of leaving Alison that day is unclear, like looking through an unfocussed lens. The pain is still very clear and sharp. Staying overnight in Corbridge, knowing I wouldn't see her until Christmas, I drank a lot of alcohol and lay awake crying for most of the night.

For most of those two years, I felt as though part of me was missing, a real physical sense of being without a limb. This was the start of years of letting go, little by little. Sometimes it was a few stuttering steps forward, then back. Today, my beautiful daughter is buying her own home, she lives on her own, with some support, makes her own life choices and makes me very proud.

ANNIE AND MAX

We are in Zimbabwe, perched at the back of a small boat, enjoying a sun downer trip, on Lake Kariba. It is a fishing holiday, and we are based on board a larger cruise ship. This is a chance for everyone to get together socially and appreciate the beauty around us.

Max is eagerly searching for fish eagle, with the possibility of hippo, crocs, baboon, black and cattle egret, pied kingfisher and blacksmith plover. He is confident he will spot lots of delights and knows he will enjoy identifying them. Gus calls him 'dead eyed Dick' as he is quick and accurate in spotting and naming even rare species. There is no competitiveness in this, it's just that birds and animals are in his 'interest areas' and he is switched on to notching them up. He and Gus will write lists of what they've seen, later. People around are praising him, accepting him, liking him. He is happy and secure. He is even singing his favourite songs to me: show tunes from Phantom, war songs, Frank and Bing, in the sure knowledge that I'll join in. Every so often, he cuddles me and kisses my cheek saying 'Guess what? I love you, Mum.'

He is being adorable and some of the adults are dabbing at tears as he sings 'Music of the Night,' simply and beautifully, here, cherished, in a small boat on a massive lake somewhere in the middle of this glorious continent. Southern Africa is tilting towards its dark hours, quitting the brazen glare of day by casting up a hoard of evocative colours, yellow of desert sands, red of blood and amber of beasts' watchful eyes. Soon the night sky will be all around and over us, a complete hemisphere of beauty, layered black with pinpricks of light beyond counting, like velvet picked out with diamante. The Milky Way is folded and draped as a magnificent diaphanous white sash, swathing across the huge expanse.

For now, he has only three things to do, all of which come easily to him: spot species, sing songs and kiss Mummy. He is content, calm, radiating peace and loveliness.

I am watching him. I have been watching him since ere this holiday began.

Before breakfast, I make sure he is clean, toileted and dressed neatly. I will help select food which is gluten and dairy free, as we've found this helps keep his bowels regular, and I will cut up his food for him. I make him hold the fork and sit next to him to prompt him to use it, rather than using fingers. I ask him to lean forward to eat so food doesn't fall on his T-shirt, and encourage him to finish and have his drink. I make him wipe his mouth, and then do it for him. I remind him to say thank you. I prompt him to reply if he's asked a question, so people don't think he's either ignoring them, or that he doesn't like them, neither of which is true. He's probably scanning the horizon for eagle, or avidly listening to a distant bird song.

He likes to pester one of our companions on the cruiser to show him the app on his phone of bird songs and images. I lean towards them both during this time to try to make sure he is polite and not overly demanding. I frequently ask the guest something about himself to make him feel valued. I don't want him to feel like a carcass that a vulture is pecking at. Sometimes, Max will say sweet or wise things, which we both will be surprised about, and enjoy.

I try to find things for him to do whilst the men are out fishing, reading mainly, and more bird-watching from the big boat. He had been out with Gus fishing on the first morning and the other men were horrified to realise he was casting with no understanding of where the hook was flicking, and nearly caught someone's ear with it. Gus is always over-optimistic about his abilities, but it was gently explained to him that Max couldn't come again.

At sleeping time, I put his plastic bed cover down on his sheets and help him put on his pull-ups the correct way round, back to the back and front to the front. Despite the pad, his pyjamas will still need to be washed by hand in the morning and hung in the cabin to dry. He sleeps soundly and for long hours. I enjoy my holiday through him as I must always do, taking care of his needs first. I am happy he is a hit with the other guests, and count this as a job well done. I can make sure he isn't a chore to have around; otherwise I wouldn't have agreed to come.

Above all, on this holiday, I am watching and making sure he doesn't fall into the water, either from the cruiser, or from this little fishing boat. There is danger all around. In Africa it is clear and apparent: – drowning, contracting bilharzia from swallowing the lake water, or being eaten by hippo or crocodile.

I will need to watch him all his life. My biggest worry at home in UK, is the more covert crocodile of abuse, and in my opinion, religious fervour is the invisibility cloak that this predator often wears. For this reason, we do not attend churches.

If those endless skies of wonder are home to the Father of the Fisher of Men, then may he protect this vulnerable boy. In the flimsy net which our child has been given, may he catch only happiness.

FAMILIAR OBJECTS

SUSAN AND KAREN

Scissors

Karen enjoys cutting paper up with a pair of metal scissors. She has done this since about the age of thirteen when she would cut comics up after she had finished looking at them. Nowadays, she cuts up copies of the TV magazines. Each week, she buys a copy of every TV programme magazine: The Radio Times, The TV Times, What's On etc. She keeps them until they are out of date, and the following day will start to cut them up. She seems to have a particular way of cutting them. I think she starts by cutting the double pages in half so that there is a pile of single pages. Then she neatly cuts each page by turn into halves, so there is a pile of halves. Then she cuts those pages in half, then half again and she continues doing this with the squares of paper becoming smaller and smaller. She is totally absorbed in this task which is like a kind of ritual. I've never actually witnessed the full process because it's something she does when she's by herself and, if anyone enters her room, she stops snipping and puts the pieces of paper down. The end result is a pile of very tiny, neat squares of paper, like mosaics, which she puts into her bin. Often, when I visit, there are piles of various sized pieces of paper on her bed and she stops snipping as soon as I've entered. Her paper bin usually has lots of tiny paper squares in it.

At times when she's unhappy or feeling stressed, she will do more cutting. Before she moved to her current residential home, she lived in 'Albert House', a home that was not well run and seemed to have a quick turnover of staff. It was not warm and inviting when you entered, the hall and staircase were dark and dingy. She had moved there at short notice after her trial as a lodger in a supported placement scheme had broken down. All seemed well at first but Karen gradually became more unhappy living in Albert House and was spending more time alone in her room. When I visited, her paper bin was full of paper snippings and I became aware that she spent all her spare cash on magazines, not just the TV ones, but expensive glossy ones too. They all ended up in her bin. I tried giving her some old magazines in an attempt to persuade her not to blow her money on the glossies but she continued buying these until she moved to her present home where she is much happier.

She no longer buys the glossies but continues to cut up the TV magazines. I believe that she finds this activity comforting and that it helps to give her a sense of control over her life.

GILLIAN AND WILLIAM

Little brown boots

I took the little brown boots from my sock drawer, and reflected on the stages of William's development that had led up to him being able to use them. He had been a floppy baby, resembling a rag doll in whom head, trunk and legs were not co-operating with one another, and was referred to the physiotherapy department when he was eight months old. Over the next year, the physio, Jenny, gradually produced a variety of equipment and suggestions of things I could make to promote his development. The first thing supplied was a corner seat with a pommel and harness to let him sit upright to explore the world; his normal position was lying on the floor, which meant that he could move around by rolling. My contribution to the corner seat was a table, modelled from a strong whisky box begged from the local off-licence, and covered with Peter Rabbit Fablon. The seat could be pushed snugly into the improvised table so that William could reach toys. Unfortunately everything was flipped onto the floor because his co-ordination was so poor. The physiotherapist's solution to this was a Dycem mat, which stayed on the table and helped to keep objects still, reducing the speed at which toys vanished – until

William learned to control his arm movements sufficiently to cause objects to disappear on purpose.

Jenny wanted to use her weighted ball, but William was not strong enough to hold it, so between us we decided to put some grains of rice into a balloon before inflating it. William was absolutely petrified by the balloon, and became a quivering wreck when it was produced. He had no previous experience of balloons, and had never had one popped near him. I still do not understand why he was so frightened. By the time he was six, he delighted in sitting on balloons and popping them to scare his sister, so his attitude had obviously changed.

William was reluctant to do any exercises at home despite being happy to co-operate in the clinic, so Jenny and I came up with other ideas so that the same goals could be achieved at home. He was reluctant to show her any of the "games" we did at home. He also had to be taught one step at a time, and could not apply what he had learned to a new situation. I guess this was an early indication of his autism, but we did not realise this at the time. People with an autistic spectrum condition can find it hard to transfer skills from one place to another, and will often associate an activity with one person, but not do it with anyone else. The problem with the balloon may well have been a sensory problem, but at that point the impact of sensory issues in people with autism was seldom recognised.

Until he was fourteen months old, William did not weight-bear, and was reluctant to attempt to stand up. He was given Valium in hospital one night, and pulled himself to standing in his cot, much to my amazement. When I reported this to the physio, she decided that it was time to practise standing, and suggested that I should make William some splints to stop his knees buckling as he tried to stand. Given that they were made from washing-up liquid bottles cut in half, exposed edges covered in tape, lined with dish cloths and secured to his legs with crepe bandages, the splints were very effective.

When William was eighteen months old, Jenny announced that she was being seconded to do further study, but measured him for some Piedro boots so that his feet and ankles could be properly supported while he learned to walk. She arranged for her colleague, an occupational therapist, to fit the boots and continue to work with William towards walking. He loved these boots, and I have kept them as a reminder of a time when he still had so many challenges to face and of the amazing progress he has made. The boots seem so tiny now. They are size two brown boots with immensely long laces. The splints had to be bandaged onto William's skinny legs, and he had to stay still long enough for his feet to go into the boots and for the laces to be tied with several bows. For me, it was odd to see my small floppy son upright – he still defaulted to rolling as his preferred means of speedy locomotion. When William took to his feet at 20 months, he was discharged from children's therapy services. He later had further physio and O.T. input when he was five, ten and twelve, to work on co-ordination for writing and balance. It seems to have been effective – he now runs, swims, skis and cycles, albeit with a slightly unusual gait. I associate the beginning of all these mature skills with those little brown boots.

PAT AND CLAIRE

Ancestral Memories

The fact that her mother is in her late 80's and not in good health is worrying her. She is panicking: "What if she dies before I have found out as much as I can? How can I have got to this age without knowing more about my roots and where I came from?" She is thinking about her mother as she picks up the file from the shelf with the label on it "Pat's Ancestry Docs and Files etc." It is a file she has been trying to collate for some time with a view to building a family tree. She has been trying to collect bits of information from her ailing aged mother, who is the only surviving member from both sides of her parents' families, and who lives some distance away from York in Bristol.

She begins to look at the photos in the file. She takes out one of her paternal grandfather, Fred, and her grandmother Priscilla, (better known as Cissy). The young serious faces look out at her. How can that pretty young woman be the old lady she knew from childhood? There is a particularly lovely one of her posing with her hand on her face, head cocked slightly to one side. Another one shows her sitting sideways on some kind of bench, with what looks like a beret on. It could be some kind of head protection of the type that woman factory workers wore during the two world wars. Had she worked in a factory, like many young women did, to keep the cogs of industry and the economy turning whilst all the young men were away fighting the wars? It is signed on the bottom "Sincerely Yours, Cis". She recognises Cissy's handwriting – always so neat and precise. Another smaller photo shows her again, head and shoulders only, in a hat with a fur collar around her neck of the type that was so popular in the earlier part of the 20th century. She has again written across the corner "Yours Aye. Cis". She finds this almost out of character compared to the old lady she recalls as a child who was always quite distant and cold towards her grandfather.

There are other photos in this collection – one of her grandfather, Fred, as a young man. It strikes her how like her brother he looks when her brother was around the same age. The photo is a small square one with a circular frame showing head and shoulders of a very serious looking Fred in a smart suit. He had a full head of hair then. Written on the back is "My Fred". She was touched when she saw this and almost moved to tears. They must have been in love once mustn't they? They had never seemed to her to be particularly happy or close in later life and she found that profoundly sad. She remembered asking her grandmother why her grandfather had no hair. She was told that all his hair had fallen out after he had returned from fighting in the First World War, due to shell shock. She only ever knew her dear "grampy" as completely bald.

How she wishes she had had the chance to understand and talk to both of them, particularly her grandfather about his war experiences. It seems such a waste to her that all the knowledge and information that both grandparents had about their lives and families has gone with them to their graves.

PAULINE AND ALISON

A Life Truly Lived

Alison is moving house again today. For someone who actively detests change of any kind, this is a massive ordeal, even though part of her is looking forward to having her own home and not having to share with anyone else. I am extremely anxious because I have been here before and know that Alison will probably be unbearable, as I attempt to persuade and cajole her into getting rid of some of her possessions, so that her new home will not be cluttered from the start.

Where on earth do I start? My eyes light on some A4 folders full of her work at Askham Bryan College. She's been left there for a long time and maybe they could go. I flick through some of the pages. There are photographs of Alison working on a sewing machine, others where she is displaying some of the articles she's made – cushions, pillow cases, pin cushions. She looks so proud, a lump comes to my throat. At the back of the folder are the certificates she received after completing her courses, and I recall the award ceremonies I attended to watch her and her peers collect them.

Some newspaper cuttings fall out of a box I'm sorting. "Open University students receive laurels" heads a picture of Alison and some of her friends from Yearsley Bridge Day Centre receiving their certificates for a course – "Patterns of Living: Working Together." Another one headlines "Play challenges prejudice".

Alison again, with other cast members from No1. Theatre Company. This one is a group of students from ABC, "Pioneering students pass with flying colours". Two more from the Day Centre – "Group enjoys a day at the races", and there they are sporting the glamorous hats they created, and "Stepping out in style" – six of them wearing fashion outfits they had painstakingly made, standing beside a stretch limo outside the Dean Court Hotel where they enjoyed a VIP lunch. Here's another one with newsreader Martyn Lewis smiling, surrounded by workers at the new Krumbs café which will provide training in catering and hopefully some job opportunities. The last one is a picture of Alison on her own, with the headline "Alison's a ray of sunshine" and an article about her nomination for Volunteer of the Year by OCAY where she helps with fundraising events.

Alison is looking very stressed and anxious, so I call her over. "Look at all these pictures of you at College and the Day Centre. These are things I'll never ask you to throw away. We'll find a special box to put them in and you can get them out whenever you like and remember all the things you've done and all the friends you used to have. Now let's look for some things you maybe can get rid of."

In relative terms, all these items of ephemera show that Alison's life experience is equal to if not greater than, any academic, employment or social success achieved by people who do not have the difficulties she has had since she was born.

ANNIE AND MAX

It's a baby! It's a boy!

I love this plastic wrist band.

'BABY MCLAREN. MALE INFANT. X41122

20-10-98 1900'

Could this have actually happened? Was that baby mine? That creature, with its own identification band, separate from me now, but mine still: see, there is my name 'McLaren', with the word 'baby'.

After 10 years of infertility problems, related treatments and seven miscarriages, it was, in the famously overused word of the Olympic athletes and commentators at London 2012, 'unbelievable.' This was no potential baby, projected from a fertilised ovum or the sight of a single blue line on a 'Clearblue' pregnancy test: he was alive and real to hold, love and care for.

This identification band was wrapped, soon after birth, round the baby's wrist, and secured with a tamper-resistant popper. The popper is still intact. I wonder if one is supposed to know how to unfasten this, or if everyone has to cut through the plastic with scissors, as I did, a few days after returning home. Even then, I wanted to leave it on, so this time would never end. I wanted constantly to be able to read and re-read the writing on the paper slip, which the midwife had carefully inserted into the plastic display pocket.

On my fortieth birthday, I had decided to give up trying for a baby, and had, at the metaphorical 'last chance saloon', conceived Max. I had no idea I was pregnant and had worn a black tie to work on my birthday to symbolise the 'Death of Youth'. This is how being forty felt to me. As the pregnancy proceeded, I knew, from the infrequent kicks I felt, that this baby was too placid. When my waters burst four weeks prematurely, I said to Sophie, our ten year old daughter, that she mustn't be upset if the baby wasn't quite right, and that we would love him nonetheless. A few years beforehand, I had said to Gus, my husband, that I was sure we could even care for a disabled child, if we were blessed enough to be given one. We had so much love to give, that when we realised he was compromised, we both felt that we would cope fine.

Wasn't it simply joyous also, to see the word 'MALE' written? Gus, my husband, dreamt of having a son. This father-needing-a-son obsession is strong in Scotland, especially in farming communities, which was his background. The male line will continue, the name live on, the fields will be ploughed. The ancient gene lines of the clan McLaren were etched into the faces of my husband's relatives. When they saw Max, their features seemed to meld into a new look, which I had never seen before: pride, deep-seated joy, and possibly some smugness. We had a daughter, but her being female had precluded her from being able to provoke that look, that smile which I now witnessed from both Gus and his family.

When Max arrived, he was of good weight for a premature baby, his breathing and alertness scores at birth were normal, and his sucking reflex was strong, so ostensibly, things were grand. For this happy time, let the bells ring out, and the trumpets sound for joy- the baby boy Max McLaren is born!!!

PAULINE AND ALISON

The Collection

Alison is an avid collector of some very specific things. Amongst her favourites are cuddly toys, anything to do with dolphins and Robbie Williams & Take That, thimbles and key-rings. Most of her collections are kept within the confines of her home. The key-rings, however, are another matter. They are probably the best example of her autistic characteristics and they go with her wherever she goes. People from far and wide who know Alison add to her collection by bringing back souvenir key-rings from holidays, and whenever we have a day out or a holiday, sure enough a few key-rings will be added. The key-rings are all clipped together and at the time of writing, are at least equal to the size of a small football. There are numerous keys as well, but no-one has any idea which locks most of them originally fitted. It is almost incredible to watch her sorting through this complete jumble to find her house key, but she knows exactly which key this is. The size of her handbag has had to increase in direct relation to the number of key-rings she carries. There is a huge variety of key-rings, some with rather grubby small soft toys attached, some with scenes from around the globe, some rather plain ones with company logos, one is a digital key-ring with moving pictures and one has a small torch incorporated into it. The latest addition, provided by her cousin who works for the National Farmers Union includes a small white plastic sheep. She loves this one.

Over the years I have tried using logic and reason to persuade her to reduce their number and at times have insisted on taking some of them off, only to find that as soon as my back was turned, every one was replaced immediately. Since she has been diagnosed as being on the autistic spectrum and I have learned more about it, I regret having tried so hard to make her fit into our world. Reason and logic are meaningless concepts to Alison. Her world does not operate that way, so now I do try to accept her idiosyncrasies as part of her character and personality. All Alison's possessions are hugely important to her, and everything has to have a particular place in her home. The drive within her to keep the status quo is quite uncontrollable. If anything becomes lost or is even moved from its usual place, her equilibrium is disturbed, which can result in some fairly challenging behaviour. It can be like lighting a firework, watching it smoulder for a while and then suddenly it explodes. Usually it's mainly verbal, including swearing and stamping around from room to room, but occasionally she has smashed things near to her.

Arriving home after a supermarket visit one day, she realised she had lost her keys. Obviously this was a major trauma for Alison. Trying to pacify her, I'm trying to find out when she last remembers having them with her, and telling her we'll go back and retrace our steps and find them. Just then the phone rang; it was the supermarket, saying they'd found some keys and believed they belonged to her. How did they know whose keys they were? They went on to say one of the key-rings had a telephone number on it, so they rang it, explaining what they'd found. Luckily, it was an organisation where Alison was a volunteer, and the office manager had told them there was only one person she could think of in the whole world, who would have such a thing and had given them her number. The keys were retrieved and calm restored.

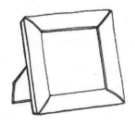

A PHOTOGRAPH

SUSAN AND KAREN

I am looking at a photograph of my daughter Karen who is wearing a red and white summer dress and is sitting on a gold coloured settee. She is laughing and is engrossed in playing with a black and white kitten, dangling my car keys in front of him. He is staring at the keys and is moving towards them before batting at the keys with a paw. It is the summer of 1991, Karen is twenty five years old and the kitten, whom Karen has named "Charlie", is about ten weeks old.

The photograph was taken in the living room of Karen's council flat. She had been living there for just over a year and had moved there after the small group home run by a charity was closed due to withdrawal of funding. In 1989, "Caring for People – Community Care in the Next Decade", a Government white paper, had been issued which stressed "the importance of helping people lead full and independent lives". The manager of the house considered that Karen was capable of living in an independent flat with support from a social worker, the Community Mental Handicap Team and home helps. Tom and I were not consulted and we were presented with the decision and the argument that Karen had expressed a wish to wish to live independently and that she "was more confident and was starting to achieve a lot more". "That's wonderful" I thought. Social services had to arrange alternative accommodation at very short notice and the City Council had offered a one bedroom flat. It sounded almost too good to be true, and with hindsight, it was.

Sometimes, if Karen is asked whether she would like to do something, she will say yes without fully understanding the wider implications. I think that because there was an urgent need to find alternative accommodation, it was dealt with too hastily and without sufficient care. I felt that the charity and Social Services had acted with expediency rather than in Karen's best interests and that Karen had been given unrealistic expectations that she was capable of living on her own and would be happy doing so. I believe that the decision had been made with good intent but was over-optimistic.

The workshop Karen had attended that was run by the same charity, closed at the same time as the house and no alternative day care was offered. Karen, like many other people with a learning disability, has great difficulty coping with changes in her life and these changes were particularly distressing for her; Karen spent a lot of time crying and saying she had nothing to do. She felt lonely and isolated when she was on her own and became withdrawn. We visited as often as we could but could not be there all the time as we both worked. Karen was not coping very well and if not for the mental handicap nurse who visited each day to assist Karen with planning her meals and cooking them, she would have gone hungry. There were times when she became muddled too, on one occasion tearing her DHSS giro cheque up and throwing it away. Eventually, after much correspondence from me to Social Services Karen was given a place at a new picture framing enterprise at a day centre and became happier but still needed a great deal of support from the mental handicap nurse and home helps.

Karen has always loved being around animals and she loved caring for Charlie. She became very efficient at feeding him and cleaning out the litter tray. Some young teenage girls had befriended Karen and one of them had given Charlie to her. Unfortunately, we later discovered that these "friends" had taken money, cassette tapes and jewellery from Karen. She is very trusting and because it is obvious to others that she is vulnerable, it is easy to take advantage of her. I think perhaps that the kitten might have been offered to her because it was a way of gaining access into her flat and to visit her. Maybe the girls had persuaded Karen to swap the tapes and jewellery in exchange for the kitten.

One evening, early the following year, the phone rang. It was Karen; she very rarely used her phone but she was distraught. "Charlie's dead.

He's been run over" she wept. I went round to her flat straightaway and she told me that the next door neighbour had told her that Charlie had been killed and that the RSPCA had taken his body away. I phoned the RSPCA to ask them if they could confirm this but the woman I spoke to was not very helpful or sympathetic. "This is important. It was my daughter's cat, she has a learning disability and she's heartbroken" I told them. The woman then confirmed that a cat had been killed but she would not give details.

When Charlie, the kitten, came into her life, he gave Karen a great deal of joy and companionship at a difficult time in her life. She gradually came to terms with her loss, finding comfort in visiting her grandparents each weekend and spending time with Ben, their golden labrador.

LINDA AND ANDREW

Baptism

As I look at my son's christening photographs my mind goes back to that day almost eighteen years ago. He was eight months old. Not for him a church service in a beautiful gown, surrounded by family and friends. We only have two photographs of this event. The most evocative one is of me and John standing next to Andrew, who is in an induced coma and on a ventilator. John and I are looking straight at the camera with dazed expressions and dead eyes.

Andrew had been in hospital with bronchiolitis for four days, having been admitted on New Year's Eve, and his condition had gradually deteriorated. On his fourth night, he took a turn for the worse and he was moved into a side ward next to the nurse's station so they could keep a close eye on him. John and I were advised to both stay the night. I slept fitfully, aware of the busy night the nurses were having with new admissions.

A nurse woke us at 6am to tell us Andrew was now critically ill and would need to be put on a ventilator. We rushed straight to his cot and I will never forget the look of pure fear in Andrew's eyes as he looked pleadingly at me. At that time they could not nurse babies on ventilators in our local hospital, but they managed to find a bed for him in one of the big Leeds hospitals. I could tell from the expressions on the faces of the doctors as they looked at Andrew's notes, and the way they avoided eye contact with me, that they did not think Andrew was going to pull through.

We are not religious people, but I felt an overwhelming need to have Andrew baptised by the hospital chaplain, who I knew very well through my work as a nurse and midwife at the same hospital. The ward sister and a staff nurse were his godparents, and they are in the second photograph. I don't know where those people are now.

We went back home to pack an overnight bag and picked a couple of toys out of his cold, empty cot. I felt numb rather than tearful. It was as though I was not in my body, but was observing everything from a distance.

John drove to Leeds and I sat in stunned silence, inwardly praying that Andrew would survive the journey. He had been transferred by ambulance with a nurse escort. Before we had left hospital, the paediatrician said they were considering the possibility he may have cystic fibrosis, and he also had a small hole in his heart, but these would be put on the back burner until Andrew was off the critical list.

When we arrived at the Paediatric Intensive Care Unit in Leeds, we were asked to sit in the waiting area as Andrew had only just arrived and the doctors were assessing him. I sat gazing into space, barely aware of the other people in the waiting room who seemed remarkably cheerful considering where we were. I just wanted to tell them to shut up and show some respect: didn't they know there were children fighting for their lives in there? How could they be so blasé?

After what seemed an eternity we were called in to see Andrew. Our son was in a hospital gown, wires and tubes snaking around him to various monitors which were beeping and flashing around the bed. They had shaved one side of his head because that was the only place they could find a vein on his shut down little body to site a drip. The doctor was very frank with us and said that he was critically ill and that it would be wrong to give us false hope. He advised us to go and have something to eat as they still had lots of tests to do and samples to take.

We crossed over the road from the hospital entrance and went into the pub which was serving meals. I stood next to John at the bar, vaguely aware of the fact he was ordering me a brandy and requesting the menu. The landlord looked in my direction and said "For God's sake love, cheer up. It might never happen". The thin veneer of strength had been breached and I burst into tears which quickly gave way to wailing and body-wracking sobs. He looked totally mortified when John explained the situation, and I can only hope he never uttered that phrase to anyone else who has since been in his pub. As tactless and cutting as his comment was, it was also cathartic and brought me back to the reality of the situation and helped me to shed tears which had been bottled up all day. As I sipped my brandy, I felt a sense of calm and my resolve to stay strong for Andrew returned. He was in good hands and he was a fighter. Whether he had cystic fibrosis, a heart problem or some kind of learning disability was no longer important. I just wanted him to survive and then we would cope with whatever condition he may have.

PAULINE AND ALISON

The ferry arrives at Craignure on the Isle of Mull and we're met by Arthur who whisks us up the island to the North and Tobermory. The B&B is quite luxurious and I have a good feeling about this holiday. Alison has always loved dolphins and this is my first attempt to make her dream come true. We are on a "Discover the World" package holiday which includes two days at sea with Sealife Surveys, when we hope to see dolphins, minke whales, porpoises, seals and even possibly a basking shark. This evening we are meeting in a pub with the eight other people on the tour to find out more about these fascinating creatures and what we can expect for tomorrow.

We're awake early and I throw back the curtains – can't wait for the day to begin. Outside, it's bright, but a bit chilly and breezy and as we near the harbour the water looks a bit choppy. We pick up our packed lunches from the local deli and I notice Alison is starting to look anxious.

I reassure her everything will be fine. Brennan, the captain, welcomes us on board and introduces us to the crew. The boat looks rather smaller than I'd expected, but there's plenty of room for the ten of us. The motor roars and we're off. There's a marine biologist aboard to answer any of our questions and they explain that we are part of a scientific project to monitor and map the numbers of cetaceans in the seas around Scotland. All Alison wants to do is see some of them, but the sea is very choppy now and the boat lurches up and down quite alarmingly. Alison is very frightened and tense and is clinging to the guard rail tightly. I'm beginning to wonder if this was really such a good idea, but we are all excited at the prospect of seeing some wild creatures and everyone is looking hard in every direction trying to spot something. After a couple of hours, Alison is very white, very quiet, looking pinched around her nose and mouth, with that almost-detached-from-everything look, so I know her fear is almost off the scale, but there's a shout – "Minke whales at 9 o'clock". We all crowd to that side of the boat and yes, there they are! The adrenaline rush is fantastic. I've never been more excited in my life. All there is to see are some black arched backs as minkes don't come very high out of the water. Alison's face is just one big smile and I have to take her picture. It has all been worth it! Later, we do see just a glimpse of a dolphin and a few harbour porpoises.

Back at the B&B, I talk to Alison about tomorrow's trip. We're going to visit some of the islands to see some of the birdlife and Alison is desperate to see puffins. Knowing what an ordeal it has been for her today and just how frightened she was at times, I explain that it is OK if she doesn't want to go out on the boat again. I will understand and I won't be cross. She doesn't answer me, so all evening I patiently keep telling her it's OK if she would rather stay on dry land tomorrow. Just as we're falling asleep, she whispers "Mum, I do want to go out on the boat tomorrow". I have never, ever, been more proud of my daughter.

ANNIE AND MAX

When I look at the photo of our home in Africa, it all comes flooding back. We spent six months in Zimbabwe, in 1990. Gus had a bursary from the organisation 'World Orthopaedic Concern' to work out there and I accompanied him, with Sophie, our daughter, age two.

In Zimbabwe, in a home, carpets are a luxury. Our house had wooden floors, with wall-to-wall ants. We soon became accustomed to walking over them en masse, with more respect than repugnance. We had learned to appreciate them as helpers in keeping a tidy house – nature's little vacuum cleaners. We also became neutral to the sight of geckos scouting the walls as they meant fewer mosquitos, and the same applied to spiders – all helpers in pest reduction, and not viewed as pests themselves.

The only public room was sparsely furnished, just two upright chairs and a small table. It was a 1930s bungalow with two bedrooms, a small kitchen and a tiny veranda. It had metal windows which opened onto a mud-patch garden, red, cracked randomly like a crackle glaze, with occasional sparse and etiolated grass stems attempting to survive in irregular clumps. Our gardener, George, commonly referred to by Violet, our maid , as "Markaye!" or "old man" in Endebele, would seemingly for hours be nurturing this dry earth with a thin stream of water from a small watering can or lying on his front cutting the grass with large scissors, slowly.

Everything in Africa is slow and goes by "Africa time". Violet and George moved slowly. She, being wide, with typical Matabele build, had a pronounced, lazy, rolling gait, and he, more typical of the Tsonga build was skinny and sat or lay down on the earth for much of the time. As she understood and could speak English better than he, she naturally fell to ordering him around and could on occasion spur him into rapid action.

I recall the day I returned home to that disgusting smell. Despite the feeling of imminent retching, I bravely followed the evidence of my nose to the kitchen. There in the small room on the old upright cooker was the culprit-something inside the large lidded saucepan. The real gag-provoking moment was upon lifting the lid to find four chicken feet sticking upright, desperately clawing at me – "Help us! Help us! Surely we are not meant to be food for someone?" But they were! Food for George! Violet screeched at him "Markaye!" and more Endebele ejaculations followed. He moved fast that day for sure, snatched up the pan and ran outside to his hut at the bottom of the garden, presumably to consume his wretched carcass cut-offs. I gave them double pay that week and only found out later that hen's feet were considered to be a delicacy.

Violet would wash clothes by steeping, then trampling them in a shallow bathtub of water using her feet, then hang them over the bushes in the garden, or peg them to the string-like washing line. When MaMac, Gus' mother, visited us, she insisted on helping Violet peg out the clothes which small act was enough to prompt Violet into embroidering a beautiful panel which read – "Thank you for what you did for me" – a fitting tribute to a Scottish lady who did not believe that one set of people should be the servant classes to another set.

We, on the other hand, had just accepted what had been arranged for our stay unquestioningly, and attempted to fall in with how the other white people lived in Bulawayo in 1990. Violet's other embroidered cloth, this time for us, read "This house may be small but the welcome is big." I think this referred to the numerous banquets we hosted in our room: one long table made of any tables all at different heights aligned and covered with white bed sheets. Guests brought their own cutlery and crockery and were treated to beef bourguignon. Beef was so tender and succulently tasty in Zimbabwe – there was no other choice for aspiring top hosts.

Although we lived in harmony with some natural housemates, like the ants, not all were as welcome. Rats were something else. At nights we would hear them running around the house, over the wooden floors as if wearing hob-nail boots. One morning we awoke to find a large hole in the skirting board in Sophie's room, rat-sized. As she was only two years old, and we had heard tales of rats nibbling the toes off babies, we moved Sophie's bed through to our room that night. We put warfarin, rat poison, into the hole in her room's skirting board. George was instructed by Violet to block up the hole after the poison had been laid, and he did so patchily, using twigs and small stick fragments. That night, as Sophie slept sweetly, there was a frenetic scuttling commotion under the floors and agonised squealing. Round and round went the rats and lurid images came to our wakeful minds of their bleeding to death with the warfarin, trying to survive by running from what they little realised, was the grim reaper within. We dropped off eventually and awoke to a solid silence.

Africa is a land of contrasts. Nature is 'raw in tooth and claw' during bursts of activity and following this, there is the quiet stillness and the languid slowness. Whilst Gus, my husband, was operating on a patient in the theatres at Mpilo, the local hospital, the rest of us at the house were lazing. Slow time is everywhere, especially during the stolen, drowsy hours of the early afternoon. Sophie was peacefully at her afternoon nap, and Violet and George were having siestas. I would lie on the bed wondering at the beauty of the stillness, when the hours passing seem to have no meaning and there will be time for all things needing doing. I have bottled this feeling and can revisit it at odd times.

I can open a secret memory box.

I am looking at the flamba tree, just outside our bedroom window.

The branches are low and covered in feather-like leaves, gently rounded, fronded together greenly. The sky beyond is, as always, a strong, constant blue, blue beyond blue in depth and complexity- you could reach right into it. The leafy branches waft in the warm and gentle air movements, so sensitive to them, that they seem to be speaking to me with loving and expressive hands.

'There is plenty time for everything,' they say, 'be calm in yourself.'

This is the true voice of Africa, and it is its essence.

PAT AND CLAIRE

I look at the photograph standing in its frame, on top of the bureau in my dining room at home. I love this photograph. It shows the faces and upper bodies of two young adults, standing in our garden, with lovely expressions on their faces. They are leaning in to each other, each with one arm around the other, and the affection between them is obvious from this body language. It is a photograph taken some years ago of my two children. My daughter was around 20 and my son 23. It brings back memories of what I perceive to have been better times.

My son had recently completed his degree at Liverpool University, and we were immensely proud of his achievements and musical ability. He was happy and carefree and enjoying life, experiencing that wonderful phase young people seem to go through – post education but not quite having to financially fend for themselves (the bank of mum and dad seemingly endless) – before they get down to the tough realities of life in the real world.

My daughter had recently been diagnosed with having Asperger's Syndrome, after years of uncertainty, and struggling to come to terms with what had been perceived as learning difficulties. We thought that was enough to be going on with in life, but unfortunately a further battle lay ahead for us all.

I love this photo because it shows my daughter when she was physically the healthiest she was ever going to be. She looks happy, well, fit and was a healthy weight. The years following have found her in a seemingly endless battle with her physical health, which would take her dangerously close to the edge before emergency surgery was performed in 2005, following a battle to control ulcerative colitis, which had been in danger of causing a perforated bowel. She has since endured several bouts of surgery and hospital stays which have left her with a permanent ileostomy. She has never been able to regain the weight she had achieved when the photograph was taken, or to look as well as she did then.

I often look at the full face and figure that she had in that photo, and wonder how she would have been today if she hadn't been blighted with the disease which has left her with periods of struggling to eat, and maintain a barely decent weight. Around the time the photograph was taken she had started to learn to scuba dive with her father. She was a keen and accomplished swimmer. Sadly she is not able to scuba dive with an ileostomy, and swimming on holiday has to be limited. The combination of this physical condition plus the Asperger's to contend with in life has been like a double dose of bad luck and a cruel trick.

It's one of the reasons why I love this photo – it's almost as if it was a perfect moment in time. My beautiful children, whom I am immensely proud of in their own achievements, look out at me from this safe happy world captured by the camera on a sunny day. It's how I will always want to remember them – happy and healthy with not too much to care about in the world.

SIGNIFICANT WORDS

SUSAN AND KAREN

'Strange'

"It's strange" Karen muttered as she gazed round the hotel room, "Don't like it. I didn't want to come here", she added. She was perturbed and her face reflected her fear. By "strange", she meant "unfamiliar" rather than "peculiar" or "odd". It is a word she has often used for people that she has not met before; prior to an appointment or a meeting for instance, "I don't know them. They're strange", she has said, clearly worried. I would reassure by saying, "But you will get to know them when you meet them and then they will not seem strange". After being introduced to them for the first time, she would be fine. Anything outside of her normal routine can make her anxious but this was the first time I had heard her apply the word "strange" to a room. "Oh no", I thought, "is she going to have an outburst? Are we going to have to leave and get the train back to York?" We had just arrived at the hotel for a long weekend in Scarborough. The twin-bedded room was light and bright and was nicely decorated. Light streamed through the French doors that led onto the balcony and there was a beautiful view of the North Bay.

I distracted Karen by pointing out the boats on the sea and the seagulls sitting on some of the nearby roofs. Then I asked if she would like to go out for a meal and then we could go to the theatre. She brightened up at that and agreed to my suggestion that we did our unpacking first and hang our clothes away. I asked if she would like to change into the pretty dress that we had unpacked; she flatly refused and her head went down. "Don't want to", she muttered. "It's okay, you don't have to wear it but it might be nice to freshen up and get changed if we're going out," I said. Karen finds it difficult to make choices so I picked out a couple of nice tops that she could wear with trousers. "Which is best?" I asked her and she pointed to the yellow one. This strategy always works better than being asked, "Which one do you want to wear?" In that situation, she usually finds it impossible to make a decision and will just keep repeating "don't know" whilst dropping her head down.

We had a lovely meal at the Stephen Joseph Theatre followed by an innovative and highly entertaining production of The Mikado where most of the male characters were cricketers, making Karen laugh. When we returned to the hotel room later that evening, Karen was happy and relaxed. The room was no longer "strange".

Another time, we stayed at a Best Western hotel at Durham. I had assumed that we would be inside the hotel building but our room was in the motel accommodation across the courtyard. When I opened the door, Karen's face fell. "It's strange" she said, and then started shouting "Don't want to be here. I didn't want to come here. Don't want to stay here. I want to go home" A full blown outburst followed with shouting and tears. She kept repeating, "Don't want to stay here". Eventually, when the storm had subsided a little, I asked "What if we try to get a different room?" She nodded and we went across to Reception and I explained that Karen was on the autistic spectrum and was not happy with the room. The receptionist was very understanding and replied that unfortunately, the main hotel was full and that all the guests had arrived. "I can offer you another motel room but it is the same layout" she said. "We can try it," I replied but I didn't feel very hopeful. We walked back across the courtyard and holding my breath, I unlocked the door. The layout of the room was identical but seemed a little less dark than the first one. "Do you think this looks okay?" I asked. Karen nodded. "So are you happy to stop here?" I continued. "Yes", she said. I breathed a sigh of relief.

For a number of years, she had been away on group holidays that her residential home had organised, usually to Blackpool or Spain, and on one occasion, she had been on a Walt Disney cruise. Although she had said that she wanted to go on these trips and had always enjoyed them, she had found the anticipation quite stressful. Staff would pack her case and hide it whilst she was out during the day to avoid any outbursts. She would become agitated if the other residents were talking about the planned holiday and she would start saying that she did not want to go. Usually, on the day itself, she would be calmer and would set off quite happily. However, on the last group holiday she had an outburst whilst being encouraged to board the mini bus shouting, "I don't want to go, you're forcing me" She lashed out at one of the staff and ran out into the road. This upset the other residents and was challenging for the staff. She didn't go on that trip and she stayed behind, seemingly with no regrets about missing out on the holiday, appearing happy to stick with her normal weekly routine. After that, she has not been invited to go away with the other residents. Initially, I felt sad about this because I felt that she was missing out on some joyful experiences.

Since then, I have taken her away for the August bank holiday weekend. She is happy with this, particularly as it doesn't interrupt her weekly routine, especially her woodwork days which she hates to miss. The two occasions with "strange" rooms taught me that some preparation is necessary. Last year, I found a nice guest house near Bridlington on the internet. I printed off some photos of the guest house from the website and when I showed them to Karen, she smiled. "Would you like me to book a room here?" I asked. "Yes, book it" she answered. When I spoke to the landlady to make the booking, I explained about Karen's autism. She was very helpful and very understanding as she had been a teacher at a special school. I asked if she could forward a photo of the room. She promised to do so along with a few other photos. When I received her email with the photos, I printed them off to show Deborah and I forwarded copies to Mike, the Deputy Manager at her home who specialised in autism. He made a booklet with the title words "I'm going on holiday to Sewerby, Bridlington" The booklet gave the dates we would be going and returning and contained the photographs with captions such as "This is my room" and "This is the dining room where I will eat my breakfast". He had also included the words "Staff will pack

my case for me on Friday" and "I will go in the car with mum at 6pm"
It worked like a dream, Karen proudly showed the booklet to staff at her
home and her day care centre. When we arrived at the guest house, and
were shown our room, Karen was very happy with it and did not find it
"strange".

ANNIE AND MAX

The tough, boorish South African fisherman said, 'You look after Max,
heh! We think he's very special.'

'Yes,' said Joan, our friend who was listening to this, 'He's a very
special little boy.'

What do they mean by the use of this word 'special'? We often,
nowadays, also use the words 'special needs.' How did this term come
into being?

The expression 'special needs' in education was introduced to try to
show that society valued and respected the child as an individual. Terms
used previously had focussed on deficit characteristics, and these were
thought to be no longer acceptable: – as generating at best, discomfort and
at worst, repulsion: terms such as moron, spastic, mentally handicapped,
retarded or uneducable.

Now, the title 'special needs' is evolving towards the term 'additional
needs' or just 'needs' on the basis that each child is an individual,
even typically developing children, and they all are individuals, with
differences. It is now felt that society is made up of a diversity of people,
with a kaleidoscope of abilities and difficulties. Education, social and life-
skill training ideally should maximise potential. Being interdependent,
sharing skills and helping each other is now viewed as best practice for
a happy and healthy society. There is supposedly a push for a 'can-do'
culture as opposed to a 'can't do' one.

Despite the change towards children with 'needs', will Max still be a
'special' little boy?

We, his parents, think so, yes. Our 'special' child, like many autistic
children, is rare in his own unique way. The usual use of the word

'special' means distinctive and distinguished in some manner. It's unusual for a typically developing child to have complete absorption, knowledge and skills in certain interest areas, without a shred of competitiveness or one-upmanship. It's rare to find a child entirely without malice. It's rare to find a non-acquisitive child, without many demands for material things. It's rare to meet a child who beams with love and happiness and is able and willing to voice and physically express these emotions without self-consciousness or reservation.

The word 'special' reflects both ways, though. It takes a special sort of person to take the time to recognise these qualities and therefore fully appreciate him. This person is not dismissive, or too quick with him, as he is slow. This person will listen and converse on his level, mindfully, in order to get the best out of him. This person will not take offence if he doesn't respond, or even if he doesn't seem to hear them the first time. They will make sure he is not distracted by something stimulatory he might be seeing or hearing. They may need to repeat themselves, slowly and clearly, and fairly loudly to be 'in his face.' They will instinctively know it's best to be open, positive, and speak plainly with him. Max should be able to respond well to this sort of person and then a confidence and dialogue will develop between them, which both will seem to enjoy.

We all have a need to have our ideas and emotions understood, despite our limitations.

One of my favourite poems is this:

'There was a man with a tongue of wood
Who essayed to sing,
And in truth it was lamentable.
But there was one who heard
The clip-clapper of this tongue of wood
And knew what the man
Wished to sing,
And with that the singer was content.'

We all sing in our own clip-clappery ways. In an ideal society we should not be left to feel completely alone. We should all be appreciated by at least one other person. I hope that Max will always be special to someone, when I am gone, as special as he is to me now.

PAT AND CLAIRE

'Special'

The pocket Oxford Dictionary definition of 'special' states: "Adjective; of a peculiar or restricted kind, of or for a particular person or thing, not generally applicable or prevalent or occurring, exceptional in degree".

These days it is a word used frequently to describe persons, children and adults, who may have some type of learning and/or physical disability. It covers a wide range of disabilities, under the guise of 'special needs'.

We have an adult daughter who has 'special needs'. It became apparent quite early on in her development that she had some kind of developmental delay. At school age she was given a Statement of Special Educational Needs, which meant she could have additional tuition at the mainstream school she attended. Later on, struggling in mainstream school we had to move her to a 'special' school which catered for school age children with moderate learning difficulties. On leaving at the mandatory age of 16 she attended York College and was able to complete a 3-year course for Special Needs students, and achieved an NVQ Level 2 in Hospitality & Catering.

The word 'special' used in this context seems to be the result of over compensating for society's attitude to anyone perceived as different or 'not normal' either in their mental development, or as having any physical abnormality present. In the cruel and not too distant past, families who had the means often hid unfortunate 'special' children and adults away from society, as demonstrated by the Royal family. The youngest son of King George V and Queen Mary, Prince John, was kept away from the public eye, living with a Nanny at Sandringham, unseen by society and not much by his family for much of his short life. (Born 1905 – died 1919). He had epilepsy which became worse as he grew older, and died at aged 13. The name 'John' has been documented as not being used since by members of the Royal Family – as if it is tainted. It was almost like a dirty secret that any family who had the misfortune to give birth to someone not perceived as 'normal' wanted to hide it by removing these persons from everyday society. The poor had no such luxury available to them and anyone falling into that category was more often than not sent to the asylum, or even the poor house.

In these enlightened times, it is now okay to have someone in the family who is labelled 'special'. This has been helped in recent years by well known people in the public eye who have made public the fact that they have a special needs child or adult in the family: the Prime Minister at the time of writing, David Cameron, for instance, Katy Price and son Harvey, Rosa Monckton – Princess Diana was godmother to her Downs daughter Domenica – to name but a few. One wonders though if this apparent complete reversal in attitude is the product of an ever increasing irritatingly PC society, so bound up in human rights laws and health & safety legislation, determined to portray that it is wholly accepting of anyone different from the perceived 'norm'.

Yes, it is very nice to have my daughter perceived as 'special' but it can be quite patronising at times in a society, which I believe to be – underneath all the PC hype and perhaps because of it – hypocritically endemically prejudiced against anyone or anything that doesn't fit in with preconceived ideas of 'normal'. Yes, my daughter is very special to me and my family and friends, but so is my son. Every one of us is unique, and we are all special to someone.

LINDA AND ANDREW

'No!'

Andrew has always loved the word "No". Like any other child, he very quickly learnt that being naughty gets mum and dad's attention. One of his favourite activities is to swing curtains or vertical blinds, often with such gusto that he takes them off the tracks. This always brings about a stern "NO!" which causes him to cackle with glee.

Andrew is 18 years old and is unable to speak or to use any communication aids or sign language, although he vocalises a lot, and has a few words such as "Yeah" and "Mum". I have never heard him say the word "No", although school staff and other friends and family members say they have. Although he clearly understands a lot of what we say, we have always been advised by the professionals working with him to use short simple sentences when we are speaking to him. We try to explain why we are telling him off, but he either repeats the activity for which he has been reprimanded, or he finds something else which will reward him with another "No".

Like most 18 year old boys, Andrew is trying to find his own identity. He automatically resists anything we ask him to do and takes great delight in doing things he knows he shouldn't do. I identify with him so much – I still remember my father telling me when I was a teenager "If I said black you would say white". At 18, I thought my parents couldn't possibly know as much as I did. Does my son now feel the same way towards me?

How much does Andrew understand about the meaning of the word "No"? I am certain he wouldn't understand the dictionary definition – 'to reject, refuse approval, or express disapproval of'. I think what he takes delight in is the way the word is delivered – the tone of voice, the facial expressions and body language that accompany it. He especially likes it when his dad is saying it, because it is invariably accompanied by a big frown, wide eyes, clenched fists and lips formed into an angry O out of which comes a barked "NO!" The louder the "No" the more Andrew laughs.

Some of the other activities which bring about a stern "No" from us include throwing any objects he can get his hands on and sweeping things onto the floor from a table. I now avoid taking him supermarket shopping following a very traumatic experience in our local Sainsbury's when he reached out from his wheelchair to knock over a display stand with his right hand. This brought about a very sharp "No" from me. Steering him away from the area just allowed him to sweep a line of tins off the opposite row with his left hand. I scooped both his arms in and held them firmly across his chest, to which he responded by lashing out with both feet, as wide as he could, trying to kick things over. All accompanied by a chorus of "No's" from me. While the staff assured me not to worry, and started putting everything back in place, I gave the shopping up as a bad job and left the store. Andrew laughed all the way home.

It is a difficult balance to get right as I view this as Andrew's frustration at not being able to tell me he doesn't want to be wheeled round a supermarket, exacerbated by teenage hormones on top of a developmental age which is probably around the "terrible twos" in some ways. We are working very closely with the professionals to help Andrew to deal with the reality of day to day life, and to continue to expand Andrew's social experiences in preparation for adulthood. We also need to learn that the word "No" is a reward Andrew actively seeks.

PAULINE AND ALISON

'Normal'

I've always had trouble with the word normal. As a child growing up in the 1940 and 50's, in a one parent family, I didn't feel we were a 'normal' family.

We didn't have a dad – that wasn't 'normal'. I've always felt different to my siblings – I was the only one to leave home and the village we'd been brought up in. I was more willing to take risks and wanted more from life than they apparently did. When I did later conform to society's expectations for women, and got married and started a family, I can say, with hindsight, that I never felt comfortable with my situation and hovered uncomfortably on the edge of our circle of friends and acquaintances. I love both my children and wouldn't ever wish that I'd never had them – but the marriage bit I could have done without. Then later, when I discovered I was lesbian I could have felt even more 'abnormal', but in fact I felt as though I'd come home, found where I was meant to be.

Whilst I was only too aware that my daughter Alison was different to most other children, I didn't want her to be "labelled" by society and brought her up as best I could, to be just "Alison". I've never been quite sure whether this was the best thing I could have done or not. She has had difficulty accepting her disability, and doesn't fully understand why she has been included in groups of people much more visibly disabled than she herself is. She hated being labelled learning disabled and now at the age of 48, (at the time of writing), having recently been diagnosed as on the autistic spectrum, she has another label to come to terms with.

Alison is very much her own person, an individualist. Watching her grow and develop into the woman she is today has been a fascinating experience.

She has a way of interacting that greatly endears her to a great many people. She lives as independently as it is possible for her to do. She belongs to groups in the community where she is certainly accepted as herself, with a great deal of affection. Yes, she is different, but who can say she isn't 'normal'. I think she is an ambassador for people with learning disabilities and is helping the slow pace of acceptance and inclusion by society at large.

Most family carers struggle with the word 'normal', when differentiating between their child and the rest of society. We haven't found a word that we find adequate or acceptable. I believe we are all different, but who is 'normal' and who is not and does it really matter? I'm glad I'm different, and I'm glad my daughter is different. Diversity adds a great deal to life, making it more interesting, colourful and exciting. Vive la difference!

GILLIAN AND WILLIAM

'Stupid'

"Oh Gillian, you are stupid!" is a refrain from my mother that I have heard repeatedly throughout my life. Mum said this in response to my clumsiness in pricking my finger and bleeding all over the skirt she had made for me – I was only allowed to do the hemming because my stitches would be out of sight. Sewing a straight seam using Mum's knee-controlled sewing machine was beyond my co-ordination. Even now I lack the skills to operate a foot-powered machine, although I have for financial reasons produced curtains, and simple clothes for the children.

Despite this I still believe that I will not be able to achieve a satisfactory result.

"Don't touch my computer. You're so stupid that you will break it," was the reaction to my attempt to sort out a gremlin caused by Mum pressing the wrong key impatiently in her frustration. I had made the same error in class the previous week, and the tutor had talked me through the steps required to sort out the problem. It was gratifying to observe the amazement on Mum's face as her useless and illogical daughter managed to restore order. Mum was working on our family tree, and her computer was normally off limits to everyone. The whole family, including my sister, who has an M.A. in computing, was deemed to be stupid where computers were concerned.

Some time later, I was surprised to hear, "Gillian, will you proof read the family history account?" As this was exclusively Mum's territory, this was out of the ordinary, and I proved to be stupid at this too, as I identified some typing errors and impossible dates. I was subsequently banned from looking at the document.

"Gillian, where did you learn to make that delicious Christmas cake?" I was asked. "From a recipe!" I replied. I was thirty, and had brought some baking with me, as my parents enjoyed the results of my culinary efforts. I had always done the baking, as Mum dismissed non-essential cooking as a stupid waste of time. At last I was considered to have accomplished something successfully.

"Will you translate this academic article from the German for me?" This was unexpected, but I worked on the paper, which was a report on the earliest research Mum could find in her specialist field of the development of plant cells. I could translate most of it, but left the botanical terms to her. After that, translation was my job. I remember a holiday in France with my parents and the children, where we collected some fossils. At the local museum I bought a booklet in French, and the afternoon culminated in a three way translation and discussion with my family and the German couple in the next door tent, who had also been looking at fossils. Translation was also to the fore when I interpreted for a group of parents at a youth brass band social event – in a mixture of

English, French and British Sign Language. I'd discovered something I could do – communicate! Just as well, given my career as a speech and language therapist.

My mother and brother-in-law stopped communicating for some time after he had taken a long time sorting out a problem with her computer. As soon as it had been repaired she put things asunder again by repeatedly pressing a wrong key. My brother-in-law told Mum that she had made a stupid mistake, and she bristled. "Don't call me stupid!" He tried to reassure her that she was a very intelligent lady, but it was too late.

I wonder who labelled Mum stupid as a child, and had such a strong effect on her later attitude and treatment of her family.

POSITIVE ENCOUNTERS WITH THE WORLD

SUSAN AND KAREN

There have been a number of people along the way who have had a positive impact on Karen's life. These include the teachers at her special school who helped create a supportive environment where she was encouraged to make the most of her abilities, and the speech therapists that helped her overcome some of her communication problems. Later, the nurses on the mental handicap team helped support Karen during the 1990s when she was having problems living independently. Nowadays, the carers employed at The Rowans, her residential home, and also the staff and volunteers at her day centre, treat her with patience, respect and love. Some people, however, will go the extra mile beyond what is required by their job description. One such person is May, Karen's key worker at her day centre.

An assessment review had been arranged at the day centre. Karen often feels very anxious before such meetings and worries about them. Sometimes, she is reluctant to attend. May had reassured her that she didn't have to attend if she didn't want to but it would be nice if she did and she could just sit and listen and she didn't have to talk if she didn't want to. Karen sat quietly to start with, her head went down a few times and she avoided making eye contact with anyone. Then May said, "You've brought your notebook haven't you?" Karen nodded. "And you've written down something that you'd like to tell everyone at the meeting", May continued. Again, Karen nodded. "Would you like to read out what you've written?" asked May. Slowly, hesitantly, Karen read, "I am not happy living at Albert House. I want to live somewhere else"

Neither the owner of Albert House, nor a staff member had bothered to turn up for the meeting. However, Joan, Karen's care manager, (social worker), was at the meeting and said "We can do something about that Karen. We could go and look at one or two places. Would you like to do that?" "Yes" Karen replied and smiled. I was amazed and delighted that Karen had found the courage and confidence to express what was on her mind, both in writing and verbally, and that she was being taken seriously and listened to.

Karen tends to bottle things up and has difficulty expressing her feelings. She either becomes very withdrawn or she will be on edge and start talking louder and louder before blowing a gasket and having an outburst. May is very perceptive and notices when Karen is worried about something or feeling unhappy. She has a gentle way of encouraging Karen to open up and say what is bothering her. In the weeks before this meeting, she had noticed that Karen had become very withdrawn and had also started shouting more than she usually did. May encouraged Karen to write down her feelings in the notebook and to say what was on her mind. Expressing her unhappiness with her accommodation was a major breakthrough. I had also noticed that Karen had been less communicative but I had been unable to ascertain what the problem was as she had answered any questions in monosyllables. I was not happy with the home and had spoken to the care staff on several occasions about Karen wearing dirty clothes or having dirty hair. I also felt that the home did not have a welcoming atmosphere when you entered; the hall seemed a bit dingy and depressing. Just a few months after that meeting, Karen moved into a pleasant residential home with caring staff where she continues to live happily today.

There were other occasions when May's support made a difference, such as when Karen had been feeling fed up with some of her activities at the day centre. She had previously enjoyed taking part in craft activities such as making jewellery and designing cards, but had become bored with them. It is sometimes assumed that people with learning disabilities enjoy doing repetitive tasks because they are easier to learn but Karen finds them monotonous. It was May that noticed Karen's frustration. "She is not being stretched enough. She's quite intelligent and needs to learn new things so we are trying to find her some new activities" she told me. This led to Karen doing woodwork with a carpenter twice a week which was a great success because she enjoys using her hands. She finds the variety of tasks such as making plant boxes, repairing fences and putting up shelves interesting and satisfying and is proud of her achievements.

I feel immense gratitude to May for helping Karen to explore her potential and make positive changes in her life.

LIZ AND SALLY

There have been many positive encounters with many caring people in Sally's life. There have been kindly teachers and trainers and social workers and good friends. But people were often bemused by Sally and found it difficult to work out what would be helpful and what they could do for her. Notable exceptions were the landlady who said to me 'You have done a lot of worrying about Sally in the past, let me do some worrying for you now'. There was the practice nurse who was so skilled and speedy at taking blood, that Sally was not all phased by this procedure which she has to have constantly. But the person who really made a difference was not in the caring professions or a friend of the family or a relative, but a woman called Sarah from the bank.

Sally has always loved shopping. She particularly likes posh shops although she has also learned to trawl round charity shops. She buys a lot of clothes, but usually wears her old favourites. Her wardrobe is full of cheerful colourful garments but she is often to be found in grey or black. She loves to buy trainers too, usually of the upmarket kind with 'labels'. Her passion is computer games, which are ridiculously expensive. She can sometimes be persuaded to buy the pre-owned variety, but she also spends a lot of time online lusting after the latest releases which are extremely costly. For whatever reason she also likes to purchase games consoles and has at various times owned most of the popular kinds. This hobby is a very expensive one for someone who cannot really add up or subtract and it means she is very liable to spend over her budget and acquire punishing overdrafts. I have tried to get her to check her bank balance before she hands over more money, but this is not often adhered to. I have tried to keep a check myself of her expenditure, but this feels intrusive and not how I really want to be with her. I tried to talk to the bank about this issue, which has been a problem since Sally got her first lot of benefits. I begged them to swallow her card when the limit was reached, but they were reluctant to do this. Maybe they liked all the additional revenue that Sally or I gave them when the overdrafts were paid off or maybe they wanted to allow their customers more freedom. Finally, Sarah, the insightful bank employee, came up with a simple solution. If you have a savings account you are not allowed to overdraw, so if Sally only had a card for such an account damage would be limited. She does have a current account into which her benefits and wages are paid, but as long as I hang on to this card all should be well. Needless to say, there are many times after suitable negotiation I hand over the card and then forget to retrieve it in time to stop Sally spending a small fortune on some boots or another computer game.

I still try to inculcate some ideas of planning and budgeting, but it has not been very successful. I have also talked about saving up for things and how rewarding this would feel. Sally doesn't seem to care much about 'deferred gratification' or indeed 'rainy days' which has been another of my tacks. She is similarly impervious to my discussions about Tory threats to those on benefits. So money and how Sally spends it will no doubt continue to be a source of aggravation between us, but I will always be grateful to Sarah, whom we never met face to face. She has since moved on. I hope she got promoted for her ability to listen, grasp an issue and provide a solution.

GILLIAN AND WILLIAM

Michael, my oldest child, looked wistfully into my eyes. "People always seem to give things to William." We were on holiday in Stoke, visiting a mining museum, and William had just been told by the elderly miner who had been our tour guide that he could keep the bright yellow safety helmet he was reluctant to return. Michael was jealous, because he wanted to go on a fossil-hunting expedition, and coveted the helmet.

Several weeks later he turned the headgear into geology equipment because William had lost interest in playing mines (i.e. digging holes in the garden and burying "treasure").

This is just one example of many positive experiences for William. People have always responded to his enthusiasm and optimistic nature. He is skilled in getting people to join in, be this Scottish dancing, or initiating a game of Trivial Pursuit with a German couple at a youth hostel. They were amazed at his general knowledge – they had realised that William had learning difficulties and so they expected to win. At another hostel he was adopted by a group of cub scouts and their leaders in the afternoon, and spent the evening playing board games with a group of adults with learning disabilities who were on holiday at the same hostel.

As an adult William has Chinese friends who are delighted to encourage him to practise his limited Mandarin, and he is now treated as one of the extended family at Chinese festivals and celebrations. When he finished the Great North Run, several organisations offered him refreshments and massages – we nearly missed the coach taking us back to our car because William was so busy socialising that he had forgotten the arrangements for meeting up. I had to summon him through the public address system. To him this was an exciting experience, which he enjoyed rather more than I did!

Holidays seem to be a prime time to develop friendships. William still meets up with a family he met in Turkey with his dad five years ago. A couple he met on his two skiing trips to Switzerland phone him whenever they come north, to arrange a day out. Another encounter led to William being invited to spend a day at a gliding club as his elderly pen-friend (another youth hostel acquaintance) was taking part in a competition locally.

Shop assistants seem keen to help William; he is greeted cheerfully wherever he goes, and he has a supportive group of friends who keep an eye on him. At college, William was on a foundation course for students with learning disabilities, and was the first from this group to access the mainstream sports course, achieving certificates at levels one and two. The tutor agreed to include him, despite initial misgivings, and an excellent package of support was developed with staff, William and me. Two years later, William was able to do a level two BTEC performing arts course, the level of support again guided by his wishes.

William has had a lot of negative encounters too, but somehow his resilience is well developed, he keeps seeing the positive side of life, and he retains his sunny nature and confidence.

PAT AND CLAIRE

Having a daughter with a learning disability has led us to encounter many people from differing professions over the years. Until a diagnosis at age 19 as being on the autistic spectrum, we endured the trials and tribulations of endless assessments in education and health. Naturally these have had a lasting effect on us, sadly sometimes not in a good way. However, there are people who have made a lasting impression on us in a positive way and have made a significant difference to both Claire's life and ours as her family.

Claire's first educational psychologist was a feisty lady called Trish. She pushed us into questioning the future possibility that Claire's perceived delayed development – at that time undiagnosed – would mean she would need to attend a special school when she was at nursery age, and we had been led to believe that we should not raise our expectations as to her future capabilities. Trish made us realise that we should not be too quick to judge her capabilities at such a young age, and that although her communication skills were poor at that time, she understood a lot more than we gave her credit for. She taught us to persevere with toilet training, and also coping strategies to deal with the many tantrums. With her encouragement, Claire started in mainstream school, where she stayed, with support, until aged ten. Trish also gave me back some of my confidence and self-esteem, which I had somehow lost in the early years of struggle and uncertainty after Claire was born. She became a family friend and I was very sorry when she left the area.

Later, there was the consultant surgeon who came into our lives when Claire was in her twenties. She was admitted to hospital as an emergency patient, following the failure of drugs to control her condition. (This has been mentioned in more detail in other chapters.) There was nothing else that could be done. She had to have the much-dreaded major abdominal surgery. We explained to Mr. C. that Claire had a diagnosis of Asperger's Syndrome, which is on the autism spectrum. He was not familiar with the details of the condition. We later learned that he had done some research on the internet the night before the surgery, and had printed information out for all his theatre staff, so that they would have some understanding of her needs before and after the operation the next morning. We were so touched that he went to those lengths and in the lead-up to the surgery all the staff she came into contact with were so caring. She was to have further surgery in the ensuing years and Mr. C also carried these out. She always felt better knowing that Mr. C. would be doing the operations. Whenever we see Mr. C. in passing at the hospital, when Claire frequently has follow-up clinics with her medical consultant, he always makes the time to stop for a catch-up, even if he is in the coffee shop, or having lunch.

Her medical consultant at the hospital, Dr. S., who she has been under for a number of years, has also shown exceptional kindness and care, not just to Claire, but to us as well. He patiently explains everything in simple English to her, including any tests or procedures that he sends her for. In these times of great strain on NHS staff in hospitals, it is a comfort to know that busy professionals can still take the time to show that they care for their patients. All it needs sometimes is for someone to show empathy and it can make a world of difference.

Her first and only employer, Sainsbury's, where she started at 18, have shown remarkable care and concern over recent years especially since she has suffered repeated bouts of ill-health that have sometimes resulted in more hospital admissions and periods of recovery at home. For a large organization they have been more than understanding about the amount of time she has had to take off her part-time job. Many of her colleagues in the workplace have also shown her touching support and understanding, sending flowers, cards and always asking after her during those difficult times.

We have a mix of special friends, not all parents themselves, both where we live and in other parts of the country. They have kept in constant touch in person or by phone, and have been an invaluable support network to us during the bad and the good times. Some are also carers for a disabled son or daughter. Most have travelled a different path to us during parenthood, but it has been a comfort to be able to share in the tears and laughter of our different experiences along the way with these special people.

Finally, when I asked my daughter, before writing this piece, whom she felt had made a real difference to her life over the years, she thought for a second before saying, "My brother". My son, soon to be married to an equally caring partner, is about to become a parent himself. I feel so proud that my son and his soon wife-to-be, although no longer living at home or nearby, feature so strongly in my daughter's world and it is a comfort to know that they will be a constant in her life, and be there to support her when we are no longer here.

LINDA AND ANDREW

There is a famous saying "It takes a village to raise a child", and it has certainly proved to be the case with Andrew. He has never had a proper diagnosis, and was given the label "Global Developmental Delay" when he was around two years old. We had to accept at a very early stage that there would be a great deal of intervention, assessment and monitoring of his needs, and at the risk of sounding ungrateful, it has sometimes seemed as if he is not our child and that we are "bit players" in his life. However, he would not have made the progress he has done without the input of a whole range of people over the years and we will always be grateful to the professionals who have worked with him.

We have also ventured outside "the village", overturning stones in a search for anything which will make a difference to Andrew's life. We have tried all sorts of complementary therapies. Impressed by the results of some of Andrew's treatments, I trained in massage and reflexology myself. I was always very selective about who treated Andrew, and could spot a charlatan from 100 yards. One therapy which made a significant difference to Andrew is called Bodybrushing. We heard about it from a friend who had taken her daughter. We first went to see Steve Clarke, the Bodybrushing therapist, when Andrew was five years old. I will never forget the first time I met Steve. A big man with kind eyes and a confident, but not arrogant, attitude. I was taken aback when he said he didn't need to hear any of Andrew's medical history before he made his assessment – a refreshing change from having to dredge all the old painful memories up again. He used what looked like a fine watercolour paintbrush and proceeded to brush different parts of Andrew's body – his face, his hands, his spine. He was looking for physiological responses to the brushing, and I was fascinated to see these physical changes occurring as he went about his assessment: colour changes around his eyes and mouth, quivering of muscles, and dilation/constriction of his pupils. At the end of his examination, Steve said that the therapy would improve Andrew's muscle tone and movement of his mouth and tongue, and that anything else would be a bonus. I appreciated his frank honesty and was overjoyed to find someone who focussed on what Andrew could do rather than what he couldn't. He gave us some brushes and sent us home with a sheet of brushing exercises which we were to carry out each day, and he said that we would see a marked change in Andrew's awareness, as he was currently "living in his head".

This appointment was just before the summer holidays, and Andrew had spent one year in the reception class. He had been a timid little boy who curled up "like a hedgehog" whenever any child came near him, or if he became overwhelmed by what was going on in the classroom. His teacher was definitely starting to bring him out of his shell, but we were concerned that the six week break would affect his confidence. We noticed during the holidays that he seemed to be taking more notice of things, especially when we were out and about, but I thought that perhaps I was wanting to think that the brushing was making the difference Steve said it would. Within a week of him returning to school, we were getting reports back that Andrew was sitting up, watching the other children and seemed much more interested in what was going on.

There is no doubt in my mind that the Bodybrushing also played a major role, along with physiotherapy and surgery, in helping Andrew to stand unsupported, and to take independent steps. Steve told me that he was enduring a lot of ridicule from the medical profession, but I went on to have a course of Bodybrushing treatment and experienced first-hand the amazing effect it had on my self-confidence and co-ordination. Steve was diagnosed with a brain tumour in 2004 and died in April that year. My world fell apart. Andrew continued to receive Bodybrushing treatment under the supervision of Steve's partner, Jenn, but his death hit me very hard.

ANNIE AND MAX

It was a chance meeting which resulted in our finding Heather. I did know of her in our village and she lived up the road, but I knew little else. My friend Sasha met her in the gym and told her about Max and that we were just about to embark upon some behavioural therapy training for him, and needed some willing helpers. As she was free at that time, Heather volunteered to help us and joined the team. So, when Max was three, a group of us, consisting of family, friends and psychology students from the University, were introduced to the ABA or Lovaas method of training. This had been found to be a success with autistic children in the States, in terms of social skills, and adapting to life in the non-autistic world. We had a timetable of sessions throughout the week, amounting to thirty hours of training for Max in all. Heather was so good at carrying out the practice drills with him, and transmitting enthusiasm when he got them right, that she soon became 'team leader.'

When he started school, he had a statement of educational needs and was awarded thirty hours of help to be provided by a Teaching Assistant. She volunteered for this job, as his TA and, luckily for us, was accepted. She remained with him for the next seven years, till he went off to secondary school. She has really been pivotal in our lives with Max. The teachers at primary school gave Heather free rein, adapting the learning objectives into a form he could grasp, and making the resources needed, for example the visual prompts to learning which help autistic children. She could put things over to him to ensure he understood what was happening, and always stood up for him. She had that ability to speak out, without any self- consciousness, or timidity and how others perceived him improved. He was viewed very positively by teachers and pupils alike, as a direct result of her positive attitude and vibrant energy in fighting and promoting his needs. When we were tired and vague, she was clear and incisive. This is the sort of positivity I would wish for all parents of a child with learning difficulties. It felt, at times, like we were brought to life using jump leads attached to her vigorous engine.

We still see Heather regularly. She always takes him out during school holidays and has him for tea quite often. She wants to continue her relationship and input into Max's life and help out in any way. She enjoys being with him, I think. We can rely on her for anything within reason, and her family would cope with having him if we needed them to. He loves her sparkly ways and she knows him so well that we don't need to hide anything from her. She thinks of things he likes and organises trips for him to bird centres and musical shows and such like. Our lives would be much poorer if we didn't have Heather, and that's for sure.

Another positive relationship we have in our lives is Sophie's boyfriend, and now fiancé, Tom. He is another person who loves Max. I remember when they first met. They both went to kick some footballs around on the trampoline together and invented a new game 'whack attack.' Tom told Sophie that he'd never met anyone like Max. He found his humour and non-competitive approach, and his 'living for the moment' style very refreshing and they were out there for ages. He always thinks to organise a 'BDO' or big day out for them both when they are together. This will incorporate a boys' treat like an air museum, fishing trip, a World War 2 songs show, or a visit to the armouries. When we were on holiday with Sophie and Tom recently, we all jumped off a boat and swam to the shore. I noticed with delight and relief that Tom was sticking near to Max; swimming alongside him in case he had difficulties and encouraging him. There are various other lovely things we've noticed. When he and Max are walking along the pavement, Tom will put him on the inside away from the kerb. These are the sort of things a mother is always alert about and to see Tom taking responsibility in this way is like being handed a feather bed and being allowed to lie on it for a while.

All positive encounters stem from a loving attitude. People would do well to remember that if they treat the persons under their care like they would a member of their own family, then they will not go far wrong.

When I worked as a doctor for twenty years at my practice, this was our attitude towards our patients. We hardly ever had any complaints and were rewarded with gratitude and loyalty from our patients.

As Henry James said, 'Three things in human life are important: the first is to be kind; the second is to be kind; and the third is to be kind.'

PAULINE AND ALISON

There are many examples of Alison's positive encounters with other people which are evident in the number of people who stop and talk to her wherever she goes. She appears to know far more people than anyone else I know.

When we are out shopping, either in town or at the supermarket, it is rare that no one comes up to her, smiling and saying how good it is to see her. Mostly I have no idea who they are and some of them knew Alison years ago, but have not forgotten her.

She works as a volunteer in the restaurant at the local hospital one morning a week and whenever I've had the occasion to visit the restaurant on a day she is working, I've been touched by the obvious affection most of the staff display towards her.

On her journey to work, she calls in to say hello to the staff at an organisation she used to work for as a volunteer and who still invite both of us to their annual Christmas dinner. She also calls in to see her hairdresser, David, who she has built up a lovely friendly relationship with.

Most of her support workers, some whom she has known for a number of years now, will bring biscuits or crumpets which they share with her for supper, making their relationship with her a bit more special.

Probably the best examples are the members of Alison's circle of support. Over the years, they have become close friends and she has learned the benefits of phoning friends regularly, something she never did before. She has also recently learned how to send texts so she has another way of keeping in contact with people and not just waiting for them to contact her.

Her latest conquests are our Zumba Gold class. I'd been doing Zumba for a while and really enjoying it, when Alison asked if she could come along, as she had nothing to do that day. I agreed she could come and watch, so she brought along one of her word-search books and sat quietly, not appearing to take very much notice of the class. The next week she asked if she could come along again, which was fine with me. This time, however, I noticed she was standing at the end of a row, looking closely at what was happening and at the end of the class she asked if she could join in the following week. The class instructor was very happy to include her and she hasn't looked back since. She now does three classes a week, is remarkably good at it, and enjoys it immensely. When she arrives at class, she goes round the whole room greeting people and giving them hugs. Some of them give her lifts home if I'm not around and everyone is very concerned if for any reason she isn't there.

Because meeting Alison is such a positive experience, ordinary people who probably have hardly ever met anyone with learning disabilities before, find their fears of people who are different to them are largely unfounded.

RITES OF PASSAGE

SUSAN AND KAREN

Leaving Home

When Karen was seventeen, she left home to go to Dilston Hall, a Social Training Centre run by Mencap. It is now designated as a College of Further Education for people with learning disabilities at Corbridge, Northumberland. The only times she had been away from home without us was when she went camping with the Girl Guides. North Yorkshire County Council had offered to fund a place for her for two years. As there was no sixth form education for "Educationally Subnormal (Moderate)" pupils at that time, this was an opportunity that was too good to miss especially as we were keen for Karen to continue her education and practise daily living skills to enable her to become as independent as possible.

We took Karen to visit Dilston Hall and we all liked the look of it. The college is in a beautiful, rural part of Northumberland and there is an old castle and chapel in the grounds. When the day came to take her to Corbridge, Karen was happy and excited. It was a beautiful September day and we had a walk round Hexham followed by a nice lunch before arriving at the college in the afternoon. When it came to saying our goodbyes, I felt quite tearful but did my best to hide my tears. It can be difficult for any parent to let go of their child when they go away to college but it can be harder for a parent of a child with special needs. I had always been very protective towards Karen knowing how much more vulnerable she was than "normal" children. There was a sense of loss because I knew that I would miss having her at home. I also knew that it was such a big step for her to leave home and all that she was familiar with and that she would miss being at home with us, but I knew that I had to let her go. However, I felt proud of her for having the courage and determination to take this journey into the unknown and very grateful that she was being given this opportunity. Karen was happy and smiling and looking forward to becoming a "college girl"; there were no tears on her part.

Karen had joined the Girl Guides when she was twelve because I wanted her to mix with "normal" children and enjoy normal activities. I remembered being told by Karen's Guide mistress that when she had gone camping with the Girl Guides, she had been one of the few girls who had not suffered from homesickness and had not cried in bed at night. I had no doubts that Karen would quickly adapt to her new life. I was not pleased, therefore, by one of the college rules. The Head of the college was an ex-military man who was quite strict and the particular rule I took issue with was that parents were not normally allowed to visit their child during the first six weeks. This was because the Head thought it was unsettling for the child to be visited during this period and that they would be upset when the parents left. I thought this rule was unreasonable, especially as Karen's eighteenth birthday in October was about four weeks after the autumn term started. Tom's mother made a fruit cake and knew someone who iced celebration cakes. The finished cake looked beautiful, with iced flowers, candles and the words "Happy Birthday Karen" with a large number 18. I phoned the military man and pleaded with him to make an exception to the rule and allow us to visit on the weekend near her birthday. "It's her eighteenth birthday, a special occasion", I pointed out. At first, he refused and said, "But what if other parents wanted to do that?" I was determined that Karen would have a proper birthday celebration so I politely persisted. "We have had a beautiful cake made for her and the other students and the staff too, will be able to have a piece at teatime". That did the trick: he agreed, reluctantly I feel, but perhaps he had a heart after all underneath his authoritarian demeanour. Tom and I drove up to Corbridge with Steven and we took Karen out to lunch that day. We left the cake at the school so that everyone could enjoy it at teatime and, as we expected, there were no tears from Karen when we departed.

The next major rite of passage came when Karen left home shortly before her twenty first birthday to move into a shared house with two other young women with learning disabilities. She was very keen to live in a place of her own, albeit with other residents and staff support and we wanted her to be as independent as possible. I remember driving to her new home, about two miles away, the boot and back seat piled with her clothes and belongings, concentrating on the road and trying to suppress the emotions that were bubbling up inside me. I did not want Karen to see how sad I was feeling that she was leaving home for good this time. It felt like an enormous step for Karen and a huge wrench for me. It was about loosening the cord and letting go, trusting that this was the right thing to do for Karen and that it would help her to grow and have a life of her own. Even though my role as "Karen's mother" was about to change, I knew that the bond of love between us would always be there. Driving home on my own, the tears I'd been suppressing poured out and ran down my cheeks.

ANNIE AND MAX

When she was carrying him, he was so content within her that she could almost feel him smiling. He was comforted by the rhythmic swooshing noises of her lifeblood system and the gentle thuds of her heart. To him, these were the sounds of a calm place, a place of peace.

After he was born, if she soothed him with a 'shhh, shhh', he would react instantly by stilling, then fall asleep. It was reminiscent of a hypnotist, who by clicking his fingers, puts the subject at once into a trance.

As a tiny baby, he used to love feeding, as it was a way of linking back to her and they were as one again. He would joyfully root for her and nestle in with small, happy, gulping swallowing noises. Sometimes he would stop to come off the nipple, look directly into her eyes and give a grateful smile spilling over with joy and white milk. She was overcome to feel he was sharing his moment of joy with her. She wondered how he seemed to be able to focus on her face, as at that time his sight was so poor he could only discern light and dark, and the edges of things, but of course, he didn't need to see her, to know she was there.

When he grew to a small child, there was an oft repeated scenario, which she would actively encourage, as they both enjoyed it. She would lie on the floor and the little one would walk up and curl into a ball next to her head and burrow back towards her heart, content to lie peacefully in her loving arms. Her sister remarked that he was trying to climb back inside her. He was like a pea, popped from the pod too soon, that says, 'Take me back, take me back, I'm not ready yet for the outside world. I'm not yet fully made!'

As he grew, he grew musical; they shared this, and would practice his choir songs together, singing into the mirror, pretending it was the audience.

He was encouraged by school to perform in nativity plays and choir performances. It was excruciating for her to watch as he unravelled on the stage, exhibiting every odd behaviour from arm gesticulations and mouth grinding to spinning and grunting. She experienced the feeling of disappointment like a sinking stone and then the usual self-blaming dictum, 'Why did I agree to put him in for this? I should have known.'

She would scuttle him quickly from the venue, head down against the glances, face set in a Mona Lisa smile to enigmatically show she was having a fine time. Walking quickly through the village, she would hold his hand, telling him how well he had done, tears streaming down her face. It was the only time she was pleased by his paucity of eye contact.

Over time, she realised, with interest, that it was the pity she loathed and came to dread. She was aware of seepage of pity rising from the audience at these events, like the sinister sign of an impending flood. Defence and pretence now futile, it was a deal too late for sandbags.

At age 15, he was asked by school to sing his first solo at the festival of performing arts. It clashed with her final rehearsal for her own choir concert and she explained to him that she couldn't miss the rehearsal, and that Daddy would be there with him. He seemed to understand, in his usual placid way. Her daughter said 'You'd go if you really wanted to, but it will be awful Mum. I don't blame you, I would do the same.'

At the last moment, she went, love triumphant as usual. They sat on the front seats at the side, ready for a quick getaway. They helped him down and watched him walk steadily round the piano where Mr Wright, the accompanist, sat, to the microphone.

'Mr Wright,' he said in a conspiratorial aside, broadcast loudly to the entire concert hall, 'Mum's got to leave straight after the applause.'

'That's alright Max' came the reply, 'Ready when you are.'

Then his deep lovely voice, clear and disarmingly note perfect sang 'Edelweiss', gaining strength and confidence as he went on. There was an immediate and rapturous applause and several people dabbed at tears. His face burst into a massive grin at Mr Wright, then at her. She asked him later why he had wanted her to be there. 'To express emotion,' he said, 'to say you were proud of me.'

PAT AND CLAIRE

My memory of starting school was a very different experience to that of my own children. I started school in the 1950s; I remember being taken by my mother to a school bus stop and just put on the bus. I remember the bus pulling away and watching my mum's worried face through the window whilst she was waving. I remember crying and feeling lost and bewildered. I'm sure there must have been other children feeling just like me but I can't recall. I was just 5 years old and simply left to get on with it. I was heartbroken at being separated from my mum and still feel sick at the thought of how barbarically the system treated small children in those times. No parents were allowed to come anywhere near the schools in those days. No breaking in gently for new children with half day visits to start with. I didn't see my mother again until the bus brought us all back after the school day, to what became that most hated bus stop. The experience I'm sure made me more needy and insecure. At the time we were living on an Air Force base, probably in the middle of nowhere, where most of the bases around the country were sited. The nearest primary school must have been some distance away, hence the bus journey. I think I hated the thought of going on that bus more than being at the school itself. My relationship with future primary schools, and the obligatory bus journeys – too many to recall due to frequent moves around the country with my father's job – left me with a determination not to put my own children through the trauma of changing schools too frequently. I also believe that my experience of being put on buses from an early age to fend for myself left me with an aversion to traveling on them. Even now, just the smell on entering a bus takes me back to those days. Needless to say I am not keen to use buses and will only do so as a last resort!

When the time came for my children to embark on their school lives my husband and I were living a short walk away from the local primary school. My eldest child, Stuart, had started school when we were living in Shropshire, and had experienced two terms in his first school when we moved back to York, where we had chosen to settle. He had seemed to take to school very well and liked going. One of the reasons my husband gave up his career in the Royal Air Force was so that our children could have the stability at an early stage in their education, which I, as a child in a service family, never had.

When my younger child, Claire, was due to start school during the late 1980s we realized that her needs were going to be different to that of our son's. She had already been statemented, having been identified with delayed speech and language development. The local primary school was happy to take her even though she had to have additional Special Needs support. She was quite a novelty in that they had never had a child in school with a Statement of Educational Needs before, and on looking back I don't think they quite knew how to deal with it. At the time I think a lot depended on the teacher who was taking the Reception class and whether or not they felt able to integrate a child with special needs into their class. Class size would have a lot to do with it. I remember Mrs. D. as being a very sympathetic and kindly lady who was willing to give Claire a chance. The Reception year that September was split into two classes, with about 16 pupils per class; quite a luxury, but more pupils were due to start in January. I discovered over the years that it makes a huge difference to a struggling child in school on how they are received by specific teachers in a mainstream setting, and I consider we were very fortunate in having Mrs. D. The school was very open about making allowances for my daughter's limited ability to understand what was happening, and encouraged me to stay with her in the classroom, in a background capacity. I busied myself helping with displays and interacting with the other children in the classroom. A discreet presence was the order of the day. This enabled Claire to become familiar with the school setting, whilst not having to be completely separated from her familiar surroundings and me at the same time.

The first term was mornings only. The second term after Christmas we began a gradual withdrawal process, with me staying for the first part of the morning, and then leaving her after initially settling her in. Even when she was able to do a full school day she was not able to stay over the school lunchtime, as she screamed in the canteen and could not cope with all the noise going on around her. I remember the first day we tried her staying for school dinners. The senior lunchtime supervisor telephoned me at home that lunchtime and more or less demanded that I come and get her as they could not cope with her distress in the canteen with the other pupils, as she was making too much noise crying. I had to bring her home and then take her back after lunch. This went on for nearly 2 years before I was finally able to leave her for a full school day. It was then that I was able to return to part-time work and claim some of my life back outside of the home. This lengthy process was quite different to how it was when I was a child!

As is often the case with Asperger's sufferers, my daughter has an ongoing obsession. This relates to buses. This started when it was time for her to move to the local college for further education at seventeen. She had to undergo supervised bus training to give her the confidence to undertake the journey alone, as at that time it was a two-bus journey. She loves using them, as long as she knows the route and which bus to get. She even collects photos and models of buses, and can recite bus numbers and which routes they relate to in our small city. I think it gives her a feeling of independence and routine, so often important in the world of autism. Unlike me, she has found using buses a positive experience and enjoys the whole process immensely.

I think my own memories of starting school made me more aware of the process for my own children, particularly my daughter. When she was much later diagnosed as being on the autistic spectrum with Asperger's Syndrome, I am so glad I was able to help her make the important transition into school life a little less painful than my own.

PAULINE AND ALISON

First School Days

It was pouring with rain, a cold, dark and windy day, matching my mood perfectly. I was on my way with Alison to a day nursery. The pushchair was something for me to hang on to. I felt bewildered and scared. Scared of what the future held for us as a family, scared about my ability to cope, scared for Alison and how she would be treated. Until recently, although Alison had been very slow in reaching the normal childhood milestones, we had managed pretty well. Our routines had adapted to whatever she needed at the time, but now that wasn't enough. Now, we seemed to inhabit a different world and we had no map to follow, no one to ask the way – it felt a very lonely place. The rain dripped down the back of my neck, my legs and feet were soaked. Alison was cocooned in the waterproof cover and I wanted a place of safety for myself. I wanted to turn round and flee back home. I wished we'd never taken Alison to be assessed by the paediatrician. All our hopes and dreams for our beautiful daughter seemed so unattainable now.

The nursery was warm, bright and welcoming – happy-looking kids, colourful toys, and young, smiling nursery nurses. The place had a nice buzz about it and I relaxed a little. After I'd filled in all the forms and paperwork, I was invited by the matron into her office and she asked me to tell her all about Alison. She said it would be good for her to have other young children to play with and I agreed, as Michael had already started his first term at infant school. Being very shy usually, I expected

Alison to be upset when I left, but she was sitting quietly, studying her new surroundings. I doubt if I could have left her if she had screamed and cried, but even so, it was hard to walk out of the building without her.

On the face of it, I was just another mum, leaving my youngster in the care of others for the first time. But this would be the first of many new assessments and services that Alison would need throughout her lifetime. I had to accept that I too was going to need help.

As Alison now carried the label 'mentally handicapped' we were also referred to the speech therapy department, because although she could speak, it was very difficult for most people to understand what she was saying. I remember at our first appointment the speech therapist saying to me, "I'm afraid you've made a big mistake moving from London. Services in the north of England are a long way behind those in the capital". My heart sank.

As Alison approached her fifth birthday, the matron at the day nursery recommended a small church school, with only three classes. She said the reception class teacher was very good and she felt Alison would do well with her help. After meeting the teacher, I couldn't believe we had been so lucky, and felt that Alison couldn't be in better hands. She welcomed Alison into her class and for the first few months everything was going well. She even made a friend of her own, Dawn, who would go on to be part of her life for a long time. You can imagine what a blow it was to hear that our wonderful teacher had cancer and in fact died within a few weeks.

The new teacher had none of the special gifts, empathy and patience of Miss Schofield, and things deteriorated rapidly. Alison was being bullied by some of the other children and a parent made a complaint about Alison being at a 'normal' school. I was called into school and a confrontation developed between me and the parent who had complained. For the first time, I experienced my ability to stand up for Alison in ways that I would never do for myself, something which I would be called upon to do many, many times in subsequent years. It was obvious to me, that without Miss Schofield the school was no longer prepared to allow Alison to attend, and she was referred to an educational psychologist.

After his assessment, the prognosis was bleak for Alison's future. By this time, I'd had enough of my child being written off at such an early age by people who didn't know her. "You are wrong. You don't know her. There is so much more to Alison than you can possibly see in such a short time", I argued. I refused to accept his assessment. I just knew he was wrong. "I insist that you do another more in-depth assessment", I demanded. This time he brought his own son along and after seeing how Alison interacted with a toddler, he agreed that the original assessment was not accurate. The outcome of his final assessment in reality made little difference, as Alison was sent to a 'special' school, for the educationally sub-normal.

I have sometimes wondered what Alison's life would have been like, if I had meekly accepted what the 'professionals' had told me in those early years – if I hadn't challenged their opinions. I do know, without a shadow of a doubt, that Alison would not be the person she is today. From being written off as almost uneducable, with very little prospect of her being able to anything very much for herself, she has grown, with lots of patience and encouragement, into a very independent woman, who wants to do everything for herself. She can read and write, although numbers and money remain difficult for her to understand. She communicates well, uses the telephone and her computer and has recently learned to send texts. She is also uniquely herself.

GILLIAN AND WILLIAM

My older son, Michael is dyspraxic, with significant coordination problems. He was allowed to start nursery a term early, as, at the age of three, he had two younger siblings and it was deemed that he would benefit from some extra attention. He had difficulty in sequencing sounds in words, and strangers found it hard to understand his speech. However his language development was advanced, and he was always keen to tell me his stories about time spent apart from me. I have written this piece in his voice from my memories of what Michael told me about his first few nursery sessions.

Mummy says that I'm a big boy now, and can go to big nursery school with Miss Smith, who goes to Sunday School with me. Miss Smith says this is because I've got my twin babies at home, and it would be nice for me to play without them taking my toys. At home I climb into the playpen to keep them away.

Mummy has made me a bag for my new black shoes, t-shirt and shorts, and sewn Thomas the Tank Engine on my special new towel. I've been practising changing my clothes really quickly. I'm getting really clever, but Mummy says I can ask for help if I need to.

I got up this morning and had a bath and dressed all by myself while Mummy ran after the babies. We had yummy porridge and bananas for breakfast, but William dropped his bowl on the floor, so Mummy was cross.

I walked like a good boy all the way to school, because William was in the pram, and Margaret was on my pram seat. When I walk with Mummy, it's really special, 'cos I can tell Mummy what colour all the cars are when they go past, and tell her their numbers and letters.

When we got to school it was a bit silly. Miss Smith the teacher was there – and Mrs. Smith, her helper – and Miss Shell, and the teacher next door is Miss Smith too! I hung up my coat and bag and Thomas towel on my very own peg, which has a picture of a train and my name beside it. My teacher said I could do some colouring and drawing, so I drew a huge bus with Humpty Dumpty sitting on top. I wrote "Humpty Dumpty" and " a hyooj bus." Mrs Smith was very pleased, and said I was a clever boy.

Then we had toilet time and played outside on bikes. That was really hard, and I couldn't manage the pedals. When we went inside again, a big boy called John was in the cloakroom moving all the towels onto the wrong pegs. That was very naughty, because he put Thomas next to a boat, and he's supposed to be by my train picture. Mrs. Smith was very kind, and helped me to put my towel back on the right peg.

It was story time next. We read the story of The Hungry Caterpillar, and I told Miss Smith everything the caterpillar ate, and did some counting. After the story, Miss Smith showed us some lovely birthday cards and Christmas cards. They all had words on the back, like dog, cat, it, is, in and red. I knew all the words.

Then it was time to go home. Miss Smith gave some of the boys and girls pretty cards with some words, but I only got a reading book. I was very sad and cried all the way home, so after dinner – cheese on toast and tiny tomatoes – Mummy drew some words on a lovely Christmas card for me, and I could read them all by myself.

Comment from Mum – "John" has autism, and moving towels and P.E. bags was one of his regular daily routines.

METAMORPHOSIS

SUSAN AND KAREN

When I was a schoolgirl, I was quite shy. I think it was partly because I was an only child. I often wished I had brothers and sisters and envied friends from large families. Their families seemed so cheerful, the children boisterous and self assured. I think my shyness and self consciousness was also partly due to bullying. When I was seven, I was often bullied walking home from school. It was more verbal than physical but a boy once put wet, sticky bubble gum down my back which stuck to my vest. Cries of "goofy teeth," followed me home. I did not receive any sympathy from my mother who was most annoyed about the bubble gum and my tears failed to move her. "It's a pity you don't have brothers to toughen you up, otherwise you'd be able to stand up for yourself", she said; she had come from a large family, four brothers and three sisters. I vowed that when I grew up, I would have a large family with four children.

At grammar school, I was part of a circle of friends but was always the quiet one and usually afraid to voice an opinion that differed to other people's because I was afraid of sounding stupid. My lack of confidence was not helped by verbal bullying from a group of very confident girls who were in my year. I had been having ballet lessons since the age of nine but felt self conscious about telling anyone at my new school and I stopped going to the classes. In 1962, when I was fourteen, Nanny, my beloved grandmother, died from a deliberate overdose of barbiturates. She was an invalid with various health problems and she suffered from depression. Her suicide was a terrible shock but my family did not discuss it. I think my dad was probably immersed in his own grief. Perhaps there was a sense of shame as he was a Catholic convert and suicide was regarded as a sin by the Catholic Church. My mother was stoical, she often kept her feelings to herself, and I think she was trying to be protective. I secretly cried myself to sleep at night and felt I could not talk to anyone about it, not even my friends.

Nanny had always called me "little beautiful" and I found this embarrassing as I thought I was anything but beautiful. For a few years, I wore braces on my teeth and I was very conscious of my pimples. I thought I would never have a boyfriend but when I was fifteen, I met Paul. We went out together for over a year and then I became pregnant. We married and five months later, Karen was born and her brother, Steven, was born two years later. It was not a happy marriage. Paul would sometimes sleep in and he lost a couple of jobs this way. We lived a fairly hand to mouth existence. One day, I hid in the cupboard in the pantry because the rent man had called and we did not have any money that day. We often argued, usually about money, and sometimes, Paul would hit me. One Christmas, he gave me a black eye for a present and another time, I had bruises on my arms and legs. I felt ashamed because I thought the neighbours knew what was happening and were talking about me. At other times, I felt invisible as if I wasn't really there. My self esteem was at rock bottom. I went with the children to my parents a couple of times but returned, hoping that Paul would change.

I sought advice from an inspector from the NSPCC because I worried about the effects on the children. "Your husband will never change", he said. One day, Paul was cuddling Steven, talking gently to him and completely ignoring Karen. She was standing at the side of the armchair gazing at Paul and was longing for him to pay her some attention. "What are you staring at?" he demanded. That was the final straw. "I need to leave him and make a life for myself and my children", I thought. I felt a cloud lift; I knew that I had made the right decision and that I had within me the strength, courage and the determination to raise my children on my own and to find a job to support them.

It was 1969, Karen was three and Steven was thirteen months old when we left. I saw a solicitor and started divorce proceedings. A year later, the divorce was finalised and I started working in the Civil Service. I had to be organised, laying out clothes and breakfast items for the following morning and rising about 5.30 am. There was a twenty minute walk to the day nursery and we would arrive there at 7.30 when it opened. I would then catch the bus, changing at the station so that I could be at work for 8.15. There were no flexi hours in those days. Things became easier after I passed my driving test the following year and bought a clapped out Fiat 600.

Karen's assessment as "educationally subnormal" (horrible expression), at the age of six was a terrible blow at that time and added to the stress that I was already under. I grieved for the loss of a "normal" little girl, hopes and expectations shattered. Life was suddenly unpredictable and I became anxious, not knowing what her potential might be or what the future might hold for her or for me. Later, I felt anger at the abrupt and unfeeling way the paediatrician had told me his verdict during a school review. "She's retarded", he had said. No advice or support had been offered; I felt as if the rug had been pulled from under my feet. My parents were a pillar of strength at the time. "Try not to worry, things probably won't be as bad as you think", said my dad encouragingly. He was the manager of a local Remploy factory and knew that Karen had the capacity to learn and develop her potential. Most of the Remploy workforce had physical disabilities but there were some there with learning disabilities too. I gradually reached a state of acceptance and was determined to do my best to help Karen live a normal life.

There have been some difficult times. In 1990, when Karen was twenty four, a charitable organisation decided to close the workshop that Karen had attended five days a week for several years and also the small group home where she had lived happily. Initially, she was not offered any compensating day care by social services; she was also moved into a council flat where she received some support from a nurse from the mental handicap team and lots of support from me. My anger at the cavalier way in which Karen had been treated galvanised me into action. In the 1980s, I had studied for an OU degree and I used some of the skills I had gained. I became a "warrior woman". I wrote to the local press, to the head of Social Services and to the MP. I also joined forces with

Pauline, another mother whose daughter had also been adversely affected by these closures and we visited the MP's surgery together. Although we were only a two woman campaign group, I feel that I really benefitted from the empathy and support we were able to give each other. Later that year, Karen was given appropriate day care but was not given better accommodation until 1992. It was not ideal but it was an improvement and I continued to advocate on Karen's behalf. Some years later, I became involved in campaigning to try and save another workshop that Karen attended. I prepared press releases, spoke at council meetings and was interviewed by local radio, something I could never have imagined myself doing when I was younger.

There have been other difficult and distressing situations and there are times when I have despaired and thought, "oh no, here we go again", but I seem to find the strength and determination of the "warrior woman" in myself to take up Karen's cause. I have always found it much easier to speak out on someone else's behalf rather than my own. Fighting Karen's corner helped to teach me to stand up and be counted, to use my anger in a constructive way and to face my fears of being in the limelight. Being part of the Caring Expressions writing group has also been an important part of my ongoing metamorphosis.

PAT AND CLAIRE

I remember the overwhelming feeling of excitement experienced as the aeroplane we had been travelling in for over 12 hours, touched down at Embakasi Airport, in Nairobi, Kenya. It was early December, the height of the African summer. The heat was dry and hot.

During the 1970's I had travelled with my husband to this far off place, which in those days was just a name on a world atlas to me. I had never been out of Europe before (except being born in Egypt where my father and mother were living at the time, whilst my father worked for the British Government), and had certainly never flown before. My husband was an aircraft engineer and had secured a sponsored post as an instructor, loaned out to the Kenyan Air Force. They had recently acquired some jet aeroplanes to enhance their Air Force, and needed to train their personnel across the spectrum in the skills they would need to maintain and fly these small jets. Amongst our party were several other families, most with small children, also on the same mission.

On the journey from the airport into the city I took in the strange sights and sounds that filled my senses. There were unusual smells and a multitude of brightly coloured plants, flowers and trees to dazzle my sight. Just watching the local population in their bright attire, many of them barefoot, even as we entered the city, was like being on a film set and seemed unreal. I could hardly believe that I was going to live in this strange exotic city for the next few years of my life.

Initially we stayed in a very nice hotel for some weeks, before all the families were housed throughout the city in quite luxurious accommodation. I quickly learned that we were expected to give employment to the local people and took on a house girl, named Tamina. She lived at the bottom of the garden in a specially made brick 'shamba' or hut, which was quite primitive. I worried quite a bit at first as it seemed so primitive but quickly learned that her accommodation was actually deemed very good. The wages we were allowed to pay were pitiful and I felt quite guilty. However, we were expected to provide employment and I like to think I treated her with respect and kindness during our time there, unlike certain other people who had arrived at the same time as us, who had quickly assumed the role of master to the servant.

We had no children at that time and were able to make the most of the time we had sightseeing and doing plenty of safaris. Kenya had only gained its independence in the mid 1960s so there was still a large contingent of ex-patriots living and working in the country, who we mixed with. There was also a large Asian community well established, mainly running many of the shops and businesses in the city. During the early colonization of Africa they had been brought over from India to provide cheap labour for the British colonial population.

I found it hard to reconcile the abject poverty amongst the native African population with the opulent and comfortable lives we had. I had never seen begging in the streets before, or maimed people left to fend for themselves by begging. In later years in our own cities throughout the UK begging and homelessness has sadly become more prominent but in those days during the 1970s in the UK, although poverty existed, it was not poverty openly displayed on the same scale. It was where I first realized how relatively well-off we were living in the UK compared to parts of the developing world and it made me more aware of how fortunate we were. The things we take for granted such as free schooling and free medical care were not available then to the local populace, and even now not wholly free.

It would be an experience that would educate and enhance my character development and help to shape me into the person I am today, some forty years later. It has helped me to deal with life as a parent, and in particular as an unexpected life long carer to my autistic daughter. I have encountered many hurdles along the way in striving to obtain the best opportunities possible for her, to help her to lead a constructive and fulfilling life. Seeing how different and difficult life can be in another culture for the indigenous population in that African country made me realise that life and its expectations should never be assumed, and to appreciate that the society we live in here in the UK does strive to protect the disabled and vulnerable in our society.

What a learning curve it was! I was a young girl of twenty when I began my life in Kenya; so naïve and unworldly. I learned about diversity, to be tolerant, and most of all human nature, sadly some of it not so pleasant. When I returned some years later I was an entirely different person – a young woman, matured and changed for the better with a knowledge of life that has surely helped and sustained me for my life's journey, with all its unexpected twists and turns.

PAULINE AND ALISON

I have gone through a few metamorphoses in my lifetime, and who knows there may be more still to come. Giving up alcohol and prescription drugs I had become addicted to, was something which changed me. Having a mental breakdown and spending time in a mental hospital was also a catalyst for change. The psychotherapy and counselling I received during my recovery quite literally saved my life. Realising in my late forties I was lesbian was another major turning point in my life.

Giving birth to a daughter who was diagnosed as being mentally handicapped was and continues to be a life-changing experience. It wasn't instantaneous as it took about three years before the reality of Alison's condition hit us. Her prognosis from the medical establishment was extremely poor which made me determined to prove them wrong Something told me there was more to Alison than they could see. I believed then that I was right and now, after 49 years of her life I know I was right. I would say that my life became a quest to help Alison reach as much of her potential as she possibly could.

Before I was married I was ambitious. I wanted to be someone. I wanted a career, not just a job. Status was important to me and I guess I wanted to reach my own potential. Becoming a life-long carer for Alison, who will always be vulnerable and who will always require help to live her life, forced me to re-think many of my values, made me realise that success is relative. I can take pleasure in Alison's achievements just as much as in my son's, although in worldly terms there is no comparison.

Certain qualities like patience and unconditional love were sadly lacking in me before I had Alison, but are qualities I now have in abundance. Having to fight the social care system to help Alison get the services she has needed has developed my ability to stand up for her rights and in turn my own. Becoming involved with voluntary organisations working to improve the lives of people with learning disabilities has gradually enabled me to be confident enough to speak in front of a room full of people, though still rather nervously it has to be said.

I think I have become a better person through having Alison in my life. I am less judgemental about other people than I used to be and I've become more tolerant of difference. I used to see things very much in black and white – now there are shades of grey all over the place. I try to see things from other people's perspectives, and know I'm not always right, although knowing this and being able to admit it are two different things!

GILLIAN AND WILLIAM

When I think of the word "metamorphosis" in relation to change, I imagine evolving into a Kafkaesque beetle, lying on my back in a hard place, waving my legs about ineffectively in an attempt to return things to normal. As an adolescent I often tried to set my world to rights, but my attempts were not particularly successful. I did a lot of leg-shaking, but eventually gave up trying to turn over.

As a mum, I was anxious about my son's development, and repeatedly metamorphosed between ineffective beetle that could not communicate effectively with others about my concerns (Kafka's beetle's voice changed beyond recognition), and someone who was listened to, and was able to access appropriate help for William. I learned to make sure that he was involved in community activities – apart from story time at the library at which he was disruptive, so we held our own exclusive club of two elsewhere in the library. William was lively but accepted at toddler group and playgroup, and enjoyed attending family Sunday afternoon coffee concerts, probably because these were sponsored by an ice cream manufacturer. An ice lolly at the end of the music if he behaved well was a satisfactory reward. He would sit and listen to music at home. The librarian had been very upset that she had not included William successfully, and she and I discussed how best to involve him in other projects as he matured. She made adjustments for the reading club by letting him tell her about books that had been read to him, as he was dyslexic. This meant that he could join in, and as a bonus, he learned to wait fairly patiently in a queue.

Liaising in advance with organisers was the key to successful activities. Nowadays that approach is known as 'personalisation', but in those days children with autism were expected to change their behaviour (a much more difficult metamorphosis than for adult professionals who have no social communication difficulties). People with autism find it hard to understand that others may not share their perspective on a situation, and can get stressed, and flounder when challenged. It is easier to teach rules of social communication when they are relaxed, which is less likely to lead to a behavioural meltdown.

As William grew older, his behaviour deteriorated. He was frustrated and aware that he was falling behind his peers at school, becoming increasingly aggressive. At that point I needed to calm my flailing insect limbs and find an ally to turn me upright again. This ally was a psychologist who assessed William, finally resulting in additional support at school. Eventually this led to a placement at a special school, where he evolved into a confident young man. He continued to perceive the world through his somewhat eccentric autistic Asperger eyes, but was friendly and accepted by most people.

The next topsy-turvy stage was when I realised that William was going to find it very hard to leave school to go to a mainstream post-16 placement. I had to rediscover my effective assertive voice again, and he was offered a place at an Independence Unit.

My subsequent beetle moment was at the next transition point for William, when he did not get funding to go to an Asperger-specific college, and I had to look for support. I found an advocate from the National Youth Advocacy Service for him, as I felt that his independent voice should be heard. A Mencap family advisor was able to help me. This stressful time resulted in me being off work for five months with anxiety and depression. There was a long series of meetings and discussions, for which I had to emerge from my despondence, having learned that I could just about be effective for short bursts before falling back again. I even got back to work gradually, but have never completely lost the panicking beetle in me. I still need allies to turn me over, to provide encouragement, and to remind me that I can produce a powerful voice when necessary. The anxiety and depression can still knock me over, and I still need to fight to keep my balance in my changeable world.

To be positive, I think that beetles can be beautiful, with their shimmering iridescent colours. They may be shunned, ignored or trampled on by much of the world, but no doubt their friends and families appreciate them, and they have a vital role in keeping ecosystems functioning. There are also an awful lot of them. Maybe it's not so bad to metamorphose between the effective human and the less obviously attractive insect. I should know – I've been there and done that frequently!

LINDA AND ANDREW

When I was younger I used to think "I will be happy when I leave school"; "I will be happy when I get married and have a home of my own"; "I will be happy if I get that job", "If I could only win the lottery I would be happy for the rest of my life". I also thought that once I was forty I would have life sussed. I have never been a materialistic person, but I was following the crowd and perceived the 'important' things in life were to earn enough money to have a nice house, the latest fashions, nights out and foreign holidays every year. I have long since given up trying to keep my ducks in a row. They are generally a very unruly lot, and seem to be breeding at an alarming rate. So I keep my fingers crossed that they will take it in turns to cause me grief. I generally choose to be happy, being the sort of person who will take the lemons life gives me and look for somebody with gin.

My natural instinct has always been to avoid conflict at all costs. I was always a pourer of oil on troubled waters, and still am to a large extent. I think this stems from my childhood, when I would keep my head down and stay quiet in the hope the bullies would not pick on me. I very quickly became used to criticising myself before anybody else had the chance, and often used humour (usually at my own expense) to defuse the situation. I became a people pleaser. This went on through most of my schooldays, and it wasn't until I joined an amateur musical theatre group at the age of seventeen that I started to develop self-confidence. I found getting up on stage and pretending to be somebody else was incredibly liberating, and the sound of 400 people applauding after I had finished singing a solo made me feel validated as a human being.

When I found out I was expecting my son, I felt that I would now be truly happy. I daydreamed about cradling my baby in my arms and singing to him; about reading to him every night to instil in him my love of books; of my little boy flinging his arms around my neck and saying "I love you mum"; of watching him play football, teaching him to ride a bike; the list of lovely times yet to come played through my mind throughout my pregnancy. Somewhere lurking in the background was an underlying sense of unease and anxiety, as if some part of me knew that many of those things would never come about.

After Andrew's premature birth and one medical trauma after another during his first year of life, I started to question what life was all about. I have never been a religious person, but I embarked on a spiritual journey of discovery which has played a huge role in my development as a human being. The phrase "When the student is ready the teacher will appear" became a lived reality for me, and I stumbled across the right book, therapy, or person just when I needed it. I vividly remember going to an evening class course called "Transform your Life" which involved us sampling things such as meditation and crystal healing each week. About half-way through the course I was chatting with one of my fellow students during a break, and we were comparing notes about our life experiences and what had drawn us to this group. She asked me if I had ever read the book "Jonathan Livingston Seagull". Although I had heard of it, I had never read it, but she said she felt it would be a good book for me to read at the time. I went straight to the library and got a copy. I started reading it that night and could not put it down. It is a very short book which is a parable about a seagull who feels there must be more to life than following the fishing boats out to sea each day, and who spends his days honing his flying skills and pushing his boundaries. He is ostracised by the rest of the flock who ridicule him and try to get him to conform. Without wishing to reveal the plot for those of you who have never read this amazing little book, Jonathan tries to help other seagulls to find the true meaning of life. I was already identifying so much with the story at this point, and when I turned the next page, I found the name of the first seagull Jonathan helps is Fletcher Lynd Seagull! I almost dropped the book! I related this to the group the following week and the tutor said it was a classic case of synchronicity. I had been guided to read that book at just the right time in my life. As wonderful a little story as it is, it would not have had the same effect on me if I had read it before my surname became Fletcher, and before I had a child with learning disabilities. Jonathan still inspires me today, as I resist my natural tendency to avoid conflict in order to make a stand on behalf of my son.

I have always been galvanised into action by anger, and find it easier to deal with a situation when I am all fired up, but that is often a recipe for disaster. I have been fortunate enough to have encountered several wise and experienced people along the way who have shared their knowledge and experience with me, helping me to develop better ways of dealing with difficult situations. The most influential people were parents who had battled the system themselves and who passed on their hard earned experience to me. I am now holding a baton and try to pass it on to anybody who will benefit from it.

My biggest teacher has been my son. He is the living embodiment of the journey being more important than the destination. On holiday in Florida, he always enjoyed the car ride to the theme parks much more than he did the experience once we were there. Andrew's fascination with trees has taught me the joy of watching the branches swaying in the breeze, and listening to the rustling of the leaves, things we all take for granted as we go about our hectic lives. Andrew truly does live in the moment and I love sharing those times with him.

I can hardly recognise my younger self now. I will fight like a tigress for my son and will stand up for his rights. I am not so good at standing up for my own, but through fighting for him, my self esteem has grown and in recent years I have a growing sense of anger at the lack of support for family carers. I matter too.

ANNIE AND MAX

Metamorphosis is change. Some changes are sudden and catastrophic, like death, but most changes in our lives, we get used to and learn to live with – a kind of living.

We've just visited the Great Wall of China. A cable car took us up high and we spilled out onto it. It is vast, a 300mile stone flagged road stepping along the mountain ridges, with high walls flanking either side. When we began to walk along it, we experienced an immediate and dramatic sense of vertigo, as if we'd had too much to drink. Everyone starting the walk felt the same sensation, as if we were plunging like

Alice through a topsy-turvy hole into Wonderland, or going through the Looking Glass, where nothing was quite what it seemed. The high walls must have been at strange angles to the road, and the road itself was also squinted, but so subtle that it couldn't be appreciated by eye, only by our inner ear balance senses. After about twenty minutes, we all became naturally accustomed to it and, subconsciously, there was an internal readjustment so none of us felt dizzy anymore. The human capacity to adapt and adjust is immense.

When we had Max it was a sudden change, of course, and we knew from the outset that he was compromised. We have, however, adjusted to our lives together. We often seem to be in a topsy-turvy land, but we manage to function and get by just the same. We are fortunate to have each other: Gus, Max and myself, as well as love and support from Sophie, his elder sister, who is now working away from home. She is mostly exempt from the day-to-day responsibilities of looking after a disabled person, but obviously becomes involved on coming home. The rest of us shuffle along through life, each having our own wants and needs which the others support, a staggering tripod of a family. Each one of us is melded with the others through family and love. Each may strike out on his own but the others skitter along behind to maintain a workable balance. Oftentimes we may want to go one way but are abruptly dragged back by the rest. Mostly it works best to placidly go along with the others, balance as balance can, and not be too overtly ambitious personally. Personal ambition will lead to inevitable disappointment so why try? We are each so accustomed to compromise, that we expect setbacks at every turn. I am no longer driven by the need to achieve, so much as the need to get by. I am more placid, slower, and take pleasure in the small things. I am less judgmental, more appreciative, and kinder. Our family has found a new internal balance with the addition of Max. We have centred ourselves again.

LIZ AND SALLY

I had always loved my job. I was a lecturer, but I was also in charge of mature students and then, later, disabled students. It fell to me to encourage people who feared that higher education was not for 'the likes of them' to have faith in themselves and apply to university. The results were nearly always supremely satisfying. These were the students who loved it all: the work, the tutors, the new friends. After initially being scared of dipping their toe in the hallowed waters of academe, after a term or two they wanted to immerse themselves deeply in theory and academic controversies. They questioned, they argued, they debated and in the process they changed and grew in confidence. The disabled students changed too. They realised they had rights, they did not need to rely on kindness. They found, in many cases, that there was much more support available to them than they had at school. They discovered they could live independently of their families, they could find their own way and by and large, they flourished. It was a privilege to witness the successes of these students, to applaud their progress and to point out to a sometimes sceptical institution how well they had done.

I retired when I was 60 because the whole work environment began to change. The institution was under pressure to cut costs. There was less time to see individual students. There were more appointments and less dropping in. There were endless meetings, a lot of Health and Safety, and Human Resources were everywhere. You couldn't get into your own office without a card and for some colleagues there was no longer a room of one's own, but only an open plan office. There was nowhere to which to retreat when you had made a complete mess of a lecture, nowhere for a desperate weeping student. There was no place for excitement, no place for spontaneity.

I also left because of pressures of home. Too often it seemed I had to rely on the goodwill of colleagues to fill in for me so I could go and rescue one of my children from some pit into which they had dug themselves. The number of grandchildren was rising and I was called upon to help, so my daughter/daughter in law could earn a living/ find themselves. Lovable babies were more alluring than facing another re-organisation.

I didn't have clear expectations of retirement. I had no burning ambitions to fulfil. I had no desire to go bungee jumping or walk the Himalayas. I'm ashamed to say I wasn't that keen to see the world and join all the other old people at the airport with my handbag slung firmly across my chest, sensible trainers on my feet and guidebook in my hand, ready for the next dose of culture.

If I had any hopes, they were of the gentler kind. I would like to do more gardening; improve my meagre sewing skills; read some good books and visit East Anglia and the Dales. Pottering was part of my plan and listening to Radio 4.

Modest as my aspirations were, it hasn't been like that. The garden is largely unloved, although my occasional forays into it are rewarding. The radio is always mysteriously tuned to something loud and local. My partner with whom I planned our pleasant rambles round rural Britain is still working hard and days away have to be argued over and prised out of a still hectic diary. Cancer, clinical depression and divorce have visited our family and remain a constant threatening presence with which to be reckoned and outfaced. The sweet babies have turned into people with views and deep voices. Toys are no longer us and even the youngest rarely wants a story but prefers the attractions of the internet and Moshie Monsters – whatever they are.

So from someone whose days were structured and whose work was stimulating, whose colleagues were interesting and courteous, whose students were grateful, I have metamorphasised into a dog walker, a nurse, a baby sitter and a kind of Butlin's Red Coat trying to keep my daughter occupied and happy. Oh yes, and I do a lot of mopping. The person who owned the house before us thought white tiles all over the ground floor were a good idea. I spend a lot of time on them.

Despite the fact that not much has been as planned and at times I wonder where the person I was before has gone, when I do get a glimpse of the retirement life I sought, these fleeting moments are all the more enjoyable for being so rare.

HOPES AND FEARS FOR THE FUTURE

SUSAN AND KAREN

The biggest question in my mind is who will advocate for Karen when I am no longer here. Who will fight any battles on her behalf, who will ensure she receives appropriate support or a fair deal or raise any health concerns? I have no siblings and I do not think it fair to expect her younger brother to take on this role although I'm sure he would play an important part. In the current economic climate with a government hell bent on making swingeing financial cuts in order to make savings, I wonder whether funding will always be available to cover the best possible accommodation and day care needs for her and to provide the necessary staffing that these entail.

At present, she lives in The Rowans, a well run home where the residents, all with special needs, are well supported and cared for. The house feels welcoming when you walk through the front door and it is very clean and beautifully decorated. The owner manager and all the staff are very caring; some of them have worked there for a number of years. I feel that this speaks volumes and is a sign that the staff, like the residents, are treated well and are valued. Karen has lived there for ten years and feels happy and secure there. It is essential that she receives the level of support that she needs from people who not only care about her but with whom she can feel comfortable and can trust.

One of my fears, based on previous experience, is that Karen could end up living in unsuitable accommodation where her needs are not met. This happened in 1990 when she moved from a small home that she shared with two other women that had learning disabilities into a one bedroom flat. She had been very happy in the shared house and there was good support there. Unfortunately, funding was withdrawn and Karen was assessed as being capable of living independently but had difficulties managing on her own and she felt lonely. The workshop that had provided her day care closed at the same time and this exacerbated her unhappiness and feelings of isolation.

About a year later, Karen moved into a group home on a six week trial basis. There were two male residents and one of them, Jim, took a bit of a shine to Karen. Four weeks into the trial, Karen was evicted with very little prior warning. I was attending a course in London and Tom received an urgent call from Anna, a nurse on the Mental Handicap team who had been helping to support Karen. Tom went straightaway to the house to find Karen's belongings on the street and a tearful Karen being comforted by Anna. Apparently, Karen had wanted to lock her bedroom door at night but there was a rule that doors should be left unlocked in case of fire. The reason she wanted to lock her door was because she did not feel safe as she was afraid that Jim might come into her room during the night. She started going into the female support worker's room during the night. The supervisor was quite opinionated and she had persuaded the other staff that the placement had broken down. I was livid that Karen had been treated in such an insensitive way and was dismayed that the eviction meant she had to move back into the flat. I hope that she is never treated in such a cavalier way again.

There was a good reason for Karen's reluctance to leave her room unlocked at night time and I felt outraged that this had not been taken into account. Before moving into the flat, Karen had broken off a relationship with her boyfriend Dave but unbeknown to us, he had been following her around and one evening, he had persuaded her to go with him to his home where he had sexually assaulted her. He was given an informal warning by the police, they were understandably reluctant to press charges because he had a learning disability and neither the police nor I wanted Karen to experience the ordeal of going to court. Some time later, Dave started stalking Karen. Her fear made her unable to be assertive with Dave, and she found it difficult to express her fears and worries to me. When I realised what had been happening, I spoke to

Karen's Care Manager and asked her, as a matter of urgency, to liaise with Dave's Care Manager so that he could talk to Dave and ask him to leave Karen alone. Karen's Care Manager, who was not very proactive at the best of times, did not seem to take my request seriously and I had to ask several times before any action was taken. I fear for Karen's vulnerability and I sincerely hope that she can be protected against any further incidents of sexual exploitation.

Karen is also vulnerable to financial exploitation. When she was living in the flat, she had money, tapes and jewellery taken by some teenage girls. In 1992, she moved into bedsit accommodation in a house that had been converted for six residents with learning disabilities. Professional support was fairly minimal, twenty hours per week shared among all the residents. Originally, there were four female residents and things seemed to go well but in 1993, two men moved in. One of them, Ian, did not appear to have a learning disability at all; he was quite "streetwise". He started stealing money from the other female residents. I could not understand why Karen was running short of cash so that I had to keep lending her some money to buy groceries. I discovered that Ian was stealing money from her room. He bought a new bicycle that I suspected had been partly paid for by Karen. When I asked his social worker why Ian had been placed with vulnerable residents, I was told that he had lost his flat so was moved in at short notice. "It was a calculated risk" the social worker said. "An unacceptable risk", I responded, "When is he being evicted?" "We have to give him six week's notice, he has rights", was the answer. "What about the rights of vulnerable females?" I asked angrily.

Shortly before she moved to The Rowans, and whilst she was living at her previous residential home, Albert House, I discovered that her mobility allowance was being misused by the owner of the home. I reported this to the Care Quality Commission who investigated my complaint but because the owner had not kept proper records, there was no proof of this. However, the owner was given a warning and required to keep accurate records.

I hope that the people working and supporting Karen continue to be trustworthy and that they look after her best interests, also that her future needs are fully met. I do my best to keep positive about the future. I also hope that she continues to receive encouragement, understanding, love and acceptance from those who spend time with her and that people will see her for the beautiful being that she is.

GILLIAN AND WILLIAM

William is a personable young man, who happens to have a variety of difficulties which have hindered him in daily living. I am concerned that he is in denial, and considers himself to be "normal". I actually agree with this positive attitude, but it has led to problems, such as losing his Incapacity Benefit after completing the form without help, despite being supposed to be receiving support with admin from an agency. William has been trying to access full-time employment for four years now without success, although he has managed to keep a part time job, given reasonable adjustments, for seven years. I am worried about his current and future financial position, and that he did not manage to access his "weekly" support for a month to enable him to appeal. The person he eventually saw did not know what to do, and it was then beyond the date to register an appeal. I was on caring duty with my parents in London, and was unable to provide practical support beyond advising him to contact the support agency. He and his care manager sent in their explanations of the delay in sending in an appeal, but this may be too late – and he is no longer receiving the benefit.

William is over-familiar with others, "talks the talk" and dresses fashionably – he is a careful observer of people. This has led to him being groomed and assaulted by another man; although the local police wished to take this to court, the CPS (Crown Prosecution Service) felt that the case rested on one man's word against another. This was despite a comprehensive report from a psychiatrist outlining the impact of William's autism on his understanding and reaction in the situation. I believe he has learned from what he refers to as "the incident." It is hard to be sure. It was something that I had tried to prepare William for, but I had not built in the scenario and script of him accepting a lift from someone he considered to be a friend into my "how to handle things" preparation.

William moved from a small town to a larger one after five years of negotiation with social services, as his work and social life were based there. He was promised the next available place in supported accommodation several times, but there always seemed to be someone else with greater needs, so he decided to move into a shared privately rented house. After three months living there he was back in his previous supported house because another tenant, who was a drug dealer, was found in William's room going through his belongings.

The second room was with a live-in landlord who was very clear about his expectations of William, and they got on well together. After a year, the rent was increased by £10 a month, and William moved out as a protest without consulting anyone, enthusiastically assisted by his new housemates. Sadly, this move was into a house where he was exploited. He lost his housing benefit during this period. He was also charged half of the rent and household bills, although there were three inhabitants. He mentioned his concerns to me after about three months, and I brought the situation to the attention of the care manager, who worked with the estate agent to find more appropriate accommodation. William has now shared another flat for eighteen months with four others, but is annoyed that his rent has recently been increased... I await further nightmares.

I am pleased that William's daily life normally runs smoothly with very little official support, and that he does inform me when he feels something is wrong. However because he wants to be independent, as is his right as an adult, he has instructed the support agency not to liaise with me as his family carer. I wish he would change this, as I feel that I have more idea about William than a rota of student social workers on placement (yes, I know they need to learn, and I was a student too). Greater continuity would be helpful, as William has a convincing "I have no problems" act and does not like to admit that he is anxious about anything. My stance is that I only contact the organisation with William's permission, as I want him to continue to trust me. I have concerns that nobody from provider services seems to have the full picture, and William tells me that they feel that he no longer needs support. It may be that he is reporting his own wishes to me, but I am worried about what will happen when I am no longer around to check that his needs are being met appropriately. I am sad that the concept of working with family carers is not being fulfilled, and that arranging to talk to William's care manager is so difficult (she works part-time), even with his permission. I do not have confidence that the "system" will support William adequately without additional pressure from the family.

I hope that support will be more consistent, but am constantly on edge, waiting for the next thing to go wrong. At least William does alert me to problems – "Hi, Mum, it's time we spent some quality time together," is a phrase that immediately raises my anxiety levels. What will happen when he no longer has that extra way of accessing help?

ANNIE AND MAX

What will happen to Max in the future? Fears and hopes are my breathing out and my breathing in. They are the involuntary preoccupation of my thoughts, sometimes brought into the forefront for examination. 'How are you all today? Are the hopes greater, the fears a little less? No? Oh, well, in my heart I knew you would be always there, more constant than a faithful lover.'

My biggest fear is that Max will be sexually abused. He is handsome, placid and loving with a gentle nature. He likes cuddles, kisses and to be stroked or tickled. He enjoys stroking my face and kissing me. He is also very demonstrative towards his sister, Sophie. Will this stop when he goes into a shared living situation, or will he transfer his affections to another? How will that person respond? I tell Sophie that we shouldn't let him kiss us on the mouth, as I view this would be inappropriate between mother and son, or sister and brother. Overall, I hope he doesn't need or come across any sexual encounters, as I feel this would be very confusing for him. If he does, I hope it's reciprocal and not exploitative or abusive. I am reassured to think that he has sufficient powers of expression to explain if he's being hurt. I hope he won't encounter anyone who urges him to keep a 'secret' or who threatens him, as it would be difficult for him to work out the sadistic intention behind such twisted and evil cajoling. Being manipulated must be the worst scenario for any vulnerable young person, and the thought of it happening to Max fills me with dread.

Sophie has asked us to move to be geographically nearer to her, when she finally settles down for good, in order that he can be settled into a supervised shared house nearby. This would mean she could more easily keep an eye on him, after our demise. This seems practical and reassures us that she will take her responsibility as his sister seriously. But what if she were to move? What then? Would she take him on holiday with her sometimes? Will she have the energy or inclination to do this? Will her husband be sympathetic or just view Max as a nuisance? When you are working, your holiday weeks are few and she may not want to spend many with her brother. I fear this may be the case, but hope it will be otherwise. We have joined the Holiday Property Bond, so some of their holidays together will be free, on us, even after we've gone.

I fear that, although he is occupied five days at school at his present age, this will change as he gets older. If he is not kept occupied he will watch TV or listen to 'You tube' excerpts from train spotters over and over till it becomes like an earworm you can't shake off. I fear hearing for the rest of my life, 'This is the 7.29, just pulling into Crewe.' Obviously, he likes the repetition of this but we don't. He will go to seed and I will be the effete seed pod, tattered and left to wither on the ground, listening to all this garbage. What use is this, when the carer is run to ground?

We want him to be occupied and his mind stretched. Most education nowadays is for education's sake. What gives typically developing children more right to study Russian or Mandarin Chinese than our child to study practical Maths and English? Are we wrong in wanting a similar life-enriching experience for our own child, even though disabled? He is still progressing with his learning, albeit in the slow lane, and we do not want him confined so early to wheelbarrow pushing.

As he reaches adulthood, I fear another gaping hole opening up to us: totally unstructured time. My life will be spent transporting him to various activities, which, as they usually seem to last only two hours or so, will mean as soon as I reach home I'm out again to fetch him. I fear my essence will be squashed away, like I've been squeezed through a mangle, till there is only a sliver of me left, the rest all wrung out and lost. I hope this won't happen, but fear it might.

PAT AND CLAIRE

The one common thing that most of us want more than anything else in life, as a carer of a son or daughter with a learning disability, is to know that they will be happy and looked after when we are no longer able to do the caring. Constantly on my mind are the hopes for my daughter's future – the long term future she will have without us, after we are gone.

She is, at the time of writing, entering her third decade. She still lives at home with us. She was diagnosed as being on the Autism spectrum, with Asperger's Syndrome at aged 19. Complications with her physical health have plagued her adult life since 2004, when she was 22. She was diagnosed eventually with ulcerative colitis, which is a vicious disease of the immune system. Since then she has endured three bouts of radical surgery to date, and has had to learn to live with what will be a permanent ileostomy. The surgery has left her with a delicate digestive system. During 2012 an abdominal abscess made her very unwell, resulting in several hospital admissions and further surgery in October that year. Recovery has been long and slow and it has required me, her mother, to become well versed in nursing skills.

Before this illness we had hoped that during her twenties she might have the opportunity to go in to some form of independent living, either into a shared assisted scheme, or on her own, with suitable support from local government Adult Services. We would love her to be able to have some kind of independent life without us having to support her emotionally, physically and financially; much the same as most parents, under normal circumstances, hope for their adult children.

It is a constant dilemma that we face most days. We know that she will be safer and happier staying with us. We do not have any other family members around us to offer help and support. Both our remaining family members live a long way away from us. We have a son who is a few years older than our daughter, but he is at present living and working in London. He is forging a career and building a life with his partner and we do not know where they will eventually settle. He says he will always look after his sister, but we don't feel it's fair that his life should have to entail caring for his sister. Eventually he will hopefully have children of his own to care for.

We know that time is running out for us and we feel helpless as the years slip away. None of us knows how long we will stay in good health or how long our lives will be. Our daughter's recent ill-health has compounded our anxieties about her future. We do not want her to end up caring for us as we become elderly and infirm. The one positive thing has been that our daughter has been able to work and maintain a part-time job for the past 12 years in a nearby Sainsbury's store. It has given her an extra layer to her life; a life outside of our home and an opportunity for her to make her own friends and to experience time away from us.

One of our main fears for the future is that, when we are no longer able to care for and protect her, she is very vulnerable and open to the various insidious forms of bullying and abuse that unfortunately prevail in our society. We already have had experience of Claire being bullied at the mainstream primary school she first attended, and then in later life, in the workplace. There have also been instances of peer group bullying out of school with 'friends' we thought were genuinely sensitive to Claire's lack of 'street' wisdom. On all occasions we have had to intervene to sort these situations out. Who will do this for her after us?

We don't want her to end up being lonely and alone in life. It would be wonderful if she could meet someone to share her life with. In the current economic climate in 2013 there are less and less options available for all children and adults with a range of disabilities so the future remains very much an unknown. We just want her to be happy and to know that she will be cared for when we are gone. We need to start making plans so that can happen and have to try and remain positive. We have encountered some wonderful people along the way who have helped

Claire so we must try and focus on the good experiences, and try not to dwell too much on the negatives.

LINDA AND ANDREW

Hopes

It is very telling that I found it much harder to write about my hopes for the future than it was to write about my fears. Is this because I find it hard to visualise a positive future for Andrew when we are no longer around? There is a TV advert which shows a cat outside a house, looking plaintively through the front room window at an empty armchair. It is for a charity which promises to care for your pet when you die, and it always strikes a chord with me. If only peace of mind was so simple when it comes to my son's future without us. His disabilities are so profound that he will always need someone to support him and to keep him safe, so I know that there will always be somebody with him. What I can only hope for is that those people supporting him will love and value him as much as we do. That they will see his potential and continue providing him with the opportunities to learn and develop, and to fill his life with pleasure and new experiences. I hope that Andrew will have an effective means of communicating, and that people will give him the time and the opportunity to be heard and understood.

Andrew has many unique characteristics – hand flapping, blowing raspberries, knocking on hard surfaces, swinging curtains, reaching out to people as they walk past, to name just a few. When he was younger most of these behaviours were endearing, but what is cute in a small child is not always readily acceptable in an adult. I hope that Andrew will continue to express himself in his inimitable way, and that people will accept him for who he is and not burst his bubble, although that is unrealistic I know, as it is something we all have to face at some point.

Although we are realistic about Andrew's disabilities, we choose not to set any limitations. As far as we are concerned, the sky's the limit. Andrew has already surprised us by taking his first independent steps at the age of 13, and regaining an interest in eating at the age of 16, eight long years after he mysteriously stopped taking anything orally. I get very angry if I feel that anyone working with Andrew does not recognise his potential, and his ability to learn, and who does not show the same level of commitment to him that we do. I constantly worry that we are not doing enough for Andrew, and I am driven by the need to overturn every stone possible to look for anything which will help him to reach his full potential. It is particularly important to us that Andrew is furnished with an effective way to communicate. On a purely selfish note, I would die happy if I could just once hear my son say, "I love you Mum". More importantly, I will feel I have done my job properly as a mother if Andrew is able to say to me one day, "Thanks for everything, but I can make my own decisions now."

Andrew is such a happy young man, we hope that he will remain so and that he will be well supported through the inevitable difficulties he will face. I hope that Andrew will always know how much he means to us, and how incredibly proud we are of him and his achievements.

I also have hopes for my own future. I hope that the government will recognise how vital it is that the vast army of unpaid carers in this country are not run into the ground physically and mentally, and will put sufficient resources in place to ensure we are supported and valued. The country would fall apart without us, but we have the right to a life too. I have many unfulfilled dreams I still intend to pursue. I want to learn to fly a plane. I want to take up painting and photography. I want to become involved in amateur theatre again. I want to write a novel. I want to find me again.

Fears

I have a recurring nightmare which always involves me, John and Andrew on a day out to Leeds by train – something we do on a regular basis in reality. In the dream, John and I are about to help Andrew to get on the train, when somebody very official-looking comes up to us and says "You two can get on, but your son will have to wait for the next train". We dutifully board the train as directed, and it is not until we sit down and look through the window at the bewildered and lonely figure of our son in his wheelchair on the platform that I start to feel panic.

The train starts to move and I jump up and shout, "Stop, I need to get off". But the train keeps going and I run up and down the carriages desperately looking for the guard. The train stops at a rural station and I get off. The platform is so long that I can hardly see the end of it, but I set off running towards a little booth at the far end. Inside the booth there is an old man with a flat cap, smoking a pipe. I ask him "How do the children get to Leeds?" "They go on a different line" he replies. "But he can't speak, how will they know where he needs to go?" With this, he blows a whistle and my train sets off without me. I burst into tears and ask the man when the next train is due. He directs me to a big wooden gate which leads to a narrow lane. At the end of the lane there is another platform with a few people waiting. Nobody speaks, but I know they have all had to leave their children on the platform too.

After what seems an eternity, a train pulls in and we climb aboard. When I get to Leeds I frantically search the station. I always wake up at this point, feeling sick and sobbing.

I don't usually remember my dreams but this one is so vivid and is always the same. There is no doubt in my mind that it is my subconscious processing my primal fear of letting go of the reins and trusting that Andrew will be OK without me. This is what drives me.

PAULINE AND ALISON

Fears

Reaching the age of 74, I look back over all the years since Alison's first diagnosis and realise I've always felt some degree of fear about her future, and it was that fear which drove me, even when she was in primary school, to try and ensure that she would be as independent as it was possible for her to be. There was a time when I actively wondered if it would be better if she died when I did. Mencap did some research some years ago, and found a large number of parent carers had feelings like this.

That isn't something I feel now, but my main worry is how Alison will cope with my death. I have always been such a huge part of her life, in terms of both her physical and emotional well-being. Over the past few years I have been standing back and letting her support agency handle much more of the day-to-day things and I know that members of her circle of support will all be there for her. A few years ago I started talking to her about death so I knew she understood what it means. Since then, one of my closest friends whom Alison knew well has died, and unfortunately a close personal friend of her own died quite recently. She has now attended two funerals, so I know she knows what to expect

I feel the only way she will get over my death is if I do everything I can to prepare her for it and I intend to leave a video of me talking to her which she can always play back if she needs to. I always wear an ankh round my neck and I have promised to leave it for her to wear when I'm gone, hoping it will provide some enduring contact with me. I've also introduced the concept of angels to her, bought her some angel ornaments and planted the idea that when I'm no longer around, the angels will be looking out for her.

I don't feel that support organisations do very much to prepare their clients for the death of close family members, or that they give their staff much in the way of training them to help people through bereavement. I've asked Alison's support agency what training they give and so far have not received a reply. I shall be following this up.

My hopes for the future are that I will stay fit and active for as long as possible and that when Alison has had time and enough support to grieve, that she will go on to live a happy and fulfilled life. Beyond that, I find it almost impossible to think of not being around for her, because I know that she will always be lonely, as there is no one who could take my place. However, she has begun to ask for help and support from friends, family and support staff as well as me, which I take as a good indication that she will eventually learn to live without me, however painful that process will be

Hopes

When we were given the topic 'Hopes and Fears for the Future', I found it easy to write about my fears – they are a constant part of my life. The difference between the reality of life for families with a learning disabled son or daughter is so far removed from my dream of how it could, and in my view should be, that I was reluctant to actually face it, let alone put it into words. I didn't want to make the comparison – I felt it would be too depressing. Then I began to think that if no-one ever says how things could be different, they probably won't ever be any different.

If you are reading this book, you will know about the reality of some families' lives – the frustrations we endure, the stresses and strains of daily life, the impact on us of the failing social care system in this country. There is no need for me to say more.

Alison's life now is better than I could ever have dreamed it could be, but that is in spite of the social care system in this country, not because of it. It is the culmination of a great deal of determination and effort by the people who care about Alison and is testament to their commitment to ensure that Alison is as happy and independent as it is possible for her to be. Many of the obstacles we have had to overcome were products of the social care system – the fact that Alison had to live in so many different places with people she didn't get on with, the fact that her autism was only diagnosed when she was in her 40's, that she didn't get Disability Living Allowance until she was in her 30's, the fact that carers get so little real support, that many of us crack-up, unable to cope with the stress of trying to do our best for our sons or daughters. My obvious hope is that Alison will be able to continue to lead a happy, fulfilling life, when I am no longer around.

My wider vision is for a different approach, a kinder, more compassionate 'system', which starts as soon as a child is born with learning disabilities or whenever that person acquires a diagnosis of learning disability. This affects the whole family – both parents, grand-parents and any older or younger siblings, and is a life-shattering experience for them all. In my new world, a professional, well-paid, well-trained support worker would be appointed for the whole family, to offer empathy, information, and support, both practical and emotional. This support would be available for as long as the family needed it.

The current financial 'benefits' system is a joke. Why do children and adults with life-long conditions – for which there is no 'cure', have to endure constant assessment and reassessment of their entitlement to disability benefits? The condition is not acquired through any fault of their own, and it is demeaning and disrespectful to everyone involved in this system. It is a constant source of anxiety to parents whose own financial situation may be diminished, due to their caring role. My hope for the future is a separate benefit system for anyone with life-long, permanent disabilities, which would eliminate the precarious financial situation for families and would make the assessed needs of the whole family of paramount importance.

A NOTE ON THE WRITING PROCESS

The unique strength of this book originates in the writing process which informed it. The Caring Expressions group was set up to provide parent carers of children with learning disabilities with a forum to write their stories, not just for some cathartic benefit in sharing and listening to each other, but with the explicit aim of making sense of their experiences in a way that would be useful to other parent carers. Thus the writing process, in common with other autobiographical accounts of health and illness which publish the personal, is a gift relationship between authors and readers, a map for those who come after the writers.

I had previously taught several life writing courses, under the title Writing Lives; as a student on one of those courses, Pauline asked me to teach the newly formed and funded Caring Expressions writing group. This was a new opportunity for me to work longer term with a group and to build on previous teaching experience to support the production of a book.

And so the group began to meet, getting together fortnightly for two hours over two years, with my tutorial guidance. For the first few months, the primary aim was to enable the seven participants to find their voices and grow more confident in their writing, and for us all to become comfortable with sharing stories. Each class had a theme: A Journey, Food and Eating, Rites of Passage, for example; I provided related reading extracts from published memoirs on the chosen topic and then participants wrote a short piece for the next class. The group reviewed each other's work after it had been read aloud, gradually becoming better able to hear what worked, and making constructive editorial corrections. Each class also included set writing technique exercises: using dialogue, the impact of tense and person, for example, which the group became able to integrate into later topic writing.

The group members' writing skills developed quickly, driven by their commitment to the project and a loyalty to each other's stories. But they also became very competent readers, listeners and editors: careful and critical, kind and firm about what made for 'good writing'. There is therefore both a reflexive sophistication to the writing, and a directness of narrative voice to be found in the telling of their stories here. The book is enriched by the narrative of connected experience; it is not a collective account of being the parent of someone with learning disabilities, but each account is both shared and unique, through the process of working together in this manner. This will enable the reader more readily to make their own connections with the stories told: there is a variety of experience recounted, many different approaches and strategies to caring, and so a number of ways to establish a productive relationship with the narratives.

For me, this has been one of the most rewarding teaching experiences in thirty five years of adult and higher education work. I have learned a very great deal about the lives of family carers, and developed insight and understanding into their lives and the lives of their children, alongside a fierce respect for their unsentimental, passionate advocacy for those children. It is no easy cliché to say that it has been an extraordinary privilege to work with the seven authors of this book.

Dr Laura Potts

AFTERWORD FOR PROFESSIONALS AND SERVICE PROVIDERS

A colleague and I were delivering some training to a group of third year nursing students. One of the students asked my colleague, who is a carer, "Why do you find it so hard to let go of your son?" With no hesitation came the reply, "I will let go when the care offered goes someway to matching the care that I give." "Well, that's an impossible dream. You'll have a long wait then, with those expectations", came a scornful retort from a mature student.

Readers, I ask you – is it an impossible dream? Is what carers are asking for an unreachable goal? No, of course it is not – it is absolutely possible. However, there are many steps for professional workers to climb, before that happens.

This book, this invaluable resource is one key to the solution. Read through these inspirational stories of love, courage, commitment and belief. Their belief that what seems impossible is indeed possible; that their commitment to their sons and daughters, a commitment to listening, observing and responding, is what makes the difference in their children's lives. Each carer passionately wants peace of mind, to know that when their son or daughter leaves home, the professional carers involved will work towards achieving the same commitment to listen, observe and respond and when eventually the family carer dies, that consistent support will continue.

I feel privileged to write this Afterword, because my journey has led me to believe that family carers are not just experts, but are expert partners, equal to professional paid workers. I listened to them, observed them, consulted them and worked alongside them and the training I delivered was devised with carers and led by them.

In reading this book it will become obvious why family carers are indeed experts in their own right. Experts with aspirations to access the most appropriate care services that will enable their sons and daughters to reach their full potential and enjoy life as equal members of our society. Each of us has the right to be treated with respect and dignity, and when that happens we grow and continue to grow and flourish.

Take notice of the stories, tips and insights offered freely to you. Your work practice will change and you can be reassured that you have contributed to enabling people with learning disabilities to live a better quality of life.

My journey began when I worked with family carers. I wanted to learn from them, so I encouraged them to tell their stories. Now I hand over to you, and encourage you all to read and take notice; then pass on your knowledge to others, so we can all contribute to making a better world.

Thank you.

Maureen Ryan

Carers Development Worker (Retired)

GLOSSARY DEFINITIONS

AUTISTIC SPECTRUM DISORDER – SIGNS AND SYMPTOMS

ASD can cause a wide range of symptoms, which are often grouped into two main categories:

- **Problems with social interaction and communication** – including problems understanding and being aware of other people's emotions and feelings; it can also include delayed language development and an inability to start conversations or take part in them properly.

- **Restricted and repetitive patterns of thought, interests and physical behaviours**– including making repetitive physical movements, such as hand tapping or twisting, and becoming upset if set routines are disrupted.

Children, young people and adults with ASD are often also affected by other mental health conditions such as attention deficit hyperactivity disorder (ADHD), anxiety or depression.

About half of those with ASD also have varying levels of learning difficulties. However, with appropriate support many people can be helped to become independent.

Children with more severe symptoms and learning difficulties are likely to need more additional care and assistance to live independently as adults, although there is no reason why they and their families cannot enjoy a good quality of life.

ASPERGER'S SYNDROME – PART OF ASD

Asperger's Syndrome is mostly a 'hidden disability'. This means that you can't tell that someone has the condition from their outward appearance. People with the condition have difficulties in three main areas. They are:

- social communication

- social interaction

- social imagination.

While there are similarities with autism, people with Asperger's Syndrome have fewer problems with speaking and are often of average, or above average, intelligence. They do not usually have the accompanying learning disabilities associated with autism, but they may have specific learning difficulties. These may include dyslexia and dyspraxia or other conditions such as attention deficit hyperactivity disorder (ADHD) and epilepsy.

With the right support and encouragement, people with Asperger's Syndrome can lead full and independent lives. *(National Autistic Society)*

BODYBRUSHING

Developed by Steve Clarke, from work done by Peter Blythe and David McGlown. It is based on the theory that many of the problems found in children with Attention Deficit Disorder, Attention Deficit Hyperactivity Disorder and with some developmental difficulties, can be related to an immature central nervous system, one that still exhibits reflexes which the child should have outgrown. The goal of brushing therapy is to mimic the movements or stimuli that should have occurred to stimulate the development of the central nervous system, and allow the development of the immature neurological reflexes, letting adult reactions come to the fore.

BRONCHIOLITIS

Inflammation of the bronchioles, the smallest air passages of the lungs. Usually caused by respiratory syncytial virus.

GASTROSTOMY

Surgical formation of an artificial opening into the stomach from the skin surface: used for feeding

GLOBAL DEVELOPMENTAL DELAY

A child may be described as having global developmental delay if they have not reached two or more milestones in all areas of development, ie motor skills, speech and language, cognitive skills, social and emotional skills.

ILEOSTOMY

An ileostomy is a surgical procedure to link the end of the small intestine to an opening in the abdomen (stoma) or to an internal pouch.

In an ileostomy, the end of the small intestine (the ileum) is disconnected from the colon (large intestine) and re-routed through a hole made in the abdomen, which is known as a stoma. An external bag (stoma bag) is attached to the opening to collect waste products. An ileostomy is needed when the colon (large intestine) is damaged, inflamed, loses function, or where it is necessary to remove part or all of the colon.

Conditions often treated using an ileostomy are Crohn's disease, ulcerative colitis and bowel cancer.

PARENTERAL NUTRITION

Feeding a person intravenously, bypassing the usual process of eating and digestion.

PMLD Profound and multiple learning disabilities

People with PMLD:

- have more than one disability

- have a profound learning disability

- have great difficulty communicating

- need high levels of support

- may have additional sensory or physical disabilities, complex health needs or mental health difficulties

- may have challenging behaviours

http://www.pmldnetwork.org/

PROGNOSIS

a.   a prediction of the course or outcome of a disease or disorder

b.   the chances of recovery from a disease

Collins English Dictionary

SHARING CARE

A short break service offered by the Local Authority to help provide regular short breaks to children and young people with severe learning disabilities or complex health needs. Family based short break foster care for anything from a few hours to a few days a month. Gives disabled children the opportunity to make new friends, gain independence and broaden their horizons whilst giving their families a break from caring.

SHORT BREAKS HOME

Offers the same opportunity for young people and their families as Sharing Care, but in a residential setting.

ULCERATIVE COLITIS

An auto-immune condition that causes inflammation and ulceration of the colon. Permanently removing the colon is usually recommended in a small number of cases when other treatments prove ineffective, involving leaving the patient with an ileostomy.

ACKNOWLEDGEMENTS

Caring Expressions would like to express their gratitude to the following people who have all helped in different ways in the completion of this book

Dr Laura Potts

Joseph Rowntree Foundation

Awards for All (The Big Lottery Fund)

York Viking Rotary Club

Dame Philippa Russell DBE

Maureen Ryan

Professor Alan Maynard

Keith Rose

Professor Marilyn Crawshaw

Briar House Resource

Izzie McKenzie

Laura Atkinson